SAILING AFTER KNOWLEDGE

SAILING
AFTER
KNOWLEDGE

The Cantos of
Ezra Pound

by
GEORGE DEKKER

Routledge & Kegan Paul
LONDON

First published 1963
by Routledge and Kegan Paul Ltd
Broadway House, 68-74 Carter Lane
London, E.C.4

Printed in Great Britain
in the City of Oxford
at the Alden Press

This book is for
J. N. S.

PREFACE

AMONG MY MANY DEBTS, there are two especially that I wish to acknowledge here. I first studied Ezra Pound's poetry under the supervision of Dr Hugh Kenner of the University of California. He has not read this book and would doubtless disagree with much that I have written; yet it certainly owes much to his sympathetic and informed instruction. Dr Donald Davie, Fellow of Gonville and Caius College, Cambridge, has read the book—several times. Having said this, I should also point out that the nature of the subject precludes any tidy work of impeccable scholarship; nevertheless, in so far as this study of Pound's poetry is readable and accurate, it is so largely because of Dr. Davie's criticism. It is only just to add that he disagrees with many of my interpretations and judgments: such disagreement does not, perhaps, say much for my good sense; but it says a great deal for Dr Davie's tact and generosity.

I am also grateful to Dr M. L. Rosenthal of New York University and Mr M. J. C. Hodgart of Pembroke College, Cambridge. They read an earlier version of this study and made many useful suggestions for its improvement. I should also like to mention the indirect, yet by no means negligible, help I have had from Professor Philip Edwards of Trinity College, Dublin, and from Dr Marvin Mudrick and Dr Homer Swander of the University of California.

To the Trustees of the Edward John Noble Foundation (New York) I wish to express my sincere gratitude. Without the research fellowship which they awarded me, I should have been unable to complete this work.

I acknowledge the permission of Mr Ezra Pound to reproduce copyright material from his poetry and prose. I also make grateful acknowledgment as follows: to Mr Gordon Leff, for permission to quote from his *Medieval Thought from Saint*

vii

Augustine to Ockham; to M. C. D'Arcy, S.J., and Faber & Faber Ltd., for permission to quote from *The Mind and Heart of Love*; and to Mr T. S. Eliot and Faber & Faber Ltd., for permission to quote from Mr Eliot's *After Strange Gods* and *Collected Poems*.

Swansea,
March, 1963.

CONTENTS

Contents

TIME AND TRADITION IN POUND'S POETRY

INTRODUCTION

MY OBJECT HERE is to explain how I approach *The Cantos* in this book and why I use this approach rather than one which might be, in the opening chapters, less tedious and difficult to follow. I also hope to anticipate and answer a few of the questions which any book on Pound is likely to prompt. I should probably say at once that this book is not intended to be an 'introduction' to Pound's mature poetry. Five such works are readily available, ranging from the advanced and sometimes bewildering discussion of Poundian poetics by Mr Kenner to the genial, intelligent, but sometimes too casual popularization of Mr Fraser.[1] On the other hand, I do not assume that my reader will have read any of these works. In fact I rather make a point of approaching the Poundian centre inductively, basing my discussion as nearly as possible on passages from *The Cantos* which I quote and comment on. I have good reason to believe that, for some readers, this is the best way of introducing Pound's mature poetry (1916–59); but the final aim of this book is to provide a reliable criticism of the poetry, not an introduction to it.

The book is divided into three sections: the first is taken up with a fairly detailed exegesis of cantos which embody the theme of Eros or which serve as useful points of entry to the poem as a whole; the second section, with a discussion of the poetic theories implicit in Canto XXXVI and, I believe, the entire poem; and the third section, with a critical and historical survey of the important poetry which Pound has published since 1916. Of course in practice I have not been able to concentrate exclusively on exegesis at one time, on poetic theory or

[1] In the order of their importance: Hugh Kenner, *The Poetry of Ezra Pound* (1951); Clark Emery, *Ideas into Action* (Coral Gables, Fla., 1958); M. L. Rosenthal, *A Primer of Ezra Pound* (New York, 1960); G. S. Fraser, *Ezra Pound* (Edinburgh, 1960); H. H. Watts, *Ezra Pound and the Cantos* (1951).

literary history and criticism at others; nor would it be desirable to do so if this were possible. But the arrangement which I outline here involves more than mere auctorial convenience.

Much of the adverse criticism of *The Cantos* is based on the fact that it is often difficult to understand exactly what Pound is saying, and on the claim that, anyway, 'what is being said [is] not much better than nothing'.[1] That the poem is difficult to understand is a matter of common experience; it is profitless to dispute the point. However, the importance which we attach to this must depend to a large extent on the justice or injustice of the claim that, if we do take the trouble to get at Pound's meaning, we shall be disappointed with what we find. Actually this claim seems to be two claims: that what Pound is talking about—usury, Chinese history, John Adams, etc.—is not interesting subject matter for contemporary poetry; less prescriptively, that Pound's response to this subject matter—his understanding and interpretation of it—is not interesting, or at any rate not interesting as poetry. Clearly, the second objection can only be met by extensive quotation and discussion; concerning the first, however, it is possible to make a brief observation here: there is little evidence that critics who object to the subject matter of *The Cantos* are very familiar with the poetic text. Dr Leavis, for example, believed in 1932 that the poem was 'Pound's *Sordello*', the game of a pedant-dilletante. In 1950 he seemed to believe that Pound's famous economic, political, and racial obsessions accounted for everything in the poem.[2] Of course certain parts of the poem fit Dr Leavis's preconceptions, and it is not possible to dismiss his strictures entirely; but the first section of my study should at least leave no doubt that Pound's interests are less caricaturable than hostile critics like to assume.

That the poem has been caricatured with relative impunity, however, must be attributed to Pound's poetic method, which makes obscurity inevitable and preconceptions difficult to overcome. Indeed R. P. Blackmur once argued, in an essay which is easily the best early criticism of the poem,[3] that we can understand Pound's poem only if we are furnished with *Pound's* preconceptions: hence, apparently, John Edwards' *Annotated*

---

[1] F. R. Leavis, *New Bearings* (new edition, 1950), p. 153.
[2] Leavis, pp. 151–7, 235–6.
[3] 'Masks of Ezra Pound', *Language as Gesture* (1954), pp. 124–54. Essay dated 1933.

Index to the Cantos[1] and Clark Emery's *Ideas into Action*, a popular but responsible exposition of the main ideas and principles upon which the poem is based. Seemingly, the more useful we find these works, the more embarrassing they become; for it would seem to follow that Mr Blackmur is right when he concludes that Pound's effort is 'scholia not poetry'. And in fact we find that Hugh Kenner, writing several years before the publication of Mr Edwards' and Mr Emery's work, attempted to forestall this embarrassment by making out a case for the self-sufficiency of the poem.[2] To make this case, he gives a number of brilliant exemplary readings and an impressive exposition of Pound's poetics, based on Pound's prose works but illustrated throughout with passages from his poetry. However, as the existence of Mr Edwards' and Mr Emery's books attests, Mr Kenner's case for the self-sufficiency of *The Cantos* is not altogether convincing; and valuable and interesting as his discussions of Poundian poetics are, they seem not infrequently to apply to a poem which exists only in the minds of Pound and Kenner.

Mr Kenner's apologia, then, does not explain away the practical difficulties which force us to accept the *Annotated Index* as a useful tool. Moreover, the poetic method which makes Pound's meaning often difficult to grasp also accounts for the startlingly uneven, apparently unpoetic surface of *The Cantos*. Nor are these disadvantages more apparent than real, especially in a didactic poem which is intended to have far-reaching social effects. Therefore, although Mr Kenner and others have explained in their own ways why Pound staked everything on such an unlikely method, I believe that the matter is so important as to warrant a fresh approach, unencumbered by Poundian jargon and the assumption that Pound is at all times a great master of poetic technique. Previous approaches along the same lines, by Mr Blackmur and Mr Watts, reach conclusions which seem to me too simple and too severe: the former is hagridden by a thesis about Pound's supposed inability to write 'original' poetry; the latter, by a thesis about a supposed usury/anti-usury dialectic which governs *The Cantos* throughout. My own discussion of Pound's poetic method, in the second section of this study, is based primarily on my reading of Canto XXXVI,

[1] *Annotated Index* (corrected edition, Berkeley, 1959).
[2] *Poetry of Ezra Pound*, pp. 191, 216–18 are particularly relevant in this connection.

which is probably the most important single canto and is certainly one of the half-dozen cantos intended by Pound to have great generalizing force for the poem as a whole. Such an approach has patent limitations, and it could not possibly result in a complete account of Pound's poetics. It does result, I believe, in a necessary supplement to, and qualification of, the accounts given by Mr Kenner and Mr Emery.

It should be clear that my discussion of Poundian poetics follows my exegesis of cantos embodying the theme of Eros because I wish to generalize about the poem which one reads, not about the various *a priori* poems which Pound's method encourages his friends and enemies alike to invent. The third section of the present study, a critical and historical survey of Pound's mature poetry, follows the first two sections because of my conviction that a reader should not be guided very far by a critic's evaluation of *The Cantos* unless that critic has first demonstrated an understanding of at least part of the poetic text. In the case of most poetry such demonstration is as unnecessary as it is impractical, for we normally accept a critic's credentials on the basis of previously established competence and responsibility. But *The Cantos* in this respect, as in so many others, seems to be a literary sport. The criticism it has received at the hands of even the most distinguished critics—Dr Leavis, Edmund Wilson, E. M. Bowra, and Yvor Winters come to mind—is often sketchy and imperceptive; Mr Eliot's observations on this subject are, I believe, among his very worst; and the generality of critics, especially those who wrote before Mr Kenner's book appeared, tend merely to paraphrase the words of Mr Eliot, Mr Blackmur, and Dr Leavis.

However, I should not fail to acknowledge that I am heavily indebted to previous critics and to the relatively uncritical followers of Pound who have during the past decade made it so much easier for a reader to gain the understanding prerequisite for sound criticism. For interpretation or criticism of *The Cantos* is at best a difficult and uncertain business, in which we need all the help we can get. I do not mean, of course, that we need a full battery of notes and commentaries to understand and appreciate much of the poem; for this, if it were the case, would offer the strongest possible argument against our needing any help at all: *The Cantos* would be a waste of our time and energy. Yet the mastery of meaning, in detail and in general, that one takes for granted in the criticism of other long poems, even one so difficult as the *Faerie Queene*, has been and probably will continue to be impossible to achieve in the case of *The Cantos*. Therefore, without either exaggerating or underestimating the difficulty of the poem, we must be grateful for the labours of Pound scholars to make it more comprehensible, as we must also be patient with critics who may not seem to have comprehended as much as they should have. In any event, the final judgment of *The Cantos* will not take place in the near future, and it will not be the work of a single critic. But this does not relieve us of the responsibility to judge the poem as well as we can at the present time.

One of the chief obstacles to just criticism of the poem is, of course, Pound's anti-Semitism and fascism. My own sociopolitical bias is more or less conventionally liberal: I detest Pound's anti-Semitism; and while I find it easy enough to forgive the misguided patriotism which led Pound to broadcast for Mussolini, I do not find it easy to forgive his association with American fascistic elements, of which the late Senator McCarthy was merely the gaudiest and most fragrant bloom. So, too, are certain parts of *The Cantos*. However, these matters count for a great deal less in the poem than is often supposed; and one should bear in mind that those who dislike Pound for other reasons are frequently willing to invoke his anti-Semitism and fascism as a more convenient argument against him. The evil, it seems to me, is obviously peripheral in *The Cantos*; the success or failure of the poem must be accounted for on other grounds.

A second problem is the issue of Pound's influence on other writers. I am not referring now to the assistance which he gave to writers ranging from Yeats to Hemingway, from Frost to Joyce: this is now well known and widely appreciated, and among those who care at all for letters it will always count for more than any harm he may have done as a fascist propagandist. What I have in mind is the question of Pound's poetry as a model for younger poets. It is an important question, but it is one which the poets themselves must answer. I personally believe that there is much to be learned from Pound in the way of diction and cadence, but that only a poet with a mature style of his own, such as Charles Tomlinson, could well afford to 'imitate' him. However this may be, I am concerned with Pound's achievement as a poet, not with the possible value of his poetry as a model. This distinction is an obvious one, but it is worth making because Pound himself rarely makes it and because Eliot, by describing *The Cantos* as 'a mine for juvenile poets to quarry',[1] has encouraged other critics to look upon the poem as 'a good influence' or 'a bad influence'.

Another, perhaps more insidious distraction from the real vices and virtues of the poem is the critic's possible concern over the poem's popular and academic reputation. I happen to share the apprehension of other observers about the kind of reputation which *The Cantos* seems to be acquiring in the United States. It appears to me quite possible that Pound is about to be enshrined along with Whitman—Whitman being the Homer, Pound the Dante of American literature. I am also aware of the argument that each new book or essay on Pound (whatever its merits) contributes toward the realization of this depressing possibility, if only because it seems to certify the importance of the subject. But if this danger really exists, the serious critic must ignore it and go ahead with his work—which is to study whatever interests him and to report his findings as accurately as possible. And I think there would be little reason to fear a wholesale uncritical acceptance of the poem, if it had not at one time suffered an almost wholesale uncritical rejection.

In any case, it *is* an important poem: because certain widely anthologized passages leave no doubt that it has moments of great beauty; because it is the only serious attempt to construct a long post-symbolist poem; and because it is the work of the author of *Cathay*, the *Seafarer* translation, *Homage to Sextus Propertius* and *Hugh Selwyn Mauberley*:

If an Author, by any single composition, has impressed us with respect for his talents, it is useful to consider this as affording a presumption, that on other occasions where we have been displeased, he, nevertheless, may not have written ill or absurdly, and further, to give him so much credit for this one composition as may induce us to review what has displeased us, with more care than we should otherwise have bestowed upon it.[2]

---

[1] *Selected Poems of Ezra Pound*, ed. T. S. Eliot (1928), p. 19.
[2] *The Poetical Works of Wordsworth*, ed. Thos. Hutchinson (revised edition, 1936), p. 741.

The Theme of Eros
in The Cantos

Section One

The Theme of Eros

in The Cantos

I

POETIC MOTIVE AND
STRATEGY IN THE CANTOS

1. Homage to Confucius

THE BEST POINT OF ENTRY to *The Cantos* is without a doubt the
first canto. A reader coming to the poem for the first time will
make little sense out of later cantos unless he has mastered the
earlier sections. However, for the purposes of this study, Canto
XIII is the best point of departure: the implications of this
canto must be grasped if we are to understand the rest of the
poem, and especially if we are to understand the so-called 'Hell
Cantos', numbers XIV and XV. For that vigorous attack on
contemporary society, disparaged by Mr Eliot and celebrated
by Miss Sitwell,[1] forms a jarring antithesis to the contemplative
ease of

> Kung walked
> > by the dynastic temple
> and into the cedar grove,
> > and then out by the lower river,
> And with him Khieu Tchi
> > and Tian the low speaking

But XIII is not a 'lyrical' canto:

> And 'we are unknown,' said Kung,
> 'You will take up charioteering?
> > 'Then you will become known,
> 'Or perhaps I should take up charioteering, or archery?
> 'Or the practice of public speaking?'

[1] Eliot, *After Strange Gods* (New York, 1934), pp. 45–7; Edith Sitwell, *Aspects of
Modern Poetry* (1934), pp. 178–214.

The noteworthy point is that Kung (Confucius) suddenly turns the question on himself.(1) We know well enough that he ought to do just what he is doing: perambulating and questioning, after the fashion of all sages. But this act of self-interrogation illustrates his own doctrine, which is shortly revealed. After each of his disciples has described his personal ambition ('What would you do to become known?')

> ... Kung smiled upon all of them equally.
> And Thseng-sie desired to know:
> 'Which had answered correctly?'
> And Kung said, 'They have all answered correctly,
> 'That is to say, each in his nature.'

It is clear that Canto XIII begins as a sort of treatise on education. The first step, apparently, is for the teacher to question his own fitness for the job: '*Or perhaps I should* take up charioteering, or archery?' The second step is to determine the student's individual aptitudes: 'They have all answered correctly, / That is to say, each in his own nature.' And the third step is to insist on the development of their talent:

> And Kung raised his cane against Yuan Jang,
> Yuan Jang being his elder,
> For Yuan Jang sat by the roadside pretending to
> be receiving wisdom.
> And Kung said
> 'You old fool, come out of it,
> 'Get up and do something useful.'
> And Kung said
> 'Respect a child's faculties
> 'From the moment it inhales the clear air,
> 'But a man of fifty who knows nothing
> 'Is worthy of no respect.'

The final step is for the state to put developed talents to use:

> And 'When the prince has gathered about him
> 'All the savants and artists, his riches will be
> fully employed.'

When the treatise on education reaches the level of the prince, it changes, by the most natural transition, into a treatise on government:

And Kung said, and wrote on the bo leaves:
    'If a man have not order within him
    'He can not spread order about him;
    'And if a man have not order within him
    'His family will not act with due order;
        'And if the prince have not order within him
    'He can not put order in his dominions.'

At first glance, this passage may seem rather repetitious, and as a matter of fact the typographical layout rather hinders than helps perception. Grammatically, the last six lines consist of three almost exactly parallel sentences. The purpose of this somewhat uncomfortable construction is to mimic the sense, which is that Everyman, prince and peasant *alike*, observes the same rule of self-government. The discomfort one experiences when reading this passage arises from one's feeling that the second and third lines state a principle that governs the fourth and fifth lines (one unit) and the sixth and seventh lines (a second unit), and that, therefore, the last four lines should be clearly subordinate to the two preceding lines. But by making the sentences parallel, Pound seeks to undermine the habit of thinking in hierarchical terms.[1]

So much for political and grammatical theory. But the treatise on government is not finished yet. Theory, if it is to be useful, is the product of careful observation within a reasonably limited field; and so, in the next few lines, we find that Kung's working vocabulary reflects a preoccupation with what is close to the world where one touches and is touched.

    And Kung gave the words 'order'
    and 'brotherly deference'
    And said nothing of the 'life after death'.
    And he said
        'Anyone can run to excesses,
    'It is easy to shoot past the mark,
    'It is hard to stand firm in the middle.'

    And they said: 'If a man commit murder
        'Should his father protect him, and hide him?'
    And Kung said:
        'He should hide him.'

---

[1] My 'Everyman' is unfortunate, since it implies a hierarchy in which the spiritual being is distinct from and higher than the worldly being; Pound is interested in 'man' rather than 'Man'.

There may be some argument as to the rightness of Kung's answer, but the distinction he makes is a humane one: to hide the son is one's duty; and this is not anti-social, because kinship is the primary social component. (Whether to *protect* the son is a separate issue, which involves the father in joining his son against society.)

Thus the study of government moves from theory to practical counsel; and, as one expects from a teacher who starts by questioning his own fitness to teach, it moves from practical counsel to personal practice:

> And Kung gave his daughter to Kong-Tchang
> > Although Kong-Tchang was in prison.
> And he gave his niece to Nan-Young
> > although Nan-Young was out of office.

Having brought order within himself, Kung's decisions are not influenced by fear of public opinion. It is clear that, though I speak of moving from theory to practical counsel to personal practice, there has been no movement: government begins and ends with, 'If a man have not order within him / He can not spread order about him'. Kung acts, counsels, and theorizes wisely because, to begin with, he has order within him.

The third part of Canto XIII contains a sort of treatise on good professional practice. Since governing is the profession which affects everybody, the prince is treated first:

> And Kung said 'Wan ruled with moderation.
> > 'In his day the State was well kept,
> 'And even I can remember
> 'A day when the historians left blanks in their writings,
> 'I mean for things they didn't know,
> 'But that time seems to be passing.'
> And Kung said, 'Without character you will
> > be unable to play on that instrument
> 'Or to execute the music fit for the Odes.

'Character' is the key word here, just as 'nature' and 'order' were the key words in earlier sections of this canto. The word 'character' as Pound uses it here implies more than moral strength, it seems to imply a firmness of outline, a clearly delimited identity—as well it might, since its Latin stem denoted a branding mark, and its Old French ancestor *charassein* denoted 'to sharpen, to engrave'. (There are far less remote usages which correspond to Pound's, but the backgrounds may serve to bring his usage into relief.) It is apparent that this definition is in line with Kung's concern to distinguish individual aptitudes and to govern oneself so far as not to be swayed by a fear of public opinion.

It is, presumably, 'character' which caused Wang to rule 'with moderation' (from *moderor*: to set bounds to, to check, to moderate, to restrain). To rule with moderation means, apparently, not to rule too much, not to impose the royal will too heavily. Likewise, the historian who has 'character' does not try to impose his will on his materials; without integrity of his own, he will fail to respect (or even recognize) the integrity of his materials. The player who has 'character', like the good historian, does not 'project': the Odes exist independent of himself, and it is his business to 'execute' the music for them, not to 'interpret'. The man who makes history, the man who records it, and the man who makes music for the eternal Odes—each must honour the integrity of his 'subject'; he must neither meddle with nor fake an understanding of it. Just as the teacher must be sure of his own vocation before he prepares others for a vocation, and as a man must have order within him before he can spread order about him, so must a man have character before he can do his job without tyrannizing his subject.

The admirable precepts which Canto XIII offers might, of course, be reduced to 'know thyself'; but the reduction merely obfuscates what I may have already obfuscated by too much commentary. Indeed, the last passage discussed might serve as a text for Pound's poetic practice in *The Cantos*. In some respects Pound was of all men the least prepared to follow the teachings of Confucius, so that, all too frequently, one recalls Canto XIII as a monument of self-deception; yet *The Cantos* would not be what it is if Pound had not taken Confucius seriously. The so-called 'Hell Cantos', which I have described as an antithesis to Canto XIII, furnish a striking example of poetry which can be best understood by the application of Pound's Confucian precepts, and which can be judged quite severely enough without recourse to other standards.

> 'The blossoms of the apricot
>   blow from the east to the west,
> 'And I have tried to keep them from falling.'

7

The Theme of Eros in The Cantos

2. A 'Hell' without Dignity or Tragedy

Some guide to Cantos XIV and XV is no doubt needed; and, as the author of *Prufrock* and *The Waste Land* has travelled extensively in infernal regions, his commentary in *After Strange Gods* ought to be attended to. Confucius, it will be remembered, 'said nothing of the "life after death" ', but Confucius had not, as Pound and Eliot had, spent years reading Dante. Eliot's discussion of Pound's 'Post-Protestant prejudice' and of his adopting Confucius as a guide immediately precedes the paragraph which I now quote (in its entirety, though I interrupt to comment at certain points).[1]

Mr. Pound's theological twist appears both in his poetry and his prose, but as there are other vigorous prose writers, and as Mr. Pound is probably the most important living poet in our language, a reference to his poetry will carry more weight. At this point I shall venture to generalize, and suggest that with the disappearance of the idea of Original Sin, with the disappearance of the idea of intense moral struggle, the human beings presented to us both in poetry and in prose fiction today, and more patently among the serious writers than in the underworld of letters, tend to become less and less real. It is in fact in moments of moral and spiritual struggle depending upon spiritual sanctions, rather than in those 'bewildering minutes' in which we are all very much alike, that men and women come nearest to being real.

Eliot clearly equates 'real' with 'individual' (i.e. when we are *not* 'all very much alike'); what distinguishes us from others is the intensity and complexity of our struggle with the Evil which is our common inheritance; for it is through this struggle that we participate in the transcendent reality, in which light *accidental* resemblances and differences (dress, class, economic status, etc.) disappear, and the individual qualities which decide individual damnation or salvation come into prominence. The construction I make is perhaps more rigidly Christian in interpretation than Eliot wished, or it may be that my reading is 'heretical', but Eliot's reasoning here is not so easy to follow as it might seem. Eliot goes on to say:

If you do away with this struggle, and maintain that by tolerance, benevolence, inoffensiveness and a redistribution or increase of purchasing power, combined with a devotion on the part of an

[1] Eliot, *After Strange Gods*, pp. 45–7.

elite, to Art, the world will be as good as anyone could require, then you must expect human beings to become more and more vaporous. This is exactly what we find of the society which Mr. Pound puts in Hell, in his *Draft of XXX Cantos*.

It must of course be recalled that the lectures entitled *After Strange Gods* were delivered in 1933, just before Pound came to be popularly associated with fascism; but in view of Pound's earlier publications, the words 'tolerance' and 'inoffensiveness' seem strangely wide of the mark as an account of his social desiderata. There is, for instance, nothing meek about Confucius. But, right or not in his account of the Poundian utopia, Eliot is certainly right in saying that Pound 'does away' with the struggle based on the doctrine of Original Sin. He is also right in describing as 'vaporous' the society which Pound 'puts in Hell'.

It consists (I may have overlooked one or two species) of politicians profiteers, financiers, newspaper proprietors and their hired men, *agents provocateurs*, Calvin, St. Clement of Alexandria, the English, vice-crusaders, liars, the stupid, pedants, preachers, those who do not believe in Social Credit, bishops, lady golfers, Fabians, conservatives and imperialists, and all 'those who have set money-lust before the pleasures of the senses'. It is, in its way, an admirable Hell, 'without dignity, without tragedy'. At first sight the variety of types —for these are types, not individuals—may be a little confusing, but I think it becomes a little more intelligible if we see at work three principles, (1) the aesthetic, (2) the humanitarian, (3) the Protestant.

Eliot's list is both inaccurate and misleading (e.g. not 'the English', but 'many English'), but it gives a reasonable idea of the miscellaneousness of Pound's hell.(2) That the figures are types rather than individuals is, as Eliot insists, most important. Though as a matter of fact individuals are named, they too are merely 'types of evil', unindividualized. But surely the point of this procedure is that the 'place' which Pound describes is a sort of hell precisely because its inhabitants are types rather than individuals.

> the perverts, the perverters of language,
> > the perverts, who have set money-lust
> Before the pleasures of the senses;
> howling, as of a hen-yard in a printing-house,

9

the clatter of presses,
the blowing of dry dust and stray paper,
fœter, sweat, the stench of stale oranges,
dung, last cess-pool of the universe,
mysterium, acid of sulphur,
the pusillanimous, raging;
plunging jewels in mud,
          and howling to find them unstained;
sadic mothers driving their daughters to bed with
                                    decrepitude,
      sows eating their litters,

                          (Canto XIV, pp. 65–6)

The canons against which this 'society' offends seem to be Confucian: the creatures are governed by lusts, so they cannot govern themselves; they are surrounded by disorder and ugliness; they betray and tyrannize kin, and thereby undermine not only 'brotherly deference' but the entire social order. One may as well allow that Pound's canons are Confucian, as he indicates by juxtaposing the materials of Canto XIII with the materials in his 'Hell'. For the allowance doesn't make these cantos any more attractive.

Eliot concludes his discussion of the 'Hell Cantos' by saying:

And I find one considerable objection to a Hell of this sort: that a Hell altogether without dignity implies a Heaven without dignity also. If you do not distinguish between essential Evil and social accidents, then the Heaven (if any) implied will be equally trivial and accidental. Mr. Pound's Hell, for all its horrors, is a perfectly comfortable one for the modern mind to contemplate, and disturbing to no one's complacency: it is a Hell for the *other people*, the people we read about in newspapers, not for oneself and one's friends.

Eliot's assault on Pound's hell is, after all, something of a masterpiece: he destroys it merely by taking it more solemnly than Pound intended it to be taken, and his assault is all the more effective because he never mentions what is nevertheless always present as the standard of excellence for this type of writing. Certainly Pound invites the comparison by quoting, as an introduction to the scene in Canto XIV:

Io venni in luogo d'ogni luce muto;

but it is quite misleading to spell Pound's hell with a capital

'H'. And the same is true of 'the Heaven (if any) implied'. Pound's hell is monstrous rather than infernal: its inhabitants are atavistic, not Evil; at worst they are rather like sharks, primitive, but efficient—streamlined appetites. They are (with one important exception) 'without dignity, without tragedy' simply because they have lost or never developed their human faculties. A glimpse of Pound's 'Heaven' is afforded in Canto XVI; and though it strikes me as rather dull, it is perfectly 'dignified':

> Then light air, under saplings,
> the blue banded lake under æther,
>> an oasis, the stones, the calm field,
> the grass quiet,
>> and passing the tree of the bough
> The grey stone posts,
>> and the stair of gray stone,
> the passage clean-squared in granite:
>> descending,
> and I through this, and into the earth,
>> patet terra,
> entered the quiet air
>> the new sky,
> the light as after a sun-set,
>> and by their fountains, the heroes,
> Sigismundo, and Malatesta Novello,
>> and founders, gazing at the mounts of their cities.
>>> (Canto XVI, p. 73)

But this paradise is not really 'dull', for there is no question of anybody having to live there: real it may be, but it is only real as an image—refreshing, recurrent perhaps, but momentary. This convention of heroes gazing at their admirable monuments is a sort of vacation from the struggle which earned them Pound's approval; just as Pound's hell is a sort of Witches' Sabbath.

Irrelevant as some of Eliot's objections appear to me, he is mostly right when he says that 'Mr. Pound's Hell, for all its horrors, is a perfectly comfortable one for the modern mind to contemplate, and disturbing to no one's complacency: it is a Hell for the *other people*, the people we read about in the newspapers, not for oneself and one's friends'. Certainly Pound does not want to excite pity or terror in his reader's mind; it appears,

rather, that we are expected to loathe the scene or to gloat over
it; for the villains eliminate each other and themselves:

> et nulla fidentia inter eos,
> > all with their twitching backs,
> with daggers, and bottle ends, waiting an
> > unguarded moment;
> > > > (Canto XV, p. 69)

And many appear to be having a rollicking good time:

> 'and the swill full of respecters,
> > bowing to the lords of the place,
> explaining its advantages,
> > and the laudatores temporis acti
> claiming that the shit used to be blacker and richer
> and the fabians crying for the petrification of putrefaction,
> for a new dung-flow cut in lozenges,
> the conservatives chatting,
> > distinguished by gaiters of slum-flesh,
> > > > (Canto XV, p. 68)

The evil these creatures do to creatures other than themselves
is hinted at occasionally (as in 'gaiters of slum-flesh'), but
Pound has segregated them all too well: they are harmless here,
obscene; and, as Pound rightly observes, such a place is 'lacking
in interest' (Canto XIV, p. 62).[1] At only one point in the 'Hell
Cantos' is an act presented which might excite our compassion
and anger:

> sadic mothers driving their daughters to bed with
> > > > decrepitude—

and, isolated as it is, it must simply be regarded as a blunder:
tragedy has no place here; and if one slips into the error of
dealing with life as it is generally lived, tragedy cannot be
avoided.(3)

Had Pound not invoked Dante as his 'precursor' in these
regions, he need not have failed so resoundingly. Pope's *Dunciad*
treats roughly the same subject; its values are roughly the same:
but how much greater is the *Dunciad*, and how much more moving! For at least in the fourth book of the *Dunciad* there is no

[1] Mr Kenner describes the effect of Pound's hell as a 'vision which exists tamed,
in an ideal order, behind glass' (*The Poetry of Ezra Pound*, p. 127). However, he
considers this a virtue.

suggestion of self-indulgence: Pope's vision there is austere and tragic; the games and fêtes of his dunces are a preparation for catastrophe. Of this there is no suggestion in the 'Hell Cantos'. Nor does this failure have anything to do with personal spite. There is infinitely more personal spite in the *Dunciad* than in *The Cantos*. What matters is that Pound's usurers are impotent, whereas Pope's dunces are not: a shot of fly-spray would eliminate Pound's 'Hell', but Pope's dunces are about to eliminate *us*.

Though it is true that in the last forty or so lines of Canto XV (pp. 70-1) Pound's vision reaches an intensity and excitement that are almost Dantesque:

> Andiamo!
>   One's feet sunk,
> the welsh of mud gripped one, no hand-rail,
> the bog-suck like a whirl-pool,
> and he said:
>   Close the pores of your feet!
> And my eyes clung to the horizon,

this last spurt cannot save the 'Hell Cantos'. To compare them with Dante's Hell is absurd, though there may be some point in comparing them with Milton's. They are possibly intended as a 'criticism' of Milton's Hell.(4) As a projection of Pound's disgust—often perfectly justified disgust—with a host of things both ancient and contemporary, Cantos XIV and XV are somewhat remarkable, though the flatness of some of the imagery, e.g. 'howling, as of a hen-yard in a printing house', suggests a defect either of interest or invention. As a revelation of infernal situations or states of mind, they are far inferior to Eliot's deadly creations.

That the author of these cantos had 'order within him' seems, to say the least, unlikely. Neither, it would appear, had he inquired very closely whether he, of all men, was fit to create a Hell, or whether, indeed, he was perhaps betraying (by coarsening and confusing) the literary convention of Hell. Worst of all, however, is Pound's betrayal of his own deepest conviction: that the activities of usurers, politicians, the press gang, etc., do affect us enormously here and now, and that they matter especially because we cannot or should not look forward to a 'life after death' where accounts will be settled. The consolation that, *if they were all bottled up together*, Pound's creatures would suffocate each other with excrement and slash each other with broken bottles, 'without dignity, without tragedy', is the merest mockery of the human predicament.

3. Antecedents and Contemporaries

Pound's 'Hell', it turns out, is rather an exposure of his own incapacities than a valid criticism of the modern world. A more effective criticism is to be found in Canto VII, where the values are rather Flaubertian than Confucian. Yet it is the essence of Canto XIII that a man should have a sense of his own range and special aptitudes: Canto VII images, though cryptically and often ambiguously, Pound's own literary predicament *c.* 1910–20 and the predicament of a society which has grown attached to *idées recues*—and there is no student of these matters more tireless and dedicated than Pound himself.

Since it is impossible to approach Canto VII without an understanding of its context, I begin by summarizing relevant materials from the preceding cantos. At a later point in this essay I treat some of them in considerable detail, but for the present a rapid survey will suffice.

Cantos I–VI deal almost exclusively with Mediterranean scenes, and their subjects are chiefly literary: i.e. they are largely a pastiche of paraphrases from Greek, Latin, Spanish, and Provençal authors—Odysseus' descent into Hades; the Trojan elders' counsel against keeping Helen; Dionysus' revenge on his kidnappers; the Cid's deception of the pawnbrokers Raquel and Vidas; and a half-dozen troubadour biographies. That accounts only for the main literary sources which Pound has plundered. These paraphrases are remarkably alive and concrete; but, when he deviates into straight history, as he does when dealing with the Italian Renaissance (though the treatment is no less vivid or concrete) the subject becomes strangely unreal:

> Tiber, dark with the cloak, wet cat gleaming in patches.
> Click of the hooves, through garbage,
> Clutching the greasy stone. 'And the cloak floated.'
> Slander is up betimes.

> But Varchi of Florence,
> Steeped in a different year, and pondering Brutus,
> Then 'Εἴγα, μαλ' αὖθις δευτέραν!
> 'Dog-eye!!' (to Alessandro)
>   'Whether for love of Florence,' Varchi leaves it,
> Saying 'I saw the man, came up with him at Venice,
> 'I, one wanting the facts,
> 'And no mean labour ... Or for a privy spite?'
>   (Canto V, pp. 22–3)

The subjects here are the assassinations of Giovanni Borgia and Alessandro de Medici, and Varchi is the historian (an honest one) with whom Pound joins to ponder the motives for these crimes: Odysseus, the Cid, and even Dionysus—their actions are out in the open, but how does one penetrate the ambiguities of this later situation? 'Whether for love of Florence ... or for a privy spite?' Or both? For the motives themselves may be ambiguous: we are nearing the realms of Henry James. (It should also be noted that the reference to Brutus suggests ironically that the Renaissance restored something besides classical art and learning.)

Having summarized this much by way of preparation, I believe that the introductory passage of Canto VII may be somewhat more intelligible than I first found it. It is not Pound at his most elliptical, but it is not easy going:

> Eleanor (she spoiled in a British climate)
> Ἔλανδρος and Ἐλέπτολις, and
>   poor old Homer blind,
>   blind as a bat,
> Ear, ear for the sea-surge;
>   rattle of old men's voices.
> And then the phantom of Rome,
>   marble narrow for seats
> 'Si pulvis nullus' said Ovid,
> 'Erit, nullum tamen excute.'
> To file and candles, e li mestiers ecoutes;
> Scene for the battle only, but still scene,
> Pennons and standards y cavals armatz
> Not mere succession of strokes, sightless narration,
> To Dante's 'ciocco', brand struck in the game.
>
> Un peu moisi, plancher plus bas que le jardin.

15

'Contre le lambris, fauteuil de paille,
'Un vieux piano, et sous le barometre ... '

What this passage amounts to is a highly condensed, peculiarly Poundian history of mimesis from Homer to Flaubert (Henry James appears shortly, bringing the history up to date). That the 'Common Reader' or even the traditionally trained literary historian would make little of it, is sure. At this point poetry becomes perilously close to cryptogram(5)—the world of *trobar clus* and 'Donna me Prega'.(6) But cryptogram though it may be, it lacks neither wit nor significance, as I hope to show.

The parenthetical remark that Eleanor (of Aquitaine) 'spoiled in a British climate' announces a shift from Mediterranean to North European focus. The association of Eleanor of Aquitaine with Helen of Troy was established as early as Canto II:

'Eleanor, ἑλέναυς and ἑλέπτολις!'
          And poor old Homer blind, blind, as a bat,
Ear, ear for the sea-surge, murmur of old men's voices:
'Let her go back to the ships,
Back among Grecian faces, lest evil come on our own,
Evil and further evil, and a curse cursed on our children,
Moves, yes she moves like a goddess
And has the face of a god
          and the voice of Schoeney's daughters,
And doom goes with her in walking,
Let her go back to the ships,
          back among Grecian voices.'
                              (Canto II, p. 10)

It is, of course, the scene where Homer compares the elders of Troy with grasshoppers, and it is one of the most justly famous strokes in the history of narrative: who could doubt after such testimony, delivered in spite of themselves, that Helen is the most beautiful of all women? The interesting point about Homer being 'blind as a bat' is that it focuses attention on his skilful manipulation of second-hand information: he had an ear for the authentic accent, a genius for turning 'hearsay' into the most convincing evidence. All of these points are recalled at the beginning of Canto VII, and all are pertinent.

Pound then shifts to the Rome of Ovid:

And then the phantom of Rome,
    marble narrow for seats
'Si pulvis nullus' said Ovid,
'Erit, nullum tamen excute.'

This development parallels the shift from Homer to Ovid which
takes place on a larger scale in Canto II, except that in this case
the shift is not to the sunlit visual world of the *Metamorphoses*,
but to the world of manners and social strategies which Ovid
celebrates in the *Ars Amatoria*. The word 'phantom' is perhaps a
bit puzzling, but it is useful to recall the earlier association
(in Canto V) of Renaissance and Roman political intrigues.
And the transition from Roman politics to amorous escapades
is provided by the public circus, where, as Pound duly notes
after Ovid, the narrowness of the seats afforded a pretext for
advances:

Proximus a domina, nullo prohibente, sedeto,
    Iunge tuum lateri qua potes usque latus;
Et bene, quod cogit, si nolit, linea iungi,
    Quod tibi tangenda est lege puella loci.[1]

The quotation from Ovid is located only a few lines away:

Utque fit, in gremium pulvis si forte puellae
    Deciderit, digitis excutiendus erit:
Et si nullus erit pulvis, tamen excute nullum:
    Quaelibet officio causa sit apta tuo.[2]

And it is precisely this latter recommendation—to make an
opportunity out of whatever comes to hand—that Ovid himself
followed as an artist. Homer made legendary material his
opportunity, Ovid made Roman society his.

    Less need be said of the lines that follow, in which Pound
sketches the relationship between subject matter and treatment
in the Middle Ages:

To file and candles, e li mestiers ecoutes;
Scene for the battle only, but still scene,
Pennons and standards y cavals armatz
Not mere succession of strokes, sightless narration,
To Dante's 'ciocco', brand struck in the game.

The Langue d'Oïl fares rather badly by Poundian standards:

[1] Ovid, *Ars Amatoria*, I, 139–42.
[2] Ovid, *Ars Amatoria*, I, 149–52.

the emphasis is on what is heard rather than seen; there is perhaps a faint allusion to the deep darkness of northern French cathedrals; and, in any case, for a description of the warfare which characterized this period, he turns rather to the Spanish *Cid*[1] ('Pennons and standards') and the Provençal de Born ('cavals armatz') than to the crusading French. The reference to 'mere succession of strokes, sightless narration' is perhaps contemptuous reference to the *Chanson de Roland*. Dante's 'ciocco' is a high point for the visual imagination.(7)

The leap from Dante to Flaubert is itself significant: the Renaissance is Pound's *bête noire*, but, more important still, according to Poundian logic the Renaissance has already had more than enough attention from other hands. Ludicrous as such reasoning would be in a general history of mimesis, it is not ludicrous here; for this history is clearly a roll call of Pound's antecedents (at least those whom he is willing to recognize). And this is an appropriate introduction to Canto VII, since the rest of the canto is concerned with problems which confronted Pound as a poet in contemporary England and France.

The quotation from Flaubert is more than a mere inventory of material objects. The exact spatial relations are noted, the state of decay is observed. The solidity of this seen material world is gross indeed compared with Dante's 'ciocco', but in its own way it is still reliable. The 'fauteuil de paille' may be cheap, a substitute, but there is little deception about it. One can still believe one's eyes.

The next passage brings the subject almost up to date:

> The old men's voices, beneath the columns of false marble,
> The modish and darkish walls,
> Discreeter gilding, and the panelled wood
> Suggested, for the leasehold is
> Touched with an imprecision ... about three squares;
> The house too thick, the paintings
> a shade too oiled.
> And the great domed head, *con gli occhi onesti e tardi*
> Moves before me, phantom with weighted motion,
> *Grave incessu*, drinking the tone of things,
> And the old voice lifts itself
>   weaving an endless sentence.

[1] The passage from which 'Pennons and standards' is lifted is quoted in *The Spirit of Romance*, p. 67.

The mere abundance of adjectives in this passage is significant: 'false marble', 'modish and darkish walls', 'Discreeter gilding', 'the panelled wood suggested'. It is as though the subject would evaporate if its attributes were dropped for a moment; for, indeed, these material objects (beside which the 'fauteuil de paille' is a pathetic but honest piece of *ersatz*) are curiously insubstantial. It is a world which the mind and art of Henry James were uniquely suited to depict; and James, himself a very substantial figure, becomes in this portrait a 'voice … weaving an endless sentence'.

The precise extent to which James's fiction reflects his own limitations or the limitations of his environment is an issue which might be raised at this point, though it cannot, of course, be answered with any certainty. It is certain, however, that during his later years James had a very strong claim to the title of 'greatest living English (or American) novelist'. From the standpoint of history, there were no doubt more reliable recorders and interpreters of that period and place. But the peculiar interest and talents (and defects) which directed him away from the public side of Victorian life—the analogy with Ovid is particularly clear and witty—and into the drawing-room with its domestic tyrannies, intrigues, and innuendoes, turned out after all to be his greatest artistic asset. Pound clearly suggests that James, whose 'endless' sentences mimicked no physical reality,[8] was uniquely gifted to deal with Victorian interiors where, as his heroines ruefully discovered, 'tone' was everything.

Certainly one of the main reasons for Pound's invoking James as one of his antecedents is that James was the Europeanized American artist *par excellence*. James, like Pound and Eliot later, was able to learn a good deal more from the French than were those writers who had been born into the English literary tradition. It is to himself and Eliot (and possibly a few other contemporaries), therefore, that Pound now turns; the scene is Paris:

> We also made ghostly visits, and the stair
> That knew us, found us again on the turn of it,
> Knocking at empty rooms, seeking for buried beauty;
> But the sun-tanned, gracious and well-formed fingers
> Lift no latch of bent bronze, no Empire handle

> Twists for the knocker's fall; no voice to answer.
> A strange concierge, in place of the gouty-footed.
> Sceptic against all this one seeks the living,
> Stubborn against the fact. The wilted flowers
> Brushed out a seven year since, of no effect.
> Damn the partition! Paper, dark brown and stretched,
> Flimsy and damned partition.

The first three lines of this passage are reminiscent of one of the recurring images in Eliot's poetry:

> ... returning as before
> Except for a slight sensation of being ill at ease
> I mount the stairs and turn the handle of the door
> And feel as if I had mounted on my hands and knees.
> 'And so you are going abroad, and when do you return?
> But that's a useless question.
> You hardly know when you are coming back,
> You will find so much to learn.'
> *(Portrait of a Lady)*

> Time to turn back and descend the stair,
> With a bald spot in the middle of my hair—
> *(Prufrock)*

> Stand on the highest pavement of the stair—
> Lean on a garden urn—
> Weave, weave the sunlight in your hair—
> Clasp your flowers to you with a pained surprise—
> *(La Figlia Che Piange)*

The odours, too ('The wilted flowers / Brushed out a seven year since, of no effect') are notable features of Eliot's world:

> Her hand twists a paper rose,
> That smells of eau de Cologne,
> She is alone
> With all the old nocturnal smells
> That cross and cross across her brain.
> Of sunless dry geraniums
> And dust in crevices,
> Shells of chestnuts in the streets,
> The female smells in shuttered rooms,
> The cigarettes in corridors
> And cocktail smells in bars.
> *(Rhapsody on a Windy Night)*

It may be observed that Eliot's treatment is infinitely more evocative than Pound's; and that, at least in part, would seem to be the point: Eliot, not Pound, is Henry James's heir, though 'we' (which is partly the 'you and I' of *Prufrock*, perhaps partly the 'we' of Eliot's criticism, partly Eliot and Pound) certainly joined forces in plundering French poetry and insisting on the difficult art of poetry—as James, under comparable influences, had insisted on the art of fiction. But the lingering odours and paper partitions which were the necessary stage properties of Eliot's poetic world are rejected here by Pound: 'Damn the partition! ... / Flimsy and damned partition'—it is a tone that never enters Eliot's poetry, and that never could enter it.

The fourteen lines that follow are, I find, not entirely intelligible.

> Ione, dead the long year
> My lintel, and Liu Ch'e's.
> Time blacked out with the rubber.
> The Elysée carries a name on
> And the bus behind me gives me a date for peg;
> Low ceiling and the Erard and the silver,
> These are in 'time'. Four chairs, the bow-front dresser,
> The panier of the desk, cloth top sunk in.
> 'Beer-bottle on the statue's pediment!
> 'That, Fritz, is the era, to-day against the past,
> 'Contemporary.' And the passion endures.
> Against their action, aromas. Rooms, against chronicles.
> Smaragdos, chrysolithos; De Gama wore striped pants in
> Africa
> And 'Mountains of the sea gave birth to troops';

The point of the first eleven lines appears to be that the physical scene is so cluttered with fakes of the past or with 'fashions' which have nothing to do with current artistic developments, that one loses one's sense of 'real' time. By 'real' time I do not mean Bergsonian time either. Pound is interested in the 'historical present', that is, 1920 as it appears to a genius in 1920 or as it will appear to a historian in 1980. In so far as 'today' is represented by a beer-bottle and the 'past' by a statue, then of course Pound is 'for' the past. But the irony implicit in such a simple-minded contrast—the contrast itself is a 'period' piece— should be obvious in a context which already included Flaubert, the man who compiled the *Dictionnaire des Idées Recues*. The point Pound is making, then, is that 'today' as represented by almost everything around him, is not today at all: Flaubert's *idées recues* have become embodied in stone and concrete and 'modish and darkish walls'. Hence Pound's glance at 'the bus behind me', which reminds one that, after all, one is living in the Machine Age. The opposition of 'chronicles' and the 'actions' they record to the 'rooms' with their 'aromas' was prepared for by 'the wilted flowers / Brushed out a seven year since, of no effect'. It is, in a way, Eliot's world of rooms and aromas (cf. 'Burnt Norton') against Pound's world of chronicles and actions. But if 'Smaragdos, chrysolithos; De Gama wore striped pants in Africa' were the best Pound could unearth, there would not be much value in following his explorations.

It may be wondered why I have taken so much trouble with a passage which, from the standpoind of articulation, is so manifestly defective. First, cryptic though it may be, testimony from within *The Cantos* as to what Pound is doing or trying to do is worth a good deal more than his own prose commentaries—which are apt to be misleading in any case. Second, Canto VII as a whole has some interest as a sequel to *Propertius* and *Mauberley*, and, as it was mostly written at about the same time as *Mauberley*, it can be used conveniently to settle disputes about the *intended* range of the ironies in the other, finer poem. Finally, the later and better sections of Canto VII cannot be understood properly without an understanding of the first part.

The next section picks up Flaubert and Eleanor of Aquitaine again:

> Le vieux commode en acajou:
> > beer-bottles of various strata,
> But *is* she dead as Tyro? In seven years?
> Ελέναυς, ἕλανδρος, ἑλέπτολις
> The sea runs in the beach-groove, shaking the floated
> > > > pebbles,
> Eleanor!
> > The scarlet curtain throws a less scarlet shadow;
> Lamplight at Bouvilla, e quel remir,

The first two lines may be taken as a clear qualification of 'Beer-bottle on the statue's pediment / ... today against the past': there have always been beer-bottles or their equivalents squatting on statue's pediments (this is also, incidentally, Pound's commentary on the Austro-German side of World War I, which he, like Henry James, saw as the force of barbarism). 'But is she dead as Tyro?' refers back to 'Eleanor (she spoiled in a British climate)'; and it prepares for the dancing woman who is to appear shortly. The words from *Agamemnon* (destroyer of ships, of men, and of cities) echo hollowly in this context, for Helen-Eleanor is herself destroyed, apparently 'drowned' like Tyro, but over a period of seven years (presumably by the British climate, which Pound likes to invest with deleterious potentialities). Though the 'she' is figuratively Helen-Eleanor, she is any woman who might inspire a poet's song—say the woman sung in *Mauberley*. But 'she' is dead as Tyro. And the sea which Homer listened to ('Ear, ear for the sea-surge') recalls the lively ghosts of literature—Eleanor who was sung by Bernart de Ventadorn, Atlanta whose body evoked Ovid's scarlet curtain simile, and the 'donna' whose body Arnaut Daniel wished to contemplate under the lamplight.

From this point to the end of Canto VII there are a series of 'visions', of scenes recollected from London (and possibly Paris; it doesn't matter too much, because this canto is directed against non-Mediterranean Europe in general). In these scenes a sexual impotence and morbidity is related to the general incrustation of dead ideas, 'fashions' which make a mockery of 'time', and 'beer-bottles of various strata'. Though the locust-casque imagery is taken from Remy de Gourmont,[1] and it alludes back to the elders of Troy ('rattle of old men's voices'), the spirit behind the images, and indeed the entire canto, is Flaubert.

> And all that day
> Nicea moved before me
> And the cold grey air troubled her not
> For all her naked beauty, bit not the tropic skin,
> And the long slender feet lit on the curb's marge
> And her moving height went before me,
> We alone having being.
> And all that day, another day:
> Thin husks I had known as men,

[1] Cf. 'The Prose Tradition in Verse', *Literary Essays*, p. 371.

> Dry casques of departed locusts
>> speaking a shell of speech ...
> Propped between chairs and table ...
> Words like the locust-shells, moved by no inner being;
>> A dryness calling for death;

The *Annotated Index* identifies 'Nicea' as a 'possible reference to the "Nicean barks" of Poe's poem *To Helen*', and for a number of reasons this seems to me a good guess. Poe was also a seeker after 'buried beauty', who found it occasionally in spite of a harrowing existence in an environment quite as dead to art as the one which Pound describes here. Any extended comparison between Pound and Poe would of course be fruitless, and the slight allusion does not solicit one. But it should be kept in mind that this canto is concerned above all else with Pound's fate as a poet and with his literary heritage; and so far as that heritage is American, it is phantom-ridden from Poe down to Henry James and T. S. Eliot.(9) Possibly there is some hint of Poe's personal disintegration in the 'Thin husks I had known as men'; but this is no doubt stretching things. There is no doubt, however, that that image is ominous (it recalls 'But *is* she dead as Tyro? In seven years?' From this point forward, there is an occasional appearance of images of death by drowning and death by desiccation).

> Another day, between walls of a sham Mycenian,
> 'Toc' sphinxes, sham-Memphis columns,
> And beneath the jazz a cortex, a stiffness or stillness.
>> Shell of the older house.
> Brown-yellow wood, and the no colour plaster,
> Dry professorial talk ...
>> now stilling the ill beat music,
> House expulsed by this house.

> Square even shoulders and the satin skin,
> Gone cheeks of the dancing woman,
>> Still, the old dead dry talk, gassed out—
> It is ten years gone, makes stiff about her a glass,
> A petrefaction of air.
>> The old room of the tawdry class asserts itself;
> The young men, never!
>> Only the husk of talk.

It is clear now that the 'locust-casques' have their counterpart in the 'shells' of houses as well as in the 'Words like the locust-shells'. So that the image is of a shell (of speech) within a shell (of a man) within a shell (of a house); and presumably this sequence goes on up to the national level. A quick shift of the image results in the dancing woman being imprisoned like a zoological specimen inside a 'petrefaction of air'. And when 'The old room of the tawdry class asserts itself', it is clear why Pound has been making such a fuss about the architecture: it is closing in! This undercurrent of grim Flaubertian humour runs throughout the locust-casque passages (there is perhaps a hint of James and Poe as well); for the 'room of the tawdry class' which asserts itself is also the dancing woman's coffin. And the young men who might take her away from the place will never 'assert' themselves, because they, too, are locust-casques or are separated by the 'petrefaction of air', the 'old dead dry talk, gassed out—'. (Pound's use of the dash here should make other poets think twice about using it for a dramatic pause.)

The lines which follow begin with a quotation which has become all too familiar to readers of the later cantos:

> O voi che siete in piccioletta barca,
> Dido choked up with sobs, for her Sicheus
> Lies heavy in my arms, dead weight
>   Drowning, with tears, new Eros,
>
> And the life goes on, mooning upon bare hills;
> Flame leaps from the hand, the rain is listless,
> Yet drinks the thirst from our lips,
>   solid as an echo,
> Passion to breed a form in shimmer of rain-blur;
> But Eros drowned, drowned, heavy, half dead with tears
>   For dead Sicheus.

The modulation to Virgil is by way of Dante, and the effect of Pound's quotation in this context is to suggest that, compared with Dante's, Virgil's boat is very tiny; and this is certainly quite true as far as the poetry of Love is concerned. The Sicheus-Dido-Aeneas triangle is sentimentality brought to the pitch of morbidity; and the marriage of death and passion is beautifully mirrored in the ambiguous syntax of

> Dido choked up with sobs, for her Sicheus
> Lies heavy in my arms, dead weight
>   Drowning, with tears, new Eros,

for it is not clear whether it is the dead Sicheus or the 'live' Dido
who 'lies heavy in my arms'. But there is, I think, no doubt
that this is Virgil superimposed on Dowson; and in fact the
entire passage that follows appears to be a valediction to the
late nineteenth century. As in a corresponding passage in *Mauberley*, there is a mixture of appreciation and somewhat reluctant
condemnation. The dead ideas, the dead architecture, and
finally an Eros which approaches necrophilia: the imagery of
prodigies ('Flame leaps from the hand, the rain is listless, / Yet
drinks the thirst from our lips, / solid as echo') describes with
remarkable adequacy the effect of, say, many a poem of Swinburne or Verlaine, in which the verbal music excites a thirst for
'content' which the poetry cannot provide. It is, in other words,
the apparition of poetry, one of the many apparitions in Canto
VII.

> Life to make mock of motion:
> For the husks, before me, move,
>   The words rattle: shells given out by shells
> The live man, out of lands and prisons,   *Desmond*
>   shakes the dry pods,   *Fitzgerald*
> Probes for old wills and friendships, and the big locust-
>   casques
> Bend to the tawdry table,
> Lift up their spoons to mouths, put forks in cutlets,
> And make sound like the sound of voices.
>   Lorenzaccio
> Being more live than they, more full of flames and voices.

The first three lines evoke the prose fiction contemporary
with, but more valuable than, Swinburne's and Verlaine's
poetry. Such writing, like that of Pound's master, Flaubert, is
not literature of the most endearing kind; but the fourth, fifth,
and sixth lines in this passage show the limit of Pound's disciple-
ship: Pound is a mortician only because his survival depends on
it; and though the move from a mausoleum to a museum may
not recommend itself to us, there are a few cantos which demonstrate that he knew what he was doing. And in any case, his

eventual confrontation with 'Life' was hard enough to satisfy most of us.

The closing lines of Canto VII fuse the description of Henry James with the figure of Alessandro de Medici, and conclude with an evocation of the 'Nicea' who appeared earlier. There is a good deal of humour involved, of course, in the grand vision of James as the central figure in an inexplicable Renaissance intrigue:

> And the tall indifference moves,
> > a more living shell,
> Drift in the air of fate, dry phantom, but intact.
> O Alessandro, chief and thrice warned, watcher,
> > Eternal watcher of things,
> Of things, of men, of passions,
> > Eyes floating in dry, dark air,
> E biondo, with glass-grey iris, with an even side-fall of hair
> The stiff, still features.

But in this 'double vision' Alessandro remains an impressive figure. At his best, Pound can indeed bring the past alive; in intention, anyway, his researches to not import into contemporary life the lifeless, merely decorative exoticism of 'Toc' sphinxes, sham-Mycenean walls, and sham-Memphis columns. Canto XIII, the Confucius Canto, may be taken as one of the better examples of 'probing for old wills and friendships', and there should be no doubt that it has a bearing on contemporary life.

Though the condensation of thought in Canto VII is so extreme as to constitute a serious defect of communication, I think I have shown that the difficulty does inhere in the condensation and *not* in any confusion or absence of thought. And this distinction is extremely important (though, of course, it doesn't make the poetry any easier). The obscurity in a bad poet's work involves a double betrayal: of himself and of his reader. At least up to and through the Rock-Drill Cantos, Pound rarely betrays himself, though there are many times, as here, when he places an unreasonable burden on his reader. In effect, Canto VII is written in a kind of poetic shorthand, which can be learned if the reader thinks it worth while; and this is by no means a matter of annotation alone. 'Smaragdos, chrysolithos', for example, is a snatch from Propertius; and as Propertius is known to be one of Pound's heroes, his appearance might be taken as a signal for Poundians to applaud; but (if my reading is correct) the context indicates that Pound is qualifying his praise of the past in general and of Propertius in particular. There may be high roads to *The Cantos*, such as Mr Emery's, but once there, one must build one's own roads.

Granted the seriousness of the obstacles, then, there is nevertheless much to be appreciated in this canto. The second half does, as it seems to me, rise to a vision of considerable poetic power, which it would be a pity not to have comprehended fully. In so far as it is a 'judgment' on England, it is certainly more viable than the 'Hell' Cantos, where Pound is too busy scandalizing himself to take account of human tragedy and waste. When, in Canto VII, he sees 'Thin husks I had known as men', he makes the crucial admission which makes it possible for us to accept the horror of the place and the need to escape from it. The terms of his rejection are chiefly literary— i.e.' What am I going to do?'—and therefore the rejection is not merely an outburst of Anglophobia or of phobias in general. But having said this, I must hasten to emphasize that Pound *did* regard England as dead and deadening at that time; and it is the peculiar strength of his treatment (and a proof of his literary seriousness) that he admits no separation of intellectual deadness from other forms of deadness: 'Still the old dead dry talk, gassed out— / It is ten years gone, makes stiff about her a glass, / A petrefaction of air.' It is the sort of idea which would have occurred only to a disciple of Flaubert, and the sort of image which would have occurred only to Pound. No doubt as a total portrait of England A.D. 1920, Canto VII 'shoots past the mark'; but the judgment Pound delivers here is not outside a poet's prerogative: it is indeed a duty to himself and his art that he should make a judgment and act accordingly. It was, after all (after *Propertius* and *Mauberley*), time to leave England —and good riddance!

NOTES TO CHAPTER I

(1) Of course this is not the exact effect which it has in the *Analects*, from which (as the *Annotated Index* informs us) Pound has selected most of the materials comprising Canto XIII. I have been unable to account for everything in Canto XIII,

but a somewhat more complete list of the passages pastiched than that given in the *Annotated Index* is as follows. Lines 1–6: Pound's own invention. Lines 7–30: a mixture of *Analects* IX, 2 and XI, 25. Lines 31–7: a paraphrase of *Analects* XIV, 46, which Pound has altered (apparently) so as to have Confucius denounce a quietist. Lines 38–42: *Analects* IX, 22. Lines 43–4: apparently a précis of XX, 12, 13, and 14 of *The Unwobbling Pivot* (*The Doctrine of the Mean* or *Chung Yung*). Lines 45–51: apparently a précis of Chapters VIII and IX of *The Great Digest* (*The Great Learning* or *Ta Hio*: chapter numbering according to Pound's arrangement in *Confucius; The Great Digest & The Unwobbling Pivot*, translation and commentary by Ezra Pound, London, 1952). Lines 52–8: a compound of characteristic Confucianisms, which probably cannot be assigned to any specific passage. Lines 59–62: *Analects* XIII, 18. Lines 63–6: *Analects* V, 1. Lines 67–75: though it is quite Confucian, this passage contains a good deal which I have been unable to trace; however, lines 69–72 are taken from *Analects* XV, 25. The *Annotated Index* assigns the passage to *Analects* XVI, 13; but, if this assignment is correct, Pound has departed so far from the original as to make any comparison pointless. The last three lines seem to be Pound's own invention.

The method of pastiching here is roughly the same as that used in *Homage to Sextus Propertius*: i.e. Pound's fidelity to the original is reflected, not in an exact translation, but in a rearrangement which argues that the author's character and spirit so penetrate each part of his work that Pound can create a new whole without violating the essential integrity of the original. Of course, some authors cannot be treated this way, but in the case of a certain kind of author (the aphoristic or epigrammatic particularly) Pound's method certainly works. It had better be added, however, that the introductory and concluding lines of Canto XIII are a hang-over from *Cathay*, and their faint odour of *Chinoiserie* is not entirely fortunate.

(2) Ezra Pound, *Letters 1907–1941* (London, 1951), p. 262. Letter to Wyndham Lewis, December 3rd, 1924: 'You will readily see that the "hell" is a portrait of contemporary England, or at least Eng. as she wuz when I left her.' But the text does not bear this out. Certainly some of the imagery is identified as English: 'greasy as sky over Westminster', for example; and no doubt Pound's Anglophobia was a major source of inspiration. But why 'many English' if the subject is in fact 'contemporary England'? Who else? The fact is that Pound was trying to persuade Lewis to leave England (cf. *Letters*, p. 242), on grounds very much like those advanced in Canto VII.

(3) Perhaps Pound's use of 'tragedy' is more exact than mine. The stage directions ('and here the placard ΕΙΚΩΝ ΤΗΣ and here: THE PERSONNEL CHANGES') possibly suggest that the 'Hell' ought to be visualized as a sort of low burlesque acted on a stage; and it cannot be, therefore, a 'tragedy'. But this possibility does not make Pound's conception of 'Hell' and its inhabitants any less trivial.

(4) There is nothing to substantiate this reading except (1) Pound's hatred of Milton, (2) his valuable but limited notion that 'The best criticism of any work, to my mind the only criticism of any work of art that is of any permanent or even moderately durable value, comes from the creative writer or artist who does the next job ... Laforgue's Salome is the real criticism of Salammbo: Joyce and perhaps Henry James are critics of Flaubert' ('Ulysses', *The Literary Essays of Ezra Pound*, edited and introduced by T. S. Eliot (London, 1954), p. 406). The absence of Milton from Pound's 'Hell', is in itself surprising, since Milton is his chief literary bogey; and I am inclined to think, therefore, that some of the incidental and irrelevant violence and obscenity is directed at Pound's great English 'precursor' in these regions.

(5) In 'How to Read' (*Literary Essays*, p. 23), Pound defines great literature as

'simply language charged with meaning to the utmost possible degree', and of course it is poetry which can be most highly charged. But it seems clear that a definition so narrow leads inevitably to cryptogram.

(6) By 'trobar clus' I mean the Provençal poetry which is intentionally obscure, accessible only to initiates. The 'trobar clus' tradition was carried on by the *Stil Nuovists*, and it was often a poetry of cryptogram. I think that Pound becomes a practitioner of the *trobar clus* in the Rock-Drill Cantos, but not before. Up to and including the Pisan Cantos, he is definitely trying to establish communication with a general reader (though on his own terms, which are frequently too demanding); but in the Rock-Drill sequence he often deals with an esoteric subject matter in a manner which suggests quite clearly that only a select few are expected to understand. Yet one can penetrate the Rock-Drill sequence, and it is sometimes (in Cantos 90 and 91) worth the trouble.

(7) The word comes from *Paradiso* XVIII, 100–2:

> Poi come nel percuoter de' ciocci arsi
> surgono innumerabili faville,
> onde li stolti sogliono augurarsi:

'Then as when burning logs are struck rise innumerable sparks, from which the foolish are accustomed to make auguries': translation and text from *The Divine Comedy of Dante Alighieri*, with translation and commentary by J. D. Sinclair, vol. 3 (revised edition, London, 1948), pp. 260–1. Though the whole of Dante's poem is characterized by an unparalleled power of visualization, it is worth noting that *Paradiso* XVIII is somewhat remarkable for the emphasis put on the act of seeing and deciphering what is seen. Dante's 'ciocco' has already appeared in Canto V, p. 21: 'Sparks like a partridge covey, / Like the "ciocco", brand struck in the game.'

(8) Ernest Fenollosa's *The Chinese Written Character as a Medium for Poetry* (*Instigations*, New York, 1920), which Pound edited and polished, makes a great point of syntax mimicking the transfer of energy that occurs in the observable world. The transfers of energy in James's world have none of the 'man-bites-dog' simplicity which (on the surface, anyway) characterized the sunny, muscular side of Victorianism. At least one of the reasons for describing James and 'his' Victorian world as phantasmal is that James was a master of the ghost story, which he used to explore traumas that he might not have been able to confront otherwise.

(9) The notable exception is, of course, Whitman, whose influence in *The Cantos* is in one sense pervasive, in another sense negligible. Certain aspects of Whitman's personality seem to have affected Pound's (both tend to be exhibitionists), and there is, of course, a somewhat misleading technical debt—misleading in that Pound's versification at its best is immensely superior to Whitman's. Among nineteenth-century American poets, however, Whitman must certainly be regarded as the closest thing to a Poundian ancestor. R. H. Pearce's view that *The Cantos* is a descendant of Whitman's *Song of Myself* is stated persuasively in *The Continuity of American Poetry* (Princeton, 1961), pp. 59-101. But ideological similarities must be treated with caution: Pound's ideas and Thoreau's (in *Walden*) are yet more strikingly alike.

II

FERTILITY RITUAL IN
THE CANTOS

1. From 'Dead Concepts' to 'Blood Rite'

THE INTRODUCTORY LINES of Canto VIII, first of the Malatesta Cantos, confirm one's suspicion that Canto VII is a sort of
Poundian 'Waste Land'.[1]

> These fragments you have shelved (shored).
> 'Slut!' 'Bitch!' Truth and Calliope
> Slanging each other sous les lauriers:

The first line is of course a parody of Eliot's 'These fragments
I have shored against my ruins'; and the general sense of the
passage appears to be that Eliot's poetic method in *The Waste
Land*, far from making the useful part of the past more available,
rather 'shelves' it again. Pound, on the other hand, will 'un-
shelve' the useful part of the past, as he does in the Malatesta
Cantos. It is this, clearly, that he has in mind when he speaks in
Canto VII of 'prob[ing] for old wills and friendships'.

This ambitious objective, and the methods which Pound
develops to achieve it, raise issues that cannot be dealt with
fully at the moment; in particular, a discussion of his use of
'documents' must be reserved until the second section of this
study. In the present chapter I shall generally limit my discussion of Pound's method to what I call, for lack of a better
term, re-creation by 'Blood Rite'.

Although Canto XXV is not a particularly distinguished
canto, it is in many respects a truer sequel to Canto VII than

[1] However, Canto VII was written before *The Waste Land*; Canto VIII was
written several years later.

31

is Canto VIII. Like the Malatesta sequence, Canto XXV is a 'documentary', but it also develops characteristic imagery from Canto VII; and this development is in terms which lead to the fertility rituals celebrated in Cantos XLVII and XXXIX. With the 'documentary' aspect I shall deal summarily: the canto begins and ends with paraphrases of several Venetian state documents, ranging in date from 1255 to 1537, which at first reveal a wide-eyed provinciality and finally a cynical cosmopolitanism. They are offered as a sort of compact history of the sensibility of Venetian officialdom; and, indeed, the earlier documents are rather interesting as evidence of a vigorous, if comical, empiricism in what was elsewhere the great age of Vision and Authority; but the later documents amount to hardly more than an *ad hominem* argument against Titian's painting. Still, there are less interesting examples of 'documentary' cantos, and even the inventories of building materials have a point: for Venice is the 'stone place' of XVII, related clearly to the 'phantom of Rome' of Canto VII (and other cantos) and to the even more phantasmal London-Paris of Canto VII.

> vadit pars, two gross lire
> stone stair, 1415, for pulchritude of the palace
> 254 da parte
> de non 23
> 4 non sincere

> Which is to say: they built out over the arches
> and the palace hangs there in the dawn, the mist,
> in that dimness,
> or as one rows in from past the murazzi
> the barge slow after moon-rise
> and the voice sounding under the sail.
> Mist gone.

This passage, roughly in the middle of the canto, introduces a lengthy digression from Venetian artifice, which, at this point in history, is growing more fantastic and unreal. The building of a utilitarian object like a stone stair for the sake of 'pulchritude' may recall the 'Toc' sphinxes and 'sham Mycenian' walls of Canto VII. In any case, the same principle is at work here where, as it were, functionless substantiality evaporates of its own pointless density. (This is perhaps putting it too strongly: Pound cannot help admiring Venice, where the phantasmal effect is an achievement, not a defect, of art; nevertheless, Venice and Rome and London-Paris each grow less real as they grow more material.) However, Pound's shift here is not, as might be expected, to London-Paris or to the 'phantom of Rome', but to a scene (purely his own creation) contemporary with Ovid's Rome. In this scene the love poetess Sulpicia is introduced, and it is well to recall that she is linked historically with the 'provincial' Tibullus rather than with Propertius and Ovid. Much as Pound may admire their urbanity, the latter are in fact too urbane for his present purposes.

> And Sulpicia
> green shoot now, and the wood
> white under new cortex
> 'as the sculptor sees the form in the air
> before he sets hand to mallet,
> 'and as he sees the in, and the through,
> the four sides
> 'not the one face to the painter
> 'As ivory uncorrupted:
> 'Pone metum Cerinthe'
> Lay there, the long soft grass,
> and the flute lay there by her thigh,
> Sulpicia, the fauns, twig-strong,
> gathered about her;
> The fluid, over the grass
> Zephyrus, passing through her,
> 'deus nec laedit amantes.'

The tactile imagery with which Pound describes Sulpicia ('Zephyrus, passing through her') is itself an illustration of the sculptural imagination he favours[1]—as opposed, for instance, to the Horatian analogy of painting and poetry. His imagination transforms her into a Latin demi-goddess of fertility reassuring her lover Cerinthus that God protects lovers. The transformation is easy and natural in Pound's scheme of things; for in *The Cantos* (as will soon be evident) the female does manifest and experience the divine through the sexual act: the idea is as

[1] Cf. Donald Davie, 'Adrian Stokes and Pound's "Cantos" ', *The Twentieth Century* (November 1956), pp. 419–36.

old as can be, of course—but then Pound is in many ways the most old-fashioned of important twentieth-century poets.

The shift to the 'phantom of Rome' does eventually come; and here, as in London-Paris, the stone imprisons rather than adorns:

> And from the stone pits, the heavy voices,
> Heavy sound:
>   'Sero, sero ...
> 'Nothing we made, we set nothing in order,
> 'Neither house nor the carving,
> 'And what we thought had been thought for too long,
> 'Our opinion not opinion in evil
> 'But opinion borne for too long.
> 'We have gathered a sieve full of water.'
> And from the comb of reeds, came notes and the chorus
> Moving, the young fauns: Pone metum,
> Metum, nec deus laedit.
>
> And as after the form, the shadow,
> Noble forms, lacking life, that bolge, that valley
> the dead words keeping form,
> and the cry: Civis Romanus.
> The clear air, dark, dark,
> The dead concepts, never the solid, the blood rite,
> The vanity of Ferrara;

Here are the equivalents of the locust casques of Canto VII, and here are the equivalents of:

> ... the old dead dry talk, gassed out—
> It is ten years gone, makes stiff about her a glass,
> a petrefaction of air.

The talk which imprisons the dancing woman as though she were a zoological specimen may be contrasted with 'The fluid, over the grass / Zephyrus, passing through her'. The image records a sensation rather than an observable effect, and it will not bear a great load of interpretation. Yet the implicit contrast with the dancing woman of Canto VII is worth insisting on even at the risk of making the Sulpicia image seem preposterous: Sulpicia is so receptive that there could be no question of young men having to 'assert' themselves ('The old room of the tawdry class asserts itself; / The young men, never!'); Sulpicia belongs to the Mediterranean world which Pound most admires, where a favourable climate (so Pound's thinking tends to run) makes one generally more receptive to influences of all kinds.

Mere passive receptivity is not, of course, enough; but with the 'dry pods' even this much is out of the question. For any kind of renewal, which is to say continuance, of life—in nature, art, social institutions—there must be a giving as well as a receiving: there must be 'the solid, the blood rite'. The most obvious and perhaps most important application of this barbarous image is to Pound's acts of imaginative translation, as expounded and practised most notably in Canto I. But the 'blood rite' of Odysseus in Hades, which Pound uses as a metaphor for translation, belongs also to fertility ritual; and fertility ritual, especially as it celebrates the story of Adonis, takes us well inside the realm of Eros.

2. *'Blood Rite': Canto I*

And then went down to the ship,
Set keel to breakers, forth on the godly sea, and
We set up mast and sail on that swart ship,
Bore sheep aboard her, and our bodies also
Heavy with weeping, so winds from sternward
Bore us out onward with bellying canvas,
Circe's this craft, the trim-coifed goddess.

In Canto XXV, then, Pound calls for 'the solid, the blood rite'; and he can justly expect his reader to recall Canto I, where the story of Odysseus' descent into Hades has been translated into the measures Pound had adapted for his early translation of the Anglo-Saxon *Seafarer*. That Pound's translation is made from a Renaissance Latin translation of the Greek—Latin being a 'dead' language, yet in the Renaissance very much a living literary language—offers a precedent for his translation into a measure modelled on the 'dead' Anglo-Saxon.

Of course, Pound is by no means the first English poet to adapt the matter and manner of 'primitive' northern European literatures, he is rather part of a tradition which goes back to the eighteenth century—a tradition including Gray, Scott, Coleridge, and Morris, which sought (often successfully) to extend the technical and emotional range of English poetry. There is not much point in calling this a 'native tradition' or in

saying that it is 'opposed' to the poetry of, say, Milton or Pope
—or the courtly Chaucer (the *Gawain* poet, for instance, is as
much at home in a courtly context as in a menacing wilderness);
yet it is different, and its virtues are not usually the virtues of the
Romance (and Latin) literatures which have so influenced our
central poetic tradition.

When Pound reaches back to the Anglo-Saxon, he is, then,
working within an established tradition (which had, admittedly, grown rather pale by the end of the nineteenth century).
This tradition was from time to time involved with strains of
self-conscious literary primitivism. And, whatever Pound's
criticism may suggest to the contrary, there is likewise a large
element of primitivism in *The Cantos*. This, in itself, is neither
good nor bad. (Or if 'primitivism' is by definition pejorative,
another term must be applied to *The Ancient Mariner* or the
best of Scott's ballad imitations or, different as they are, certain
of Pound's cantos.) When Pound translates Andreas Divus's
Latin translation of Homer into a measure based on the Anglo-
Saxon, he is, as it were, reversing the historical process by which
Renaissance Latinism spilled over into a vernacular literature
whose Anglo-Saxon elements of style and subject had long
since been dismissed as barbaric: but so, by courtly or Renaissance standards, is Homer barbaric.

Barbaric indeed is the 'blood rite' by which Odysseus gains
knowledge from Tiresias:

> And Anticlea came, whom I beat off, and then Tiresias
> Theban,
> Holding his golden wand, knew me, and spoke first:
> 'A second time? why? man of ill star,
> 'Facing the sunless dead and this joyless region?
> 'Stand from the fosse, leave me my bloody bever
> 'For soothsay.'

Homer's conception of the 'Life after death' (about which Confucius said nothing—Canto XIII) is generally conceded to be
primitive, much more so than Virgil's where the idea of reward
and punishment is well developed. But as we have seen in connection with the 'Hell Cantos', Pound is quite incapable of
the kind of thinking and feeling that goes with a sophisticated
religious vision: his attempt to use the convention of Hell only

results in a conceptual, hence moral and poetic, muddle. Homer's conception of Hades is, however, more amenable; and the very fact that it is not so well mapped out makes it possible for Pound, in Canto XLVII, to associate Odysseus' voyage to Hades with the rape of Proserpina. How important that association is, of Eros and Knowledge, I have already noted.

3. Sailing after Knowledge

If there can be such a thing as an 'answer' to *The Waste Land*, Canto XLVII is that answer. Eliot's Tiresias, as the epigraph from Petronius strongly suggests, would like to die; he is, it is intimated, the symbol of a worn-out cultural heritage which is cursed to linger on after its vitality has been spent. The erotic basis of Western ritual and spiritual knowledge has, in the central figure of Tiresias, been reduced to a mechanism: he 'throbs' like a bruised member, like an internal combustion engine, 'like' a body engaged in sexual intercourse. The knowledge which Eliot's Tiresias—the former seer, 'the mind of Europe'—can give us, is an eerie blend of voyeuristic revelation and glamorous, superficially plausible, yet wildly unjust literary 'parallels' from the past. For Eliot's Tiresias, the past exists to spice up the present and to provide a self-justifying illusion of satiric commentary: as in the boudoir scene from 'A Game of Chess'.

I do not claim that the whole of *The Waste Land* can be explained in the terms which I suggest above, and indeed I do not believe that any coherent account of that poem has been or can be given. Neither, for that matter, would Ezra Pound— sometime editor of *The Waste Land*—agree with each of the points that I make above (at least, I feel sure, he would not have in 1922 when his editing of the poem was just completed). But, from one point of view, Canto XLVII can be read as a partial repudiation of *The Waste Land*—partial in that, as we have seen in Canto VII, Pound agrees with Eliot that the contemporary scene is desolate. But Pound's Tiresias is robust, Homeric:

> Who even dead, yet hath his mind entire!
> This sound came in the dark
> First must thou go the road
> > to hell

> And to the bower of Ceres' daughter Proserpine,
> Through overhanging dark, to see Tiresias,
> Eyeless that was, a shade, that is in hell
> So full of knowing that the beefy men know less than he,
> Ere thou come to thy road's end.

There is nothing dead about *this* past, however dead the present may be. And, of course, the past can only be brought back to life if one admits its pastness; if the past is to be anything more than a covey of obscene ghosts haunting the present, like Eliot's Tiresias and Eliot's Cleopatra, one must 'go the road to hell' and hold discourse with a Tiresias who is something more than an 'Old man with wrinkled female breasts'. One must, in other words, make that act of communion with the past which brings both past and present back to life.

The sound that 'came in the dark' in the passage quoted above is, of course, the instruction that Circe gives Odysseus while they are in bed, and it seems most likely that the sexual act and Odysseus' voyage to hell after knowledge are the same thing, or at any rate not to be confidently differentiated.

> Knowledge the shade of a shade,
> Yet must thou sail after knowledge
> Knowing less than drugged beasts. *phtheggometha*
> *thasson*

Before he can return and restore his lands to order, Odysseus, like the vegetation god, must descend after knowledge that is 'the shade of a shade'. Odysseus, the most intellectually capable of men, must join all men in raising his voice (*phtheggometha thasson*) to the creature who is 'either a goddess or a woman' (Canto XXXIX). She changes men to 'drugged beasts': very well, that is the metamorphosis which gives one access to the most vital knowledge, common to all men, nutriment to each according to his individual nature and abilities.(1)

Pound shifts then to the fertility rites of Tamuz (Adonis), and quotes from Bion's 'Lament for Adonis', in which Aphrodite is called Diona after the name of her mother (Diona was wife to Zeus and, in fact, his feminine counterpart; therefore Aphrodite, when invoked as Diona, as she is in the *Pervigilium Veneris*, represents much more powerful forces than one normally attributes to her).

The small lamps drift in the bay
And the sea's claw gathers them.
Neptunus drinks after neap-tide.
Tamuz! Tamuz!!
The red flame going seaward.
  By this gate art thou measured.
From the long boats they have set lights in the water,
The sea's claw gathers them outward.
Scilla's dogs snarl at the cliff's base,
The white teeth gnaw in under the crag,
But in the pale night the small lamps float seaward
        τυ Διώνα
        TU DIONA

και Μοῖρα τ' Ἄδονιν
KAI MOIRA T' ADONIN
The sea is streaked red with Adonis,
The lights flicker red in small jars.
Wheat shoots rise new by the altar,
  flower from the swift seed.

Here 'Scilla's dogs' signify the purely destructive element in nature threatening the perilous offerings of mankind, but 'the sea's claw gathers them outward', surely, to the gods. The fates preside over this world (KAI MOIRA T' ADONIN) but apparently offerings made with good-will are answered: 'Wheat shoots rise new by the altar / flower from the swift seed' in the Garden of Adonis. The precise meaning of 'By this gate art thou measured' does not become clear until later, but in the present context 'this gate' refers, apparently, to a river mouth. As such it may have a secondary commercial significance; and it certainly signifies the purification of the river, any part of which, like any member of the human race, has a limited term.

The theme of the 'goddess or woman' and her 'drugged beasts' is developed in new terms:

Two span, two span to a woman,
Beyond that she believes not. Nothing is of any importance.
To that is she bent, her intention,
Whether by night the owl-call, whether by sap in shoot,
Never idle, by no means by no wiles intermittent
Moth is called over mountain
The bull runs blind on the sword, *naturans*
To the cave art thou called, Odysseus,

By Molü hast thou respite for a little,
By Molü art thou freed from the one bed
    that thou may'st return to another
The stars are not in her counting,
    To her they are but wandering holes.

Surely such verse speaks incomparably well for itself. Most
people would agree that female subjectivity is not so extreme as
Pound asserts in the last two lines; but this is a poetry of first
principles. It is a world in which the masculine principle is
heroic, brutal even, but not necessarily dominant:

Moth is called over mountain
The bull runs blind on the sword, *naturans*

Those who claim that logical and grammatical connections are
a *sine qua non* of poetry must deny what seems to me the absolute
rightness and adequacy of these two lines. But all of the lines in
this canto have the absolute rightness and adequacy of great
poetry.

    In the next block of verse Pound introduces Hesiod and the
Beowulf, but annotation of this sort is strictly additional information.

Begin thy plowing
When the Pleiades go down to their rest,
Begin thy plowing
40 days are they under seabord,
Thus do in fields by seabord
And in valleys winding down towards the sea.
When the cranes fly high
    think of plowing.
By this gate art thou measured
Thy day is between a door and a door
Two oxen are yoked for plowing
Or six in the hill field
White bulk under olives, a score for drawing down stone,
Here the mules are gabled with slate on the hill road.
Thus was it in time.

And the values expressed in these lines are very much 'in time',
i.e. permanent, though of course the poetry lacks the bustling
modernity of the earlier cantos. The important point here, I
think, is the juxtaposition of the image of man's life ('Thy day

is between a door and a door') with the instructions for the proper use of oxen; and the moral of this juxtaposition is, certainly, that just as one uses oxen according to a careful estimate of their capacities relative to the task at hand, so does one gauge the treatment of human beings according to one's knowledge of their life span—which is, as the Anglo-Saxons told better than any, painfully short. There is, of course, no question of Christian after-life here, just as there is no question of Christian morality in the rest of this canto. In its concern with fitness, ritual and, above all, harmony between man and his environment, this canto is surely one of the fruits of Pound's Confucianism—though, of course, it is deeply Western in its imagery and feeling.

Before going on, however, I think it is worth insisting on the centrality of a canto in which Pound says 'Thus was it in time'. It is, indeed, a variation of 'Once upon a time', and it may be said that the world Pound reconstructs in this canto is nearly as remote as Faery Land. Of course, 'Once upon a time' is simply a convention which allows us to step outside time into a world from which natural law is conveniently excluded, and one may agree that the mind is such a place, since, in one sense, time past and present (and perhaps time future) are simultaneously present. But that is an Eliotic, not a Poundian, approach to reality. For Pound things do definitely exist in a temporal order (Pound frequently gives dates, chronology does not matter in Eliot's world); it is the mind that moves up and down history in *The Cantos*: the events have an existence outside the mind. The freedom Pound takes, chiefly in Cantos I–XLI, is simply to range up and down history, unrestricted by the sequence in time and place which is history. This freedom confers great advantage, of course, but disengagement from a temporal order, though it may suit the poet-scholar and the muckraker, is an approach to reality that fails finally to deal with Pound's deepest convictions and sympathies. One may grant that this disengagement is necessary to Pound's project during its early stages, but there is surely a note of deep satisfaction, perhaps even of relief, when in Canto XLVII he says: 'Thus was it in time'. At last, though temporarily, he has reached a resting point in time (though it is before history) a world in which time matters as much as it matters to Pound. In such a world one may discover values which endure simply because they are based on a recognition of temporal limits and, therefore, the need to renew from season to season.

The contrast between the moth and the bull is developed in a new way now, chiefly in terms of quarrying imagery:

> And the small stars now fall from the olive branch,
> Forked shadow falls dark on the terrace
> More black than the floating martin
>   that has no care for your presence,
> His wing-print is black on the roof tiles
> And the print is gone with his cry.
> So light is thy weight on Tellus
> Thy notch no deeper indented
> Thy weight less than the shadow
> Yet hast thou gnawed through the mountain,
>   Scilla's white teeth less sharp.
> Hast thou found a nest softer than cunnus
> Or hast thou found better rest
> Hast'ou a deeper planting, doth thy death year
> Bring swifter shoot?
> Hast thou entered more deeply the mountain?

Exegesis here is, I take it, irrelevant. Donald Davie has already explored the connections between the imagery of this passage and the sculptural imagery which occurs so frequently in *The Cantos*.[1] One thing I can add to his discussion: in the essentially pre-Christian context of this canto, it is clear that a masculine principle (the sculptor, the ploughman) works *with* a feminine principle (the mountain, Tellus). It is only partially true, therefore, that the feminine principle is passive and the masculine principle active. In the first of the Pisan Cantos Pound comments somewhat cryptically on this relationship:

> that the drama is wholly subjective
> stone knowing the form which the carver imparts it
> the stone knows the form
> sia Cythera, sia Ixotta, sia in Santa Maria dei Miracoli
>   where Pietro Romano has fashioned the bases
>   (Canto LXXIV, p. 457)

[1] Donald Davie, 'Adrian Stokes and Pound's "Cantos" ', *The Twentieth Century* (November 1956), pp. 419–36.

There is, apparently, a mystical identity between the stone, the goddess of Eros, Sigusmondo Malatesta's mistress, and the Mother of Christ: the sculptor transfers his love from the goddess, the woman, or the saint *to* the stone, which, because of the identity shared through the feminine principle, 'knows the form' which the lover-sculptor wishes to impart. The stone co-operates, as the woman co-operates in the sexual act. It is true and it is not true, therefore, that the female is passive and the male active. In fact, the attitude Pound takes toward the female part of the world is that she yearns for the form which the male alone can give her.

The important thing to note here is that this view of the relationship between male and female is very far from original or eccentric. (It is perhaps eccentric in the twentieth century.) It is a view that antedates Christianity by many centuries. By what I assume is a coincidence, M. C. D'Arcy, in his monumental study of *The Mind and Heart of Love,* uses an almost identical sculptural analogy in describing a pre-Christian kind of love which, though inferior to Christian *Agape,* is not as entirely selfish and egocentric as the *Eros* of Plato or the mystery cults. Fr D'Arcy discovers a clear formulation of the principle in Aristotle:

… His predecessors had been puzzled by the apparent contradiction that if a thing changes it must both be and not be at the same time. What is not turns into what is, and what is ceases to be and is not. The earliest thinkers, like Heraclitus, had tried their hand at an answer, an answer which is both scientific and poetical; they had used striking images, such as hate and love, which have more than archaic value, and they played with a theory of numbers. But Aristotle tackled the problem seriously, and he used for its solution two principles which, whatever we may think of them in the precise formulation Aristotle gives to them, have proved indispensable in any philosophic explanation of nature. I will call them the determinant and the determinable. It was Aristotle's conviction that both of these must be present in any object which can suffer change … a piece of marble is in the rough; it is taken hold of by a sculptor and given a form of a man. Unless the marble in some mysterious way was of a material which could be so shaped, the change would be impossible, and that means that there was more in the marble than we imagined, though before the work of the sculptor upon it, it was actually nothing more than a lump of marble. This seems to force us to admit that there is something really there, which is not nothing and not actual. This is what Aristotle called the determinable, something which is not actual, but which can be actualized.[1]

D'Arcy admits that this is essentially a metaphysical distinction, and that Aristotle might resent its application to the terms of Eros and Agape; but the application is, as he says, illuminating.

Aristotle's aim is wholly other from that which Freud, for example, had in mind when writing of the life and death instinct. Nevertheless, the image of matter as a female desiring the male and the great discovery that there is an element of non-being in every finite reality, are suggestive and helpful.

The determinable and the determinant, the matter and the form make up every living being. The one gives notice of death to come, the other sticks to itself and keeps chaos at bay, and neither can be without the other. Life therefore is an affair of two principles and by their marriage it persists. Let us go further and say that in the receptivity and going out of itself of one, and the embrace and possession by the other, the mingling of these two together has its analogies with breeding in nature and marriage among human kind. The duality which is fundamental to nature expresses itself, when nature has separated itself off into two distinct beings within a species, into a determinant and a determinable, a masculine and a feminine. These latter are the separate types of what is in a lower and more fundamental level of nature a rhythm and duality present together as positive and negative, form and matter. It does not matter at all whether, in fact, in certain species the feminine is the dominant and the masculine the patient, so long as the two are there. The point is that, however assigned, these roles are necessary and universal; they are always present and it is by their marriage that life proceeds, dies and comes to be.[2]

This, it seems to me, is an excellent philosophical gloss for Canto XLVII,(2) though I must hasten to add that Fr D'Arcy would certainly regard this picture as sadly incomplete. In his view, of course, Christian Agape reforms and completes this pre-Christian picture, and the mystical union which Pound goes on to celebrate is a union which leads finally—however much Pound

---

[1] M. C. D'Arcy, s.j., *The Mind and Heart of Love* (London, 1945—second edition, 1954), pp. 185–6.
[2] D'Arcy, pp. 188–9.

himself loves life—to the dark passion of romantic love, which is the love of death. But these are matters which I am certainly not qualified to discuss: suffice it to say that, in Canto XLVII, Pound has done an astonishing job of reconstructing an enlightened pre-Christian view of sexual experience. Or, if you like, it is a form of Poundian 'translation'. The Christian is, of course, bound to regard it as, at best, a feat of regression.

Pound moves from the quarrying and planting imagery to the mystic illumination proper (the description is obviously related to the initiation ritual of the Eleusinian mysteries):

> The light has entered the cave. Io! Io!
> The light has gone down into the cave,
> Splendour on splendour!
> By prong have I entered these hills:
> That the grass grow from my body,
> That I hear the roots speaking together,
> The air is new on my leaf,
> The forked boughs shake with the wind.
> Is Zephyrus more light on the bough, Apeliota
> More light on the almond branch?
> By this door have I entered the hill.

This perhaps owes something to Whitman, but Whitman could never have written it so well. Pound then begins a short but beautiful recapitulation of the themes which he has explored:

> Falleth,
> Adonis falleth.
> Fruit cometh after. The small lights drift out with the tide,
> sea's claw has gathered them outward,
> Four banners to every flower
> The sea's claw draws the lamps outward.
> Think thus of thy plowing
> When the seven stars go down to their rest
> Forty days for their rest, by seabord
> And in valleys that wind down toward the sea
> κ αι Μοῖρα τ' "Αδονιν
> KAI MOIRA T' ADONIN

A burst of new imagery occurs, and then the canto closes solemnly with lines which remind one that Circe, too, had 'the power over wild beasts':

When the almond bough puts forth its flame,
When the new shoots are brought to the altar,

τυ Διῳνα, και Μοιρα

TU DIONA KAI MOIRA

και Μοῖρα τ' ᾿Αδονιν

KAI MOIRA T' ADONIN

that hath the gift of healing,
that hath the power over wild beasts.

NOTES TO CHAPTER II

(1) In a quite early essay, 'Psychology and Troubadours', *The Quest*, vol. IV, no. 1 (October 1912), pp. 46–7, Pound has this to say about the relationship between Eros and Knowledge, between the flame and the light: 'Sex, that is to say, of a double function and purpose, reproductive and educational, or, as we see in the realm of fluid force, one sort of vibration produces at different intensities heat and light. No scientist would be so stupid as to affirm that heat produced light, and it is into a similar sort of false ratiocination that those writers fall who find the source of illumination, or of religious experience, centered solely in the philo-progenitive instinct.'

(2) Cf. 'Psychology and Troubadours', *The Quest*, p. 45: 'At any rate, when we do get into contemplation of the flowing [in the vital universe, as opposed to mere society] we find sex, or some correspondence to it, "positive and negative", "north and south", "sun and moon", or whatever terms of whatever cult or science you prefer to substitute.'

III

TROUBADOUR BIOGRAPHY
AND MYTH

1. Testimony: Canto II

THE FULL SIGNIFICANCE of Canto XLVII cannot be appreciated unless it is read in conjunction with those other great cantos
of the 'Fifth Decad', numbers XLV and XLIX. However, considered in the light of the cantos which we have so far examined,
Canto XLVII has an obvious importance for the poem as a
whole: it celebrates, in particular, a lively and unself-conscious
sexuality which is in sharp contrast to the deadly frustration
depicted in Canto VII; it celebrates, in general, a natural order
and harmony related to that which was recommended for
human society in the Confucian canto, number XIII; and it
re-creates a living and life-giving image of the past, just as, by
implication, Pound promised to do in Canto I. At least in the
case of Canto XLVII, then, Pound succeeds in providing the
'nutrition of impulse'[1] which the societies of Cantos VII and
XXV so badly needed, and in making good the implied boast at
the beginning of Canto VIII that he would 'unshelve' the past.

It is true of Canto XLVII, as of the cantos which I shall
discuss in this and the following chapter, that 'nutrition of
impulse' consists largely in restoring an active awareness of the
mystery and sacredness of procreation and the sexual relationship. So far as direct social relevance is concerned, it had better
be noted in advance that Pound seems to have very little of,
say, D. H. Lawrence's interest in, or understanding of, the
moral and emotional complexity of contemporary sexual

---

[1] 'How to Read', *Literary Essays*, p. 20.

relationships. Pound's diagnosis of sexual ills—which for him, as for Lawrence, are inseparable from spiritual ills—is not subtle, though it is incisive:

> sadic mothers driving their daughters to bed with
>   decrepitude
> sows eating their litters,

Therefore, any curative value which Pound's treatment of sexual themes might have will be more indirect still than the indirect value which, it may be, *Women in Love* has for contemporary society. What should be looked for in the cantos about to be discussed is testimony as to the sacred and, when it is thwarted, often violent character of the sexual instinct. Perhaps the only moral attitude which Pound can be said to endorse clearly is that sexual love, being a mystery, must not be prostituted for the sake of social convenience.

Canto II, which consists largely of an extended paraphrase from Ovid's *Metamorphoses*, is generally conceded to be an unusually important and beautiful canto. And since it has been commented on frequently and well, I shall limit my remarks to an aspect of the canto which has an important bearing on my discussion of other parts of the poem. In the first place, one should note that Pound provides here a working demonstration of the attitude towards nature, and the way of seeing it, which he favours:

> So-shu churned in the sea, So-shu also,
>   using the long moon for a churn-stick ...
> Lithe turning of water,
>   sinews of Poseidon,
> Black azure and hyaline,
>   glass wave over Tyro,
>
>   (p. 13)

These are examples, one from China and the other from the Mediterranean, of the mythopoetic imagination at work, seeing in the moon a churn-stick for the gods or in a twisting wave the live sinews of a god. The passage is also an example of Pound's eclecticism at its best; for what interests him here is that this valuable way of viewing natural objects and activities is shared by oriental and occidental civilizations. Of such eclecticism there are many examples in the cantos which I am about to discuss: these represent Pound's effort to find a 'permanent basis in humanity' which exists regardless of place or time; along with this effort, there is an equally important effort to preserve the cultural integrity of his materials, the qualities inseparable from place and time.

Indeed, Canto II is concerned throughout with the gathering of materials from distant times and places:

> Hang it all, Robert Browning,
> there can be but the one 'Sordello'.
> But Sordello, and my Sordello?
> Lo Sordels si fo di Mantovana.

Anybody who has dipped into Provençal literature will experience a strange emotion when he reads the line 'Lo Sordels si fo di Mantovana'. The formula is familiar. 'Peire Vidals si fo de Toloza'; 'Bertrans de Born si fo de Lemozi', and so on, with but minor variations, through almost all of the troubadour biographies.(1) But it does not require a knowledge of Provençal literature to see what Pound is about. Against the quibbling voice of Pound—'there can be but the one "Sordello". / But Sordello, and my Sordello?'—comes this ghostly voice, in a dead (but intelligible) language, doggedly putting first things first: 'Lo Sordels si fo di Mantovana.'(2) How important this bit of information was to the medieval man can be shown easily enough by recalling *Purgatory* VI, where, Virgil having identified himself as a Mantuan, Sordello embraces his compatriot with joy, and Dante delivers a passionate attack on the civic disorder which separates countrymen from each other and himself from his Florence.

This voice out of the Middle Ages—'Lo Sordels si fo di Mantovana'—is the first of a series of contemporary testimonies as to the character, identity, or power of some historical or mythical personage. Canto II is especially the canto of testimony:

> And the wave runs in the beach-groove:
> 'Eleanor, ἑλέναυς and ἑλέπτολις!'
>   And poor old Homer blind, blind, as a bat,
> Ear, ear for the sea-surge, murmur of old men's voices:
> 'Let her go back to the ships,
> Back among Grecian faces, lest evil come on our own,
> Evil and further evil, and a curse cursed on our children,

Moves, yes she moves like a goddess
And has the face of a god
      and the voice of Schoeney's daughters,
And doom goes with her in walking,
Let her go back to the ships,
      back among Grecian voices.'

Here the testimony is most telling because it is delivered in spite of the speakers' will: we, who have not seen Helen, could not comprehend her beauty from any description; but the Trojan elders' grudging admiration—they speak as eyewitnesses—convinces us of what we have missed. After this powerful testimony Pound moves on to Book III of the *Metamorphoses*, a poem made up of events no less miraculous than Helen's beauty:

Lifeless air become sinewed,
      feline leisure of panthers,
Leopards sniffing the grape shoots by scupper-hole,
Crouched panthers by fore-hatch,
And the sea blue-deep about us,
      green-ruddy in shadows,
And Lyaeus: 'From now, Acoetes, my altars,
Fearing no bondage,
      Fearing no cat of the wood,
Safe with my lynxes,
      feeding grapes to my leopards,
Olibanum is my incense,
      the vines grow in my homage.'
The back-swell now smooth in the rudder-chains,
Black snout of a porpoise,
      where Lycabs had been,
Fish-scales on the oarsmen.
      And I worship.
I have seen what I have seen.
      When they brought the boy I said:
'He has a god in him,
      though I do not know which god.'
And they kicked me into the fore-stays.
I have seen what I have seen:
      Medon's face like the face of a dory,
Arms shrunk into fins. And you, Pentheus,
Had as well listen to Tiresias, and to Cadmus,
      or your luck will go out of you.

                        (pp. 12–13)

The situation is archetypal: Acoetes can explain, vividly, his experiences; but to go beyond description is impossible; he can only say, 'I have seen what I have seen'. (This, perhaps, is to be taken as a corollary of 'I am what I am'.) The communication gap between him and Pentheus is absolute; for Pentheus has not experienced the same thing, and his inquisitorial attitude makes it impossible for him to sympathize with, let alone share, the experience.

It should be clear how this applies to 'Lo Sordels si fo di Mantovana': though fabulous in certain respects, Sordello's Provençal biography is the most nearly contemporary report on him that we have, and, in so far as it expresses the mental experience of Sordello's age, it is also the most authentic report we have. If other civilizations, particularly that of the troubadours, have something to say to us, then we must be prepared—as Browning was not—to listen carefully and humbly to the voice of first-hand experience. We must also try to find out what mattered to these unfamiliar civilizations, even to the extent of pondering the significance of 'Lo Sordels si fo di Mantovana.' Admittedly, the full significance cannot be grasped at once, but a reader who goes on to Canto VI will find:

> E lo Sordels si fo di Mantovana,
> Son of a poor knight, Sier Escort,
> And he delighted himself in chançons
> And mixed with the men of the court
> And went to the court of Richard Saint Boniface
> And was there taken with love for his wife
>   Cunizza, da Romano,
> That freed her slaves on a Wednesday
> Masnatas et servos, witness
> Picus de Farinatis
> and Don Elinus and Don Lipus
>   sons of Farinato de 'Farinati
> 'free of person, free of will
> 'free to buy, witness, sell, testate.'
> A marito subtraxit ipsam ...
>   dictum Sordellum concubuisse:
>   'Winter and Summer I sing of her grace,
>   As the rose is fair, so fair is her face,
>   Both Summer and Winter I sing of her,
>   The snow makyth me to remember her.'

And Cairels was of Sarlat ...
>   Theseus from Troezene,
> Whom they wd. have given poison
> But for the shape of his sword-hilt.

(pp. 26–7)

The only part of this passage of any striking poetic interest is Pound's rendering of the quatrain beginning ' "Winter and Summer ..." ': a rendering which suggests why we are at all concerned with Sordello the medieval Mantuan. Indeed, what Sordello did as a poet is rightly more important to us than who he was or what he did as a lover; and so it is to Pound as well. But Pound is also struck by the intense interest which both the ancient Greeks and troubadour biographers took in the places of origin of their heroes. Here Pound recalls just as much of the Theseus legend as suits his purposes: the loyalties and licences of the provincial mind are dangerous in any age, any place; but the Greek and medieval Mediterranean provincials created a language of craftsmanship which transcended these limits. And it may even be that, as Vlaminck is reported to have said (in Canto 87, p. 30), art 'is local'. In any event, Theseus from Troezene was recognized in Athens because of the unique shape of his sword; and Sordello from Mantua was recognized in provincial courts in Spain, France, and Italy because Provençal was then a nearly universal poetic language, and because he shaped it like the best of the local troubadours.

Before going on to Canto IV where Greek myths and troubadour biographies are again, more memorably, related, I should perhaps re-emphasize the lesson of Canto II. It is especially important to keep in mind the principles implicit in 'Lo Sordels si fo di Mantovana' and in 'I have seen what I have seen'. The first phrase should help us to remember Pound's desire to preserve the cultural integrity of materials, which yet, in juxtaposition with other such materials, may help us to locate 'a permanent basis in humanity'. The second phrase should prepare us to respect, or at any rate suspend disbelief in, Pound's idea of a mythological basis of reality, first revealed in Canto II and developed more elaborately in the cantos which we are about to examine. I should add that Acoetes' impenetrable (to some minds, infuriating) statement has a much wider significance in *The Cantos* than I am able to discuss here: it, together with 'Lo Sordels ... ', might take the place of Canto XXXVI as a text on which to base a discussion of Poundian poetics.

2. *Canto IV: Myth, Troubadour Biography, and Metamorphosis*

Canto IV begins with that image of destruction which is, to Western minds, the archetypal image of destruction:

> Palace in smoky light,
> Troy but a heap of smouldering boundary stones,

There are two extreme ways of viewing this somehow glorious catastrophe: as a triumph of arms, of public right over entrenched immorality; or as a triumph of love, which rather accepted destruction than surrender the beloved:

> ANAXIFORMINGES! Aurunculeia!
> Hear me. Cadmus of Golden Prows!

'ANAXIFORMINGES' is an epithet from Pindar and it represents the former view; 'Aurunculeia' is the name of Catullus' bride and it represents the latter. The idea that the Greeks were moralists while the Romans (as descendants of Aeneas) were lovers is a cliché of antiquity, and it was especially popular during the Middle Ages (when the Greeks were the type of the cuckold). However, 'Cadmus of Golden Prows' seems to be invoked here as an alternative to the rival views represented by Pindar and Catullus. That is, Cadmus is the founder and builder of Thebes; and the constructive principle emerged from a context of destruction, since Cadmus' builder-citizens were the survivors of a fratricidal strife: in order to build the city, one must sow the dragon's teeth. Likewise, out of the destruction of Troy came the basis of Western civilization (Homer who created the ethos of Greek civilization, and Aeneas who founded Rome). This is not so much an alternative view of the event, perhaps, as a more distant view, which does not exclude the other two.

This seems to me the most plausible reading of the four introductory lines of Canto IV: the most plausible reading, anyway, within the context of the entire poem.

In the following passage Pound shifts to a sort of Ovidian Eden, the country of myth:

> The silver mirrors catch the bright stones and flare,
> Dawn, to our waking, drifts in the green cool light;
> Dew-haze blurs, in the grass, pale ankles moving.
> Beat, beat, whirr, thud, in the soft turf
>   under the apple trees,
> Choros nympharum, goat-foot, with the pale foot alternate;
> Crescent of blue-shot waters, green-gold in the shallows,
> A black cock crows in the sea-foam;

Then Pound returns to the matter of Thebes and the subject of cannibalism. The speaker is, I take it, Oedipus, whose house has been cursed because of that crime; but the tale he tells comes out of thirteenth-century France, replete with cries of 'Ityn!' which recall Philomela's vengeance on Tereus. (A snatch from Horace is tossed in as well.) Time does not matter here, we must assume, for the tales are timeless:[1]

> And by the curved, carved foot of the couch,
>   claw-foot and lion head, an old man seated
> Speaking in the low drone ... :
>   Ityn!
> Et ter flebiliter, Itys, Ityn!
> And she went toward the window and cast her down,
>   'All the while, the while, swallows crying:
> Ityn!
>   'It is Cabestan's heart in the dish.'
>   'It is Cabestan's heart in the dish?'
>   'No other taste shall change this.'
> And she went toward the window,
>   the slim white stone bar
> Making a double arch;
> Firm even fingers held to the firm pale stone:
> Swung for a moment,
>   and the wind out of Rhodez
> Caught in the full of her sleeve.
>   ... the swallows crying:
> 'Tis. 'Tis. Ytis!

I am not sure that Pound's impressionistic version of the troubadour biography of Guillem de Cabestanh is as good as the

---

[1] Cf. Warren Ramsey's valuable 'Pound, Laforgue, and Dramatic Structure', *Comparative Literature*, vol. III, no. 1 (Winter 1951), pp. 47–56. This is perhaps the best brief commentary on this much-discussed canto.

original, but his judgment in joining it with the legend of
Tereus, Itys, Procne, and Philomela was sound enough:

Nous pourrions multiplier les exemples de biographies fantaisistes.
La légende du troubadour Guillem de Cabestanh, tué, dit son
biographe, par un baron jaloux qui lui arracha le cœur et le fit
manger a la femme infidèle, est commune au folklore de plusieurs
pays.[1]

The terrifying punishment exacted for infidelity in each of
these stories, of the unfaithful husband eating his son and the
unfaithful wife eating her lover's heart, has a savage 'poetic
justice' that has not lost its affective power. And surely Soremonda's reply to her husband (neatly telescoped by Pound)
must rate among the grand gestures of that gesture-hungry age:
'Seigner, ben m'avetz dat si bon manjar que ja mais no · n
manjarai d'autre.'[2]

The troubadour biographies, it should be noted, have a place
in literary history of the first importance:

Ce sont de petits morceaux d'allure dramatique, coupes de
dialogues, ou il y a un embryon de psychologie et parfois de
remarquables qualités de style; ces premiers specimens de l'art de
conter en prose, fort semblable aux nouvelles italiennes du xive
siècle, auxquelles ils ont servi de modelès, sont les humbles et
lointains ancêtres du roman moderne.[3]

No wonder Pound delighted to retell these stories, some of
which have been retold by such diverse writers as Boccaccio,
Heine, and Swinburne. At a moment like this, when one sees
what Pound is driving at, one may well feel that Pound has
some right to that favourite image of himself: the scholar-poet
sailing after knowledge, having 'speech with Tiresias, Thebae'.
For Pound is in touch here, surely, with primary manifestations
of the human imagination which, peculiar to no one race or
time, may change their shape slightly with each metamorphosis, yet retain an archetypal identity and power.

---

[1] Pierre Belperron, *La joie d'amour* (Paris, 1948), p. v.
[2] *Anthology of Provençal Troubadours* (New Haven, Conn., 1941), p. 112.
[3] Alfred Jeanroy, *La poésie lyrique des troubadours* (Toulouse-Paris, 1934), vol. I,
p. 103. Though by now out of date in certain respects, Jeanroy's great work is
still the general authority in troubadour matters.

In the next 'metamorphosis' from Greek to Provençal, however, the parallelism is by no means so exact. The myth is that of Actaeon and Diana, and the troubadour biography is that of Peire Vidal, who (so the story goes), because he loved a lady by the name of 'la Loba', dressed himself as a wolf and ran around the countryside in that guise; after being nearly killed by shepherds and their dogs, Vidal was carried back to la Loba. She took no pity on him, but her husband was so taken with Vidal's gesture that he ordered la Loba to receive Vidal kindly. The connection between this tale and the myth of Actaeon and Diana cannot, in fact, bear very close examination, though the two stories have notable resemblances.

> Actaeon ...
>   and a valley,
> The valley is thick with leaves, with leaves, the trees,
> The sunlight glitters, glitters a-top,
> Like a fish-scale roof,
>   Life the church roof in Poictiers
> If it were gold.
>   Beneath it, beneath it
> Not a ray, not a slivver, not a spare disc of sunlight
> Flaking the black, soft water;
> Bathing the body of nymphs, of nymphs, and Diana,
> Nymphs, white-gathered about her, and the air, air,
> Shaking, air alight with the goddess,
>   fanning their hair in the dark.
> Lifting, lifting and waffing:
> Ivory dipping in silver,
>   Shadow'd, o'ershadow'd
> Ivory dipping in silver,
> Not a splotch, not a lost shatter of sunlight.
> Then Actaeon: Vidal,
> Vidal. It is old Vidal speaking,
>   stumbling along in the wood,
> Not a patch, not a lost shimmer of sunlight,
>   the pale hair of the goddess.
>
> The dogs leap on Actaeon,
>   'Hither, hither, Actaeon,'
> Spotted stag of the wood;
> Gold, gold, a sheaf of hair,
>   Thick like a wheat swath,

Blaze, blaze in the sun,
    The dogs leap on Actaeon.
Stumbling, stumbling along in the wood,
Muttering, muttering Ovid:
    'Pergusa ... pool ... pool ... Gargaphia,
'Pool ... pool of Salmacis.'
    The empty armour shakes as the cygnet moves.

The ecstatic vision of Diana is, apparently, being experienced by Vidal; his legendary 'folie', then, is the madness of a visionary in touch with the mythical world of Ovid. On a more prosaic level, it is true that the troubadours owed something to Ovid,(3) but the main point seems to be that the medieval imagination, as expressed in the troubadour biographies, was possessed by what Pound calls 'mythopoeia', and that it was therefore close to the creative springs of life and art.

This conception of the troubadours, as having discovered an almost mystical 'joie d'Amour', has some truth. But the biography of Vidal is not only a product of the later period of courtly decadence, but also, in so far as it owes anything to pagan mythology, a very degraded thing. The fierce old legend of Actaeon and Diana, which causes Ovid to exclaim:

at bene si quaeras, Fortunae crimen in illo,
non scelus invenies; quod enim scelus error
    habebat?[1]

is conceived with religious awe and artistic authority; whereas the story of Vidal's madcap adventure is an amusing but trivial entertainment, whose possible connection with the Actaeon and Diana myth only reminds one of the degeneration which often occurs during oral transmission. It may be objected that, since Pound calls attention only to that part of the Vidal biography which resembles the Greek myth, the rest of the biography can be ignored. But if 'Ityn!' is sufficient to recall the Tereus myth in its entirety, then the same must be true of 'Then Actaeon: Vidal, / Vidal'. Besides, Pound is constructing a weighty parallel between the Greek and troubadour worlds on the basis of this not so very weighty resemblance. In fact the parallel is so weighty that it evokes an ecstatic vision of creativity:

---

[1] Ovid, *Metamorphoses*, III, 141–2.

> Thus the light rains, thus pours, *e lo soleils plovil*
> The liquid and rushing crystal
>   beneath the knees of the gods.
> Ply over ply, thin glitter of water;
> Brook film bearing white petals.
> The pines at Takasago
>   grow with the pines of Isé!
> The water whirls up the bright pale sand in the spring's
>   mouth
> 'Behold the Tree of the Visages!'
> Forked branch-tips, flaming as if with lotus.
>   Ply over ply
> The shallow eddying fluid,
>   beneath the knees of the gods.

The imagery of creative light (which is not to be entirely distinguished from the destructive light of Troy in flames) is especially important in *The Cantos*, as may be recalled from Canto XLVII:

> The light has entered the cave. Io! Io!
> The light has gone down into the cave,
> Splendour on splendour!

And it is yet more important in the Pisan and Rock-Drill Cantos. In this canto the imagery of creative light (a manifestation of the Divine Mind?) gives way to the imagery of human love:

> Torches melt in the glare
>   set flame of the corner cook-stall,
> Blue agate casing the sky (as at Gourdon that time)
>   the sputter of resin,
> Saffron sandal so petals the narrow foot: Ὑμην,
>   Ὑμεναι ὦ, Aurunculeia! Ὑμην, Ὑμεναι ὦ,
> The scarlet flower is cast on the blanch-white stone.

It is possible, too, by going a number of lines ahead, to find an image which links the imagery of creative light with this passage about Aurunculeia, the bride who is waiting for her husband:

> … upon the gilded tower in Ecbatan
> Lay the god's bride, lay ever, waiting the golden rain.

The reference to the rites of Hymen may perhaps be taken as an approval of chastity, if only a pagan chastity, but that is far from Pound's mind. The punishment for adultery may be brutal, as in the Tereus legend or the story of Cabestan, but procreative instinct does not observe these taboos, which are not so primitive as it nor so cunning:

> So-Gioku, saying:
> 'This wind is the king's wind,
>> This wind is wind of the palace,
> Shaking imperial water-jets.'
>> That Ran-ti opened his collar:
> 'This wind roars in the earth's bag,
>> it lays the water with rushes;
> No wind is the king's wind.
>> Let every cow keep her calf.'
> 'This wind is held in gauze curtains ... '
>> 'No wind is the king's ... '
>
> The camel drivers sit in the turn of the stairs,
>> Look down on Ecbatan of plotted streets,
> 'Danaë! Danaë!
>> What wind is the king's?'

One of Pound's (and Dante's) favourite women, Sordello's mistress Cunizza, was also like the wind:

> And Sordello subtracted her from that husband
> And lay with her in Tarviso
> Till he was driven out of Tarviso
> And she left with a soldier named Bonius
> nimium amorata in eum
> And went from one place to another
> 'The light of this star o'ercame me'
> Greatly enjoying herself
> And running up the most awful bills.
> And this Bonius was killed on a sunday
> and she had then a Lord from Braganza
> and later a house in Verona.
>
> (Canto XXIX, p. 147)

Not only was she amorous—the star whose light overcame her was Venus, of course—but she was also notably generous: she 'freed her slaves on a Wednesday', as Pound duly notes in a passage quoted above.

However, the meaning of the passage from Canto IV which

concludes with the question, 'What wind is the king's?' is not exhausted by this simple analogy. One should recall another, and in fact the main, component of Canto IV—the folk tradition, which is connected in ancient Greece with the name of Tereus or Atreus, and many centuries later, with the name of Guillem de Cabestanh. This tradition (which Pound will later call 'sagetrieb') is conceived as a force that expresses itself at various times and places through individuals, legendary or otherwise; and parallel with this force, it seems, is the divine procreative force, which no amount of cunning can thwart.

This is a very primitive view indeed, and not one which recommends itself to a society, Christian or otherwise, confronted with problems of overpopulation. Pound's world is based on the recommendation to 'be fruitful and multiply'. In this respect, as in many others, Pound is a die-hard, and it is possible that *The Cantos* may be the last great unqualified affirmation in English poetry of fertility and procreation, of the life force expressing itself through *both* man and nature, and, as such, harmonizing their wills. This affirmation expresses itself in many ways, some of them coarse (or, by Christian standards, immoral, or both), yet often the result is poetry, as in Canto XLVII, or as in:

> 'Danaë! Danaë!
>   What wind is the king's?'

Where it seems to me that his shift of Ran-ti's assertion that 'No wind is the king's' into a question which Pound asks Danae —does for a breath-taking moment collapse all barriers of time, language, and civilization. It is an effect which Pound has been striving for throughout this canto. Once is nearly enough, or might have been if the conclusion of the canto were not so dismally mechanical in its attempt to illustrate the principle, implied here but stated clearly in Canto XXI, that 'confusion [is] the source of renewals'.

> Polhonac,
> As Gyges on Thracian platter set the feast,
> Cabestan, Terreus,
>   It is Cabestan's heart in the dish,
> Vidal, or Ecbatan, upon the gilded tower in Ecbatan
> Lay the god's bride, lay ever, waiting the golden rain.

By Garonne. 'Saave!'
The Garonne is thick like paint,
Procession, —'Et sa'ave, sa'ave, sa'ave Regina!'—
Moves like a worm, in the crowd.
Adige, thin film of images,
Across the Adige, by Stefano, Madonna in hortulo,
As Cavalcanti had seen her.
    The Centaur's heel plants in the earth loam.
And we sit here ...
       there in the arena ...

NOTES TO CHAPTER III

(1) Jeanroy, *Poésie lyrique des troubadours*, vol. I, p. 102: 'Les Biographies, écrites d'un style uni, sans prétention, mais non sans charme, son jétées dans un moule uniforme: elles nous renseignent sur le pays d'origine du troubadour, sa condition sociale, les circonstances de sa vie, parfois, et très longuement, sur ses aventures amoureuses; elles se terminent généralement par un jugement sommaire sur son talent de poete et de musicien.'

(2) Jeanroy, *Poésie lyrique des troubadours*, vol. I, p. 132: 'Les historiettes concernant la vie amoureuse des troubadours sont sorties de l'imagination des biographes, interprétant très librement les textes et rattachant a leurs héros des thèmes connus, pour des raisons qui souvent nous échappent; néanmoins, en ce qui concerne la patrie, la famille, la condition sociale de ceux-ci, ces chroniquers, si peu scrupuleux par ailleurs, ont essayé (et ils y ont souvent réussi) a se procurer des informations précises qu'il serait téméraire de rejeter sans examen.'

(3) However, Jeanroy finds little evidence of a direct influence by Ovid on the troubadours (*Poésie lyrique des troubadours*, vol. II, pp. 64–8). But the influence, directly or not, of the *Ars Amatoria* is certainly important. A useful discussion of the relationship between the troubadours and Ovid can be found in the first chapter of C. S. Lewis's *The Allegory of Love* (London, 1936).

IV

MYTH AND METAMORPHOSIS

1. Two Aspects of Myth in The Cantos

POUND'S PAGAN GODS have already appeared several times in
the course of this study, especially in the examinations of Cantos
XLVII and IV. On most of these occasions they have appeared
in the context of a myth or legend which Pound wishes to retell
or recall. At other times, however, they seem to be making a
personal appearance which does not occur for the sake of some
story in which they figure. Bearing these distinctions in mind,
it must nevertheless be confessed that the significance of these
gods and of the myths in which they figure is sometimes rather
obscure; indeed, the whole mythological apparatus in *The Cantos*
recedes inevitably into the arcane regions of Acoetes' 'I have
seen what I have seen'. In the next section of this chapter I shall
do my best to explore these arcane regions. For the present,
however, it will be most useful to consider two aspects of myth,
which may be described briefly as 'myth as [im]moral fable'
and 'myth as a record of a delightful psychic experience'. It is
not always possible to make a hard and fast distinction between
these, and the passages I select for discussion are not the clearest
examples that I might give. My previous expositions will, I
believe, help me to get around this difficulty.

In the later cantos Pound occasionally refers, rather enig-
matically, to the powers of myth:

> Remove the mythologies before they establish clean values
> (Canto 88)

> Bernice, late for a constellation, mythopoeia persisting,
> (now called folc-loristica)
> (Canto 97, pp. 27–8)

It is not until very late in *The Cantos* that Pound formally recognizes that myth has an independent status as an instrument of communication, roughly comparable to the categories he had established much earlier of 'logopoeia, melopoeia, and phanopoeia'.[1] There is no doubt, however, that his earlier use of myth was based on a recognition, if not of the myths' special virtue as a poetic instrument, at least of their potency as exemplary fables. The idea that they help to 'establish clean values' involves a good many things, such as religious awe in Canto II and sexual morality in Canto XXX.

One discussion of myth which may help to define Pound's use is to be found in Denis de Rougemont's *Passion and Society*, a book with whose central argument Pound would disagree emphatically:[2]

... we are no longer at the stage of supposing that the mythical is tantamount to unreality or illusion. Too many myths now display their indisputable power over us. And yet abuse of the term has made a fresh definition needful. Speaking generally, a myth is a story—a symbolical fable as simple as it is striking—which sums up an infinite number of more or less analogous situations. A myth makes it possible to become aware at a glance of certain types of *constant* relations and to disengage these from the welter of everyday appearances.

The immediate importance of this definition of myth is the way it seems to apply to the myths and troubadour biographies examined in Canto IV. The relations depicted in those fables certainly are, as de Rougemont says, '*constant*'; and Pound's treatment of them is certainly designed to focus attention on just that quality of 'constancy'.

The fables themselves are '[im]moral', which is to say that they deal memorably with archetypal human situations which give rise to moral problems. If they are taken as guides to conduct, their influence is of course 'immoral'; in the Cabestan tale, for instance, we see one crime after another—adultery, murder, suicide: the stark and (as de Rougemont would say) '*compelling*' plot of romantic love. Dante recognized this problem in the Paolo and Francesca story, and Plato had recognized the

[1] 'How to Read', *Literary Essays*, p. 25.
[2] de Rougemont, *Passion and Society* [L'Amour et L'Occident], (revised edition, London, 1956), p. 18.

general problem long before him. But in this violent little fable (which we remember, no doubt, because it is violent) there is an unforgettable sequence of clearly motivated yet blindly egotistical acts: at no point does one of these monoliths inquire whether he or she is damaging anybody else; each is a law unto himself, gesturing grandly in a world not unlike that of Jacobean tragedy. We shall see that in Canto XXX Pound develops these ideas in an unexpected and powerful way.

Before going on to Canto XXX, however, I should define the second aspect of myth which I mentioned—myth as 'the record of a delightful psychic experience'. This, it is obvious, is something quite different from myth as a moral fable; and it may be that 'myth' is a misnomer for what I have in mind. But my authority for this is Pound himself, and the idea has an interesting history:

> Poetry is a sort of inspired mathematics, which gives us equations, not for abstract figures, triangles, squares, and the like, but for the human emotions. If one has a mind which inclines to magic rather than science, one will prefer to speak of these equations as spells or incantations; it sounds more arcane, mysterious, recondite.[1]

Mario Praz was, I believe, the first critic to suggest that this passage from *The Spirit of Romance* was the seed from which Eliot's 'objective correlative' sprang.[2] Another development is this:

> I believe in a sort of permanent basis in humanity, that is to say, I believe that Greek myth arose when someone having passed through delightful psychic experience tried to communicate it to others and found it necessary to screen himself from persecution. Speaking aesthetically, the myths are explications of mood; you may stop there, or you may probe deeper. Certain it is that these myths are only intelligible in a vivid and glittering sense to those people to whom they occur. I know, I mean, one man who understands Persephone and Demeter, and one who understands the Laurel, and another who has, I should say met Artemis. These things are for them *real*.[3]

'I have seen what I have seen', says Acoetes in Canto II; and it will be recalled that mad Peire Vidal seems to be experiencing

[1] Pound, *Spirit of Romance*, p. 5.
[2] Mario Praz, 'T. S. Eliot and Dante', *Southern Review*, vol. II, no. 3, pp. 525–48.
[3] Pound, 'Psychology and the Troubadours', *The Quest*, vol. IV, no. 1, pp. 43–4.

such a vision in Canto IV. The essay from which this passage is extracted, though written as early as 1912, has in fact proved an invaluable confirmation of many of my readings. As a very early essay, however—written before Pound began *The Cantos*—it has only a limited usefulness as a commentary on the poem as it now stands. It is clear, for instance, that the definition of myth which he gave there proved too limited. Yet the idea of a 'permanent basis in humanity' does obviously apply to myth as a moral fable as well as to myth as the record of a 'delightful psychic experience'.

I shall return later to this second aspect of myth in *The Cantos*, but it is time now to examine Canto XXX. The first part of that canto leads into the thickets of courtly doctrine, but this route will give a new perspective on Pound's use of myth as moral fable.

What Pound discovered in courtly poetry was something quite different from what Coleridge, Rossetti, and Morris discovered:

> Compleynt, compleynt I hearde upon a day,
> Artemis singing, Artemis, Artemis
> Agaynst Pity lifted her wail:
> Pity causeth the forests to fail,
> Pity slayeth my nymphs,
> Pity spareth so many an evil thing.
> Pity befouleth April,
> Pity is the root and the spring.

This would appear to contradict Chaucer's *Complaint unto Pity*, in which he makes it quite clear all other courtly virtues are worthless unless 'Pity' is alive. In fact the convention of Chaucer's poem is that Pity is dead (lines 36–42):

> About hir herse there stoden lustely,
> Withouten any woo, as thoughte me,
> Bounte parfyt, wel armed and richely,
> And fresshe Beaute, Lust, and Jolyte,
> Assured Maner, Youthe, and Honeste,
> Wisdom, Estaat, Drede, and Governaunce,
> Confedred both by bonde and alliaunce.

Nothing could be more conventional. The important point of this stanza, however, is that all of the courtly virtues are 'Confedred both by bonde and alliaunce', and that Pity, now dead, is an essential, indeed the chief, member of this confederacy. But by the same token, the death of 'Youth' would equally disrupt this allegorical confederacy. If 'Pity' were alive, in other words, and allied herself with 'Elde' or some equally uncourtly attribute, she would disrupt the entire courtly world. And this, very nearly, is what has happened in Canto XXX.

The Pity which Chaucer valued so highly is, then, quite a different creature from the Pity who 'spareth so many an evil thing'. But lest Pound's complaint against Pity be taken as a wholesale rejection of compassion and sympathy, I must point out at once that there is a crucial ambiguity in the line 'Pity is the root and the spring': in context, of course, the words 'of all that causes my complaint' are implied as an appendage to this line, but taken by itself, the line says something quite different —it says simply that 'Pity is the root and the spring'. The justification for detaching the line from its context is provided by the syntactical pattern, which consists essentially of a parallel series of transitive sentences (Pity causeth ... Pity slayeth ... Pity befouleth ...), followed by a sentence built around a copula (Pity is ...). Pity, in essence, is 'the root and the spring' of any number of things, some good, some bad; and it is even, for that matter, the 'root and the spring' of *The Cantos*. But, like love itself (as we shall see shortly), what is essentially desirable can be perverted by indiscriminate use.[1]

> Now if no fayre creature followeth me
> It is on account of Pity,
> It is on account that Pity forbideth them slaye.
> All things are made foul in this season,
> This is the reason, none may seek purity
> Having for foulnesse pity
> And things growne awry;
> No more do my shaftes fly
> To slay. Nothing is now clean slayne
> But rotteth away.

These lines have apparently caused their author considerable worry, because we find him qualifying them in both the Pisan and Rock-Drill Cantos:

[1] Pound may very well have had in mind *Inferno* XX, where Virgil reproaches Dante for having pity on the damned; however, as I have occasion to explain later, Canto XXX is probably based on the *Pervigilium Veneris*.

> J'ai eu pitie des autres
> Probablement pas assez, and at moments that suited my own
> convenience
> (Canto LXXVI, pp. 488–9)

> Pity, yes, for the infected,
> but maintain antisepsis,
> let the light pour.
> Apollonius made peace with the animals
> Was no blood on the Cyprian's altars
> (Canto 94, p. 95)

Though I do not believe that these second thoughts in any way contradict the lines from Canto XXX, there is an apparent danger that a careless or ignorant reader might misconstrue them. Their first target is, no doubt, the Romantic Mediaevalists who sentimentalized and thus obscured the Middle Ages. The second target is the misuse of the word 'pity' and of the emotion it signifies. It is clear that this misuse involves a good deal more than erotic subjects: it includes, for instance, Wilfred Owen's famous and misleading dictum about his own poetry; and it includes generally those aspects of humanitarianism which had grown into an unassailable moral posture rather than an active force of social reform. But the handiest and least pretentious formulation of what Pound is driving at, I have found in Kingsley Amis's *Lucky Jim*, where Jim decides at last to abandon his neurotic girl friend in favour of a quite unpitiful beauty:

> For the first time he really felt that it was no use trying to save those who fundamentally would rather not be saved. To go on trying would not merely be to yield to pity and sentimentality, but wrong and, to pursue it to its conclusion, inhumane.

Pound then shifts to the classic triangle of Mars, Venus, and Vulcan. The 'Compleynt against Pity', which has rather general significance, is illuminated by a specifically erotic misuse of Pity:

> In Paphos, on a day
> I also heard:
> ... goeth not with young Mars to playe
> But she hath pity on a doddering fool,
> She tendeth his fyre,
> She keepeth his embers warm.

This, however, is classical myth as it was used by the Middle Ages, and one cannot do better than consult the Chaucerian translation of the *Roman de la Rose*: outside the garden of the Rose, the lover sees portrayed the 'Deadly Sins' of courtly love; one of them is 'Elde', and I quote at some length, for reasons which will soon be apparent:

> The tyme, that may not sojourne,
> But goth, and may never retourne,
> As watir that doun renneth ay,
> But never drope retourne may,
> Ther may nothing as tyme endure,
> Metall, nor erthely creature,
> For alle thing it fret and shall,
> The tyme eke, that chaungith all,
> And all doth waxe and fostred be,
> And all thing destroieth he;
> The tyme, that eldith our auncessours,
> And eldith kynges and emperours.
> And that us alle shal overcomen,
> Er that deth us shal have nomen;
> The tyme, that hath al in welde
> To elden folk, had maad hir elde
>
> But natheles, I trowe that she
> Was fair symtyme, and fresh to se,
> When she was in hir rightful age,
> But she was past al that passage,
> And was a doted thing bicomen.
> A furred cope on had she nomen,
> Wel had she clad hirsilf and warm,
> For cold myght elles don hir harm.
> These olde folk have alwey cold;
> Her kynde is sich, when they ben old.[1]

Possible though it may be, I do not claim that Pound had this passage in mind when he wrote:

> She tendeth his fyre,
> She keepeth his embers warm.

(It is more likely to be simply an allusion to Vulcan's occupation.) But it is certainly in keeping with the spirit of this passage when Pound goes on immediately afterwards to write:

[1] Geoffrey Chaucer, *Works*, ed. by F. N. Robinson (second edition, London, 1957), p. 569, lines 381–96 and 403–12.

Time is the evil. Evil.
                  A day, and a day
Walked the young Pedro baffled,
             a day and a day
After Ignez was murdered.
Came the Lords in Lisboa
             a day, and a day
In homage. Seated there
                dead eyes,
Dead hair under the crown,
The King still young there beside her.

The shift to Camoens's Portugal is violent and 'illogical', but emotionally it is right; for the terrible homage exacted by Pedro, insane flourish that it is, is as poignant as it is morbid. And though it is perhaps most ghastly because of its inadequacy as a revenge for the Lords' assassination of Ignez, it has an almost archetypal adequacy as an expression of human loss and of the irrecoverability of time:

> The tyme, that may not sojourne,
> But goth, and may never retourne,
> As watir that doun renneth ay,
> But never drope retourne may,

But Pedro's grief, terrible and affecting in itself, has by this ceremony become translated into a perverted, if 'poetic', gesture of the same order as Soremonda's 'No other taste shall change this', or her husband's savage revenge on her and Cabestanh. Memorable these acts are, and memorable their actors intend them to be—as monuments to their own outraged feelings and their own self-conscious capacity for outrage. In the sense that they act violently they are quite the opposite of the 'Pity' which Pound attacks in the first part of this canto; but they are quite alike in their assumption of a nearly unassailable moral posture. There is somewhat the same thing in Pound's Dido (Canto VII), where the suggestion of necrophilia anticipates Pedro's exhumation of his dead mistress or Pity's care for 'foulnesse' and 'things grown awry'.[1]

However, I might just as well acknowledge what is certainly true about the Middle Ages and its 'Pite': that the courtly

---

[1] Pound's point of view here might usefully be compared with the point of view in *Lady Chatterley's Lover*, though the differences are perhaps more interesting than the similarities.

society (so far as it existed) and its doctrine were a bizarre mixture of fantasy and ruthless 'realism'; and that mediaeval
heroes like Richard Cœur-de-Lion committed mass atrocities
and grand seigneurial gestures with equal ease. It would be
foolish to suppose that Pound gives these things their due weight
in his total evaluation of the Middle Ages. But he is not suggesting here or anywhere else in *The Cantos* that we should model
ourselves on the Middle Ages or on China or on early-nine-
teenth-century America: but we *can* learn from them in certain
areas, such as 'Pity', where the courtly doctrine exhibits a
certain honesty of response or where the Confucian doctrine
recommends that one save one's self before saving others.

Yet this argument will hardly satisfy the reader who recalls
Pound's record as a fascist and anti-Semite (and who, at the same
time, perhaps recalls Chaucer's Prioress: 'a Jewerye, / Sustened
by a lord of that contree / For foule usure and lucre of vileynye'[1]).
I introduce this topic only because it is unavoidable; I deny,
however, that the unavoidable associations are invited or immediately relevant to Canto XXX. It is not true (it is in fact anti-
Semitic to argue) that intolerance towards sentimentalized
ugliness and unnaturalness leads to Dachau and Buchenwald.
What is probably more true is that a little more of the ruthless
enlightenment recommended in Canto XXX might have
eliminated Pound's vulgar, typically American Legion, prejudices. But it is futile to argue the point: Canto XXX is poetry of
a high order, it is 'mediaeval' in the best, not Romantic, sense of
the word; and as a 'criticism of life' it is considerably better than
most of Pound's own work in an overtly 'contemporary' vein.

I have discussed this first half of Canto XXX as though it
were an independent poetic unit; and so, it seems to me, it is.
The second half is rather a coda to the entire first book of thirty
cantos;[2] and if I were an anthologist, I should feel quite justified
in printing the first half by itself. Outside the Pisan Cantos—
where it is necessary if one is to select at all—this practice is
rarely justified. It is a misfortune that Pound's prejudices and
our own make the anthologizing of this admirably self-contained
passage an unlikely event.

[1] Chaucer, *Works*, p. 161, lines 1679–81.
[2] However, Mr Emery makes out a fair case for the coherence of the whole
canto. *Ideas into Action*, pp. 120–3.

Many myths, including some treated by Pound, enshrine sexual taboos. The taboos are still with us, necessary no doubt, for the old mythological violence is dangerous now as ever:

> and Till was hung yesterday
> for murder and rape with trimmings plus Cholkis
> plus mythology, thought he was Zeus ram or
> another one
>
> Hey Snag wots in the bibl'?
> wot are the books ov the bible?
> Name 'em, don't bullshit ME.

 OΎ ΤΙΣ

> a man on whom the sun has gone down
> the ewe, he said had such a pretty look in her eyes,
> and the nymph of the Hagoromo came to me,
> as a corona of angels
> (Canto LXXIV, p. 456)

Pound's evident sympathy for Till is partly a matter of propinquity: as inmates in the Pisa D.T.C. they were both men 'on whom the sun has gone down'. But there is a recognition, too, that in a section of society where the search for knowledge is reduced to a quiz contest, one cannot expect moral scruples to hold the old mythological violence in check. A knowledge of the myths does not so much 'establish clean values' as remind us that a man like Till isn't necessarily an incomprehensible fiend, even when his 'trimmings' are carved with a switchblade or a straight razor.

But if the myths still have a real force as embodied in Till, they have a very different reality as embodied in the 'nymph of the Hagoromo' who visits Pound in the D.T.C. This, apparently, is the sort of thing he had in mind when, thirty years earlier, he wrote: 'I know, I mean, one man who understands Persephone and Demeter, and one who understands the Laurel, and another who has, I should say, met Artemis. These things are for them *real*.' Until the Pisan Cantos, I am not convinced that these things are '*real*' for Pound. The impressionistic evocation of an Ovidian Eden in Canto IV is admirable in its

71

own way, but it is chiefly an evocation of a scene; it rates, perhaps, as an 'explication of mood'. The same thing can be said about Canto XVII, which Yeats selected for the *Oxford Book of Modern Verse*. There are in fact many such passages scattered about the first thirty cantos, and they are rightly admired. But the goddesses do not come alive until the Pisan Cantos.

The 'Lynx' passage in Canto LXXIX is probably the best example of its kind in *The Cantos*, it is already famous, and it requires very little explication. I shall merely quote two passages from it which, in themselves examples of the best of Pound's work, will serve to advance my general discussion of Eros:

> Ἴακχε, Ἴακχε, Χαῖρε, ΑΟΙ
> 'Eat of it not in the under world'
> See that the sun or the moon bless thy eating
> Κόρη, Κόρη, for the six seeds of an error
> or that the stars bless thy eating
>
> O Lynx, guard this orchard,
> Keep from Demeter's furrow
>
> This fruit has a fire within it,
> Pomona, Pomona
> No glass is clearer than are the globes of this flame
> what sea is clearer than the pomegranate body
> holding the flame?
> Pomona, Pomona,

This should certainly recall Canto XLVII very vividly to mind, for both are concerned with the Eleusinian Mysteries. Most remarkable about this passage, however, is Pound's oblique and very beautiful treatment of a young girl's fascination with sex. The symbolism is, of course, traditional, but it is Pound's particular approach to the Persephone story that makes it so radiant.

Aphrodite appears frequently in the Pisan and Rock-Drill Cantos, and she is the chief among many deities in the 'Lynx' passage:

> O lynx, guard my vineyard
> As the grape swells under vine leaf
> Ἥλιος is come to our mountain
> there is a red glow in the carpet of pine spikes

Myth and Metamorphosis

O lynx, guard my vineyard
As the grape swells under vine leaf
    This Goddess was born of sea-foam
    She is lighter than air under Hesperus
        δεινὰ εἶ Κύθηρα
terrible in resistance
        Κόρη καὶ Δήλια καὶ Μαῖα
trine as praeludio
        Κύπρις' Αφρόδιτη
a petal lighter than sea-foam
        Κύθηρα.

It is not clear why Maia, mother of Hermes, is chosen as the representative of motherhood to set beside Delia the virgin and Kore the daughter, but the implication of 'trine as praeludio' appears to be that Aphrodite is 'three goddesses in one'—the Poundian Trinity. The element of silliness in this conception should not, however, distract one from the importance which Pound attaches to Aphrodite. In the next section, indeed, we shall see that she is (in some not entirely penetrable sense) the controlling force in Pound's world and thus in *The Cantos*.

2. Metamorphosis

The general subject of metamorphosis, or even the subject of metamorphosis as a principle of construction in *The Cantos* (which is not to say a principle of organization), cannot be treated adequately in this essay. Yet any lengthy exposition of the poem necessarily involves an attempt to explain why Pound is so much concerned with metamorphoses.

One kind of metamorphosis is that which involves the transmission and translation of knowledge—an idea, an image, an archetypal figure or deity—through various languages and cultural situations. The legends of Tereus and Cabestanh seem to be a case in point: though the circumstances of the stories are in many respects dissimilar, the central episode, the revenge for adultery, remains much the same; apparently there is something in the cannibalistic feast-revenge which, however times and customs change, remains fascinating to the folk imagination. Perhaps the idea inevitably recurs, or perhaps it is retained and reshaped in oral tradition, or perhaps it is taken

73

from a written source, i.e. Ovid, and translated by the mediaeval mind into mediaeval terms; but in any case it is a constant element in a world characterized by change, and its constancy would seem to be a guarantee of its intrinsic validity as an index to a 'permanent basis in humanity'.

Speaking broadly, this kind of metamorphosis is the basis of Pound's poetic method in *The Cantos*. And yet to say so may be misleading, since he is equally concerned with, say, the mediaevalism of the Middle Ages—as reflected in, for instance, the unvarying sequence of details in the troubadour biographies. The Middle Ages can be useful for our time only if we try to understand them with some precision, as we have seen in the case of the mediaeval use of the word 'Pity'. Likewise, when Pound attempts to translate Homer by 'blood rite', he uses the nearest equivalent to Homer that he can find in English literature. It is at root a Confucian concern, or Confucian as Pound understands it. And there is nothing more central in *The Cantos* than this effort simultaneously to capture the constant element in the flux and yet to honour the thing *as it was* at the point where it was captured. In Canto 90, which I shall examine shortly, there is an effort to define the conception of reality which is behind this concern; it is a conception in which a second kind of metamorphosis plays an important part.

This second and more fundamental kind of metamorphosis is the kind that Ovid used as an organizing principle for his compendium of mythology, the *Metamorphoses*. The one constant, that is, which Ovid could use to bring his supernatural tales together was the constant change of form which his legendary characters underwent—from a man to a hawk, from a woman to a swallow. And, indeed, to a primitive mind the guarantee of the supernatural nature of a subject is its capacity to alter form dramatically. The result of Ovid's method in the *Metamorphoses* is a restless and fluctuating surface which is very much like Pound's picture of life. This kind of metamorphosis, it is clear, takes us again into those arcane regions concerning which Acoetes says, 'I have seen what I have seen'.(1)

Canto 90 begins with a mediaeval Latin epigraph which asserts that the human soul is not love but that love issues from it, and therefore the soul does not delight in itself, but in the love which flows from it:

> Animus humanus amor non est,
> sed ab ipso amor procedit, et
> ideo seipso non diligit, sed amore
> qui seipso procedit.

The point here seems to be (to use a familiar Yeatsian distinction) that the dancer is admirable in so far as she dances. It is, in effect, a repudiation of the subject-attribute conception of reality, where the colour of an object is an attribute, somehow distinct from its essence. The introductory lines of the canto pick up this idea:

> 'From the colour the nature
> & by the nature the sign!'
> Beatific spirits welding together
> as in one ash-tree in Ygdrasail.

On this showing colour is the active mode of being of an object, just as love is the active mode of being of the soul; and it is by the colour or the love that we know and value an object or the soul—that is, by its manifestations. Translated into mythological terms, as in the tree of Ygdrasail, this approach to reality instructs us that, though the roots of things are in heaven, we worship best by understanding their particular manifestations on earth.

The connection between pagan polytheism and this view of the world is quite clear. On the psychological level we observe, say, that sacred to Dionysus are the vine, the ivy, the rose, panthers, lions, lynxes, dolphins, etc. They are, as in Canto II, manifestations of his power and affection; and they are, each of them, to be valued accordingly. This clearly suggests a form of Neo-Platonism (derived chiefly, probably, from Erigena);(2) but in its assignment of values it differs radically from Platonism proper and from many forms of Neo-Platonism (Christian or pagan) which stress the inferiority of 'created things' and the desirability of turning away from them toward the Prime Mover. For Pound it is always *this* world that matters; and from his point of view the pagan gods are always, whether by patronage or metamorphosis, more concretely involved with this world than is the Christian god or the Neo-Platonic one.

Committed as he is to the world of particulars inside time, where each decays, dies, or is subject to destruction, Pound is nevertheless deeply concerned with permanent values. On the one hand, permanence is achieved through the gods (in this case Hermes), who express their supernatural will through perishable particulars:

> Templum aedificans, not yet marble,
> 'Amphion!'

Or, less esoterically, through an oral tradition:

> to the room in Poitiers where one can stand
> casting no shadow,
> That is Sagetrieb,
> that is tradition.
> Builders had kept the proportion,

Admittedly, this is cryptic, but the legend of Amphion driving stones into order with the music from his harp has already appeared in *The Cantos*, as has a reference to the church in Poitiers whose remarkable construction has left a room in which one may stand without casting a shadow. The power which, through Amphion's harp, compelled the stones into place in the wall of Thebes creates the temple, as yet a place of worship and not a monument of civic pride: the religious and creative force are united here, as they are in the 'Sagetrieb' which combines practical knowledge with a knowledge of religious symbolism. Stones or men may perish, but the wisdom of the race is handed down, or, lacking that even, the religious impulse reasserts itself.

Dropping down a few lines, we find in Latin (the closest thing to imperishability in language) a cryptic but central statement of Pound's conception of the world:

> Kuthera δεινά
> Kuthera sempiterna
> Ubi amor, ibi oculus.
> Vae qui cogitatis inutile.
> quam in nobis similitudine divinae
> reperetur imago.

Here are four separate phrases, grammatically unlinked, but not impenetrable. The goddess of Love has, as one of her epithets, 'eternal'; and this is not quite the same thing as saying that 'Love is eternal'. For the copula 'is' contains a suggestion of assertion which Pound does not want; 'sempiterna' and 'Kuthera' simply go together. This is the permanent element in Pound's universe, and it is typical that he prefers the goddess Kuthera to the abstraction Amor. It is still more typical that he shifts quickly from the supernatural to the natural: 'Ubi amor, ibi oculus.' For, following the logic of the introductory lines of this canto, it is not the soul (or 'Kuthera') that delights, but the love that flows from it; and love, in flowing, manifests itself in actions, through concrete particulars. We respond to this love worshipfully by observing its manifestations, i.e. by directing our attention *outside* of ourselves. Hence the jeremiac 'Vae qui cogitatis inutile'—which is made meaningful by recalling 'Cogito ergo sum'. On the Poundian view of reality, Descartes's (or any Skeptic's) introspective method, of positing the universe on the basis of his own mental activity, is sacrilegious as well as perverse. And of course 'quam in nobis similitudine divinae / reperetur imago' is not merely the chief argument for human self respect; its corollary is the mediaeval 'Doctrine of Signatures', which holds that all created things contain the 'signatures' of divine forms and, as such, should be respected. Moreover, if the image of the divine is indeed found in us, we should act accordingly: i.e. reveal this kinship by an outflowing of love.

A brief summary may be useful at this point. Pound seems to envisage a natural world of more or less perishable particulars, which are not to be despised because they are perishable, but to be studied with affection because they are manifestations of divine love. Besides 'Kuthera sempiterna' there is a body of wisdom (practical and spiritual) which survives from generation to generation, and which is our guarantee that, whatever dark ages descend, civilization will rebuild. The capacity to renew is, of course, a capacity that each of us has, as a member of nature:

> 'Mother Earth in thy lap'
> said Randolph

(This is juxtaposed directly with 'quam in nobis similitudine divinae / reperetur imago'.) And, as we shall see, this view of the world is extremely hospitable to metamorphosis.

Pound then recalls Cunizza's liberation of her slaves and goes on to less congenial 'liberators':

> liberavit masnatos.
> Castalia like the moonlight
>   and the waves rise and fall,
> Evita, beer-halls, semina motuum,
>   to parched grass, now is rain
> not arrogant from habit,
>   but furious from perception,
>   Sibylla,

Castalia is the fountain on Mount Parnassus dedicated to Apollo in which pilgrims to the Delphic shrine purify themselves. And though there is a certain element of humour in the notion of Hitler as a sybil, it is a sorry pilgrimage which leads to such oracles. However, it is useful to note that the conception behind this passage and the actual imagery were in Pound's mind as early as 1912:

And with certain others their consciousness is 'Germinal'. Their thoughts are in them as the thought of the tree is in the seed, or in the grass, or the grain, or the blossom. And these minds are the more poetic, and they affect mind about them, and transmute it as the seed the earth. And this latter sort of mind is close on the vital universe; and the strength of the Greek beauty rests in this, that it is ever at the interpretation of this vital universe, by its signs of gods, and godly attendants and oreads.[1]

The idea of resurrection is not present in this passage, but it clearly indicates the basis of resurrection. In the lines from Canto 90 there is also the image ' … the waves rise and fall', which might be illuminated by this brief passage from Canto XLII:

>   wave falls and the hand falls
> Thou shalt not always walk in the sun
>   or see weed sprout over cornice
> Thy work in set space of years, not over an hundred.
>   (p. 218)

It is in the nature of things, of men and civilizations, that they rise and fall. The serenity with which Pound contemplates this

---

[1] Pound, 'Psychology and Troubadours', *The Quest*, vol. IV, no. 1, p. 45.

rise and fall of civilizations is one of the attractive features of
the Rock-Drill Cantos—and yet how strangely it contrasts with
the savage utopianism of Hitler, which was to have produced a
world order that would last for a thousand years.

In the next block of verse Pound elaborates the theme of
resurrection, though the active figure this time is (apparently)
himself:

> from under the rubble heap
> > m'elevasti
> from the dulled edge beyond pain,
> > m'elevasti
> out of Erebus, the deep-lying
> > from the wind under the earth,
> > > m'elevasti
> from the dulled air and the dust,
> > > m'elevasti
> by the great flight,
> > m'elevasti,
> > > Isis Kuanon
> from the cusp of the moon,
> > m'elevasti

It is not at all surprising that Pound turns from 'the rubble heap'
to a natural world which he believes to be penetrated by a divine
and vital force. (This occurs frequently in the Pisan Cantos.)
How far the Chinese goddess of mercy Kuanon (Kwannon)
shares the attributes of Isis, I don't know; but it is certain that
Isis, goddess of the moon and the underworld (among many
attributes), represents a type of divinity common to almost all
peoples of the ancient Mediterranean and Asiatic worlds. In this
context she represents the natural cycle of death and rebirth, as
does 'the great flight' (of migratory birds, presumably, whose
annual squadrons attest the persistence of the regenerative
instinct).

Next Pound turns to one of the most ancient symbols of
renewal and wisdom, then to fertility rites which echo Canto
XLVII, and at last to a region of mythological serenity:

> the viper stirs in the dust,
> > the blue serpent
> glides from the rock pool
> > And they take lights now down to the water

the lamps float from the rowers
              the sea's claw drawing them outward.
'De fondo' said Juan Ramon,
                    like a mermaid, upward,
but the light perpendicular, upward
and to Castalia,
                    water jets from the rock
and in the flat pool as Arethusa's
                    a hush in papyri.
Grove hath its altar
                    under elms, in that temple, in silence
a lone nymph by the pool.

It is again characteristic of Pound's world that serenity comes after (derives from) a period of intense creative activity. In fact many individual cantos, for instance Canto XLVII, follow this emotional curve. But, as Canto 90 is the canto of rise and fall, the action begins again with even greater vigour:

              Wei and Han rushing together
two rivers together
              bright fish and flotsam
torn bough in the flood
              and the waters clear with the flowing
Out of heaviness where no mind moves at all
              'birds for the mind' said Richardus,
'beasts as to body, for know-how'

One could preach a lengthy sermon on this text from Richard of St Victor (from whom most of the Latin quotations in this canto are taken); but as I must limit myself to the present context, I note only that, though the bird moves more rapidly and freely, through a different element, his flight depends on the same physical principles as does the movement of a beast. So it is with metamorphosis and natural growth in Pound's world: the sudden appearance of Dionysus' pards out of the aether may indeed be a revelation, but, for the mind accustomed to seeing individual lynxes, leopards, and roses as manifestations of divine forces, such metamorphoses belong to the same order of reality. And it is well to underscore what has already been said: that the soul (stasis) is not love; that love is a flowing, the perception of which requires the eye; and that, of course, there is a visionary eye as well as a natural eye.

The architect from the painter,
>   the stone under elm
Taking form now,
>   the rilievi,
>   the curled stone at the marge
Faunus, sirenes,
>   the stone taking form in the air
>   ac ferae,
>   cervi,
>   the great cats approaching.
Pardus, leopardi, Bagheera
>   drawn hither from woodland,
woodland ἐπὶ χθονί
>   the trees rise
>   and there is a wide sward between them
οἱ χθόνιοι myrrh and olibanum on the altar stone
giving perfume,
>   and where was nothing
now is furry assemblage
>   and in the boughs now are voices
grey wing, black wing, black wing shot with crimson
and the umbrella pines
>   as in Palatine,
as in pineta. χελιδών, χελιδών
For the procession of Corpus
>   come now banners
comes flute tone
>   οἱ χθόνιοι
to new forest,
>   thick smoke, purple, rising
bright flame now on the altar
>   the crystal funnel of air
out of Erebus, the delivered,
>   Tyro, Alcmene, free now, ascending
e i cavalieri,
>   ascending,
no shades more,
>   lights among them, enkindled,

It may be doubted whether, as a matter of historical fact, architectural form necessarily or even often follows the visual lead set by painting. But it is an idea which helps one follow the development of this passage: the experience of metamorphoses (of the god's presence) leads to the institution of ceremony and places of worship, and these lead to the deliverance of vital spirits from the earth. The connection of this imagery with that of the fertility cults (especially the cult of Isis and the Eleusinian Mysteries) is sufficiently clear.

It is well to remember that 'Kuthera sempiterna' is behind all of this, for the shades are liberated through 'the crystal funnel of air', and crystal is the sphere of love where Cunizza was placed by Dante. One shade only, it seems, is not liberated by love:

> and the dark shade of courage,
> Ἠλέχτρα
> bowed still with the wrongs of Aegisthus.

Elektra remains behind, still trapped inside, incapable of forgiveness or regeneration. Then Pound closes Canto 90 with a reassertion of the main principles on which it is based.

> Trees die & the dream remains
> Not love but that love flows from it
> ex animo
> & cannot ergo delight in itself
> but only in the love flowing from it.
> UBI AMOR IPI OCULUS EST.

There are other cantos, notably the second, in which metamorphosis as such bulks larger; but there is no other canto, I think, in which metamorphosis is so clearly related to other, equally important components of Pound's world. For Pound metamorphosis is a revelation of the godhead, but it is not something that exists apart from the natural world; it is, rather, a more dramatic sign of the divinity which is immanent in the objects around him, whether they be works of art or works of nature. The creative force that reveals itself through metamorphosis is the same force that drives the tree or the temple upwards. Or, in more human terms, we perceive that there is a permanent body of wisdon which survives in myth, in ritual, and in the craftsman's lore; and this wisdom survives to a large extent because it can assume new forms according to the demands of a new time and locality. But whatever form it takes, it embodies something of the divinity which may be discovered by a loving observation of the growing world.

NOTES TO CHAPTER IV

(1) In the middle of the canto appears the formula 'Ubi Amor, ibi oculus est'. I think that Pound may have in mind, as a parallel, 'Ubicunque Lingua Romana, Ibi Roma' (quoted in the *ABC of Reading* (London, 1934), p. 17). Spelled backwards, 'Roma' is 'Amor'—a favourite device during the late Middle Ages, signifying the opposition of the Church of Love and the Church of Christ. It would not be possible on the basis of this indication alone to pronounce Canto 90 a Poundian version of 'trobar clus', i.e. a hermetic writing in the style of 'Donna me prega'. But in fact the entire canto deals with the stuff of mystery:

> did Jacques de Molay
> know these porportions?
> and was Erigena ours?

The 'proportions' [spelled 'porportions' in the text, presumably a typographical error?], I suppose, are to be traced finally to Pythagoras. 'And was Erigena ours?' Was he, that is, an initiate? (He was, of course, condemned as a Manichean; he was, in any case, an adventurous Neo-Platonist). Like most readers, I suspect, I find myself not a little impatient with the 'trobar clus' convention, and ready to cry, 'Hum-bug!' One thing, however, is certain: my exposition of Canto 90 leaves many of its secrets intact.

Of course, Pound's poetry, at least from the time of *Mauberley*, has shown a marked tendency toward 'trobar clus' all along; however, I am inclined to think that Canto 90 marks its first appearance in the poem. As I argue in later sections of this essay, many of Pound's poetic assumptions can be traced to (or explained in terms of) 'Donna me prega'. It is not at all surprising that, eventually, these assumptions drew him back to 'trobar clus'.

(2) Clearly a philosophical gloss would be helpful here. Just how far Pound can be said to believe in any philosophy (other than that of Confucius) is a baffling problem. One oddity in Pound's philosophical position is that he found his 'practical' philosophy in the Far East and his 'spiritual' philosophy (so far as he has one) in the Near East and Mediterranean. The latter is not odd in itself, of course, but what he found there is only slightly less odd than what Yeats put into *A Vision*. The compound of Neo-Platonism, Pythagoreanism, and Gnosticism which is so important in the Rock-Drill sequence seems to have been acquired by Pound during the early years of his association with Yeats. It was perhaps through Yeats that Pound came into contact with G. R. S. Mead, editor of *The Quest* (in which Pound's 'Psychology and Troubadours' first appeared) and author of such works as *Apollonius of Tyana* (London, 1901) and *Thrice-greatest Hermes: Studies in Hellenistic Theosophy and Gnosis*, 3 vols. (London, 1906). Apollonius of Tyana is one of the chief heroes of the Rock-Drill sequence, and there are occasional references to other heroes and heroines of Gnostic mythology. But it is unlikely that Pound would accept many of the Gnostic doctrines, in so far as they stress asceticism and the inferiority of created (particular) things.

In fact, what Pound apparently found most congenial in Neo-Platonism was the 'Doctrine of Signatures':

> 'We have', said Mencius, 'but phenomena.'
> monumenta. In nature are signatures
> needing no verbal tradition,
> oak leaf never plane leaf. John Heydon.

> (Canto 87, p. 33)

It was from Heydon, the Rosicrucian, that Pound learned the doctrine that each particular, as a 'signature' of an eternal form, was an expression of divine power.

And in Erigena Pound discovered an elaborate argument in favour of this view of reality. The following summary of part of Erigena's theory may serve as a partial gloss of Canto 90 (Gordon Leff, *Mediaeval Thought from St Augustine to Ockham*) (Harmondsworth, Middlesex, 1958), pp. 69–70.

'When we regard the created world, therefore, we are regarding God's manifestations. From what we have observed above, we can see that all that exists—as opposed to sin which is (following Augustine and Denys) a deprivation of being—is both good and from God. Everything is a participation in God's nature as expressed in creation; it is like the rays of light which reflect the sun. Because all creatures both derive from God as principle, and move towards Him as end, the whole of nature is a movement powered by love of God. This view of all being as originating in and returning to God was one of the most markedly Dionysian influences in John's outlook, and was to be of the utmost importance in succeeding centuries. In John's case, it led not simply to a personal attempt by the soul to grasp its connections with God, but also to an objective analysis of the created world.

'In the first place, the created world is a world of essences derived from the Ideas of archetypes in the Word. Thus knowledge of anything is through the forms which inform it: in looking at anything we are aware of its colour, its size, its shape, its quality, these are all essences by which we judge it: only matter cannot be recognized separately. Ideas, then, are the cause of all being and of all our knowledge of being. "There is, I hold, nothing visible or corporeal which does not signify the invisible and the incorporeal." Matter itself, far from being the means by which we can know the essence in things, is quasi-being, the cause of nothing. For John the problem of the relation of the universal to the particular did not arise. Each individual portrayed the natures of which it was composed and in turn belonged to genera and species with their source in divine Ideas.'

V

EROS: AN INSTIGATION

1. Earlier Influences and Achievements

SINCE POUND'S STUDIES of the troubadours date back to his university days, we must assume that one of the earliest ingredients of his thought was the notion that 'fin amors' was an instigation of poetry, good manners, and even chastity. This idea appears constantly in his early prose and verse:

> The light became her grace and dwelt among
> Blind eyes and shadows that are formed as men;
> Lo, how the light doth melt us into song:
>
> The broken sunlight for a healm she beareth
> Who hath my heart in jurisdiction.
> In wild-wood never fawn nor fallow fareth
> So silent light; no gossamer is spun
> So delicate as she is, when the sun
> Drives the clear emeralds from the bended grasses
> Lest they should parch too swiftly, where she passes.

Mr Rosenthal has rightly noted that this is one of the earliest 'of the shining moments of exultant vision, suffused with imagery of light, in Pound's poetry'.[1] And certainly this poem, 'Ballatetta', represents one possible line of development of the idea of Eros as an instigation—a line of development which, not uninfluenced by Pater and the Pre-Raphaelites, appears in *The Cantos* in the form of a translation of Cavalcanti's *Canzone d'Amore* (Canto XXXVI) and throughout the poem in the form of Pound's goddesses (e.g. Diana in Canto IV).

However, since the sexual passion in this case is very highly

---

[1] Rosenthal, *A Primer of Ezra Pound*, p. 6.

subtilized indeed, this line of development—though most impressive in its results—appears to have presented few problems to Pound: it is his personal development of the radiant visions of Guinicelli, Cavalcanti, and Dante; its origin in sexual passion therefore goes without saying, and it leads clearly to the Kuthera sempiterna of Canto 90 (as it led Dante to the God of Love—and, incidentally, with the same assistance from Richard of St Victor). Another, less lofty, development of the troubadours' idea of Eros as an instigation is associated in Pound's scheme of things with Sextus Propertius; and it was a development which was not accomplished without a certain self-consciousness and awkwardness on the way:

> O my fellow sufferers, songs of my youth,
> A lot of asses praise you because you are 'virile,'
> We, you, I! We are 'Red Bloods'!
> Imagine it, my fellow sufferers—
> Our maleness lifts us out of the ruck,
>   Who'd have foreseen it?

> O my fellow sufferers, we went out under the trees,
> We were in especial bored with male stupidity.
> We went forth gathering delicate thoughts,
> Our 'fantastikon' delighted to serve us.
> We were not exasperated with women,
>   for the female is ductile.

> And now you hear what is said to us:
> We are compared to that sort of person
> Who wanders about announcing his sex
> As if he had just discovered it.
> Let us leave this matter, my songs,
>   and return to what concerns us.

Here Pound's style veers crazily from the predominantly rough-and-tumble colloquial style of *Lustra*, to the pseudo-courtly style of the juvenile poetry that he is talking about, and finally, in the last two lines of the second stanza, to the suave latinity of *Homage to Sextus Propertius*. But this self-consciousness is not to be found in *Propertius*, perhaps chiefly because Propertius himself was not self-conscious.

Here is a passage from *Propertius* which reveals the connection

between this Latin author and the troubadours which so fascinated Pound:

> Yet you ask on what account I write so many love-lyrics
> And whence this soft book comes into my mouth.
> Neither Calliope nor Apollo sung these things into my ear,
>> My genius is no more than a girl.
>
> If she with ivory fingers drive a tune through the lyre,
>> We look into the process.
> How easy the moving fingers; if hair is mussed on
>> her forehead,
> If she goes in a gleam of Cos, in a slither of dyed
>> stuff,
> There is a volume in the matter; if her eyelids sink
>> into sleep,
> There are new jobs for the author;
> And if she plays with me with her shirt off,
>> We shall construct many Iliads.
> And whatever she does or says
>> We shall spin long yarns out of nothing.
>
> Thus much the fates have allotted me, and if,
>> Maecenas,
> I were able to lead heroes into armour, I would not,
> Neither would I warble of Titans, nor of Ossa
>>> spiked onto Olympus,
>
> And my ventricles do not palpitate to Caesarial *ore
>> rotundos,*
> Nor to the tune of the Phrygian fathers.
> Sailor, of winds; a plowman, concerning his oxen;
> Soldier the enumeration of wounds; the sheep-
>> feeder, of ewes;
> We in our narrow bed, turning aside from battles:
> Each man where he can, wearing out the day in his manner.

The line 'My genius is no more than a girl' is a paraphrase of
one of Pound's favourite quotations—*ingenium nobis ipsa puella
fecit*—which he habitually links with the troubadours. Although
there is an obvious distinction to be made between Propertius'
robust sexuality and the 'fin amors' which led to Cavalcanti's
canzone and ultimately to the *Paradiso,* there was in fact an
occasional sign of less subtilized sexuality in the troubadours'

poetry (particularly in that of Arnaut Daniel).[1] There was enough, at least, to indicate that their kinship with Propertius was not merely a Poundian illusion.

This line of development was further influenced by Remy de Gourmont, whose curious blend of highly scientific and highly aesthetic eroticism appears as an important element in *Mauberley*. Speaking of the difference between Gourmont and Propertius, Pound once wrote:

> ... one wants merely to show that one has himself made certain dissociations; as here, between the aesthetic receptivity of tactile and magnetic values, of the perception of beauty in these relationships and the conception of love, passion, emotion as an intellectual instigation; such as Propertius claims it; such as we find it declared in the King of Navarre's
>
> 'De fine amor vient science et beauté';
>
> and constantly in the troubadours.[2]

In *Mauberley*, however, Pound brought Gourmont and the troubadours into a very close and ingenious association. The second sequence of that poem, it will be recalled, is concerned with the life of a fictional minor poet whose career is a failure partly because of a hostile environment and partly because of inherited defects. One of Mauberley's defects, and the one which is most disastrous for him, is pointed to in this epigraph:

> 'Qu'est ce qu'ils savent de l'amour, et qu'est ce qu'ils peuvent comprendre?
>
> S'ils ne comprennent pas la poésie, s'ils ne sentent pas la musique, qu'est ce qu'ils peuvent comprendre de cette passion en comparaison avec laquelle la rose est grossière et le parfum de violettes un tonnerre?'
>
> CAID ALI

Poor Mauberley has some understanding of poetry all right, but he has little of Gourmont's 'aesthetic receptivity of [the] tactile and magnetic values' of sexual love. For an Anglo-Saxon like Mauberley, indeed, Gourmont's point of view seems so exotic that Pound has attributed this epigraph (written by himself, of course) to one Caid Ali. And Mauberley's blindness to these

---

[1] Pound, *Literary Essays*, pp. 136–7.
[2] Pound, *Literary Essays*, pp. 343–4.

values is catastrophic—his tragic flaw—for when his chance
comes, he does not see it:

> He had passed, inconscient, full gaze,
> The wide-banded irides
> And Botticellian sprays implied
> In their diastasis;

> Which anaesthesis, noted a year late,
> And weighed, revealed his great affect,
> (Orchid), mandate
> Of Eros, a retrospect.
>   . . .
> Mouths biting empty air,
> The still stone dogs,
> Caught in metamorphosis, were
> Left him as epilogues.

The general meaning of this passage is clear enough—Mauberley, having failed to note a flirtation, comes later to perceive
what he has missed and is left with a sense of frustration which
is both artistic and sexual. In other words, lacking Gourmontian
awareness, he misses his chance to utilize artistic resources discovered by Propertius and the troubadours. Also to be noticed
is that each of these three quatrains is based on one of Pound's
erotic/creative touchstones: the Botticellian goddess who reveals
herself in a vision to the true artist (cf. Canto I) and who is
immanent in particular human female beauties (cf. 'Envoi' in
Mauberley); the second of these quatrains is a parody of Cavalcanti's theory of Love (cf. Canto XXXVI), which holds that
the essential form of Love is held in the memory, and that
human passion is an 'accident' (translated by Pound as 'affect')
which occurs when the ideal form seems to be embodied in a
particular woman;[1] and the third quatrain is based on an image
which is closely related to the quarrying imagery of Canto
XLVII and which Pound quotes in connection with Cavalcanti: 'the god is inside the stone, *vacuos exercet aera morsus*. The
force is arrested, but there is never any question about its
latency, about the force being the essential, the rest "accidental" in the philosophical technical sense. The shape occurs.'[2]

[1] I am simplifying Cavalcanti's theory a great deal: cf. note (1).
[2] Pound, *Literary Essays*, p. 152.

Alas, it does not occur for Mauberley, he does not release any latent force either of love or art.

In *Mauberley*, then, there is a remarkably successful fusion of the various elements in Pound's Eros,[1] and the idea of Eros as an instigation is particularly well developed. Another aspect of *Mauberley* which should be noted in this connection is the Odysseus motif:

> His true Penelope was Flaubert,
> He fished by obstinate isles;
> Observed the elegance of Circe's hair
> Rather than the mottoes on sun-dials.

This is an ironic 'criticism' of Pound himself; but merely to observe 'the elegance of Circe's hair' is a Mauberleyan, not a Poundian, activity. The author of *Propertius*, *Mauberley*, and *The Cantos* knows very well that Circe has important secrets to divulge if she is handled properly. And in Cantos XXXIX and XLVII Odysseus-Pound is shown to be profiting from the sexual awareness which poor Mauberley lacked—both of these cantos are developed largely in terms of the ideas and images already present in the three quatrains from *Mauberley* which I have just discussed. These ideas, especially as they are embodied in *Mauberley* and Canto XLVII, seem to me at the very centre of Pound's conception of art and love. An exegesis of Canto XXXIX would perhaps clarify these ideas still further; but I must now turn to another development of the idea of Eros as an instigation. Suffice it to say here that XXXIX looks backward to *Mauberley* and forward to XLVII; it can best be regarded, I think, as a half-way point between two major integrations of forces.

2. Gourmont and the Troubadours in Canto XXIX

Canto XXIX falls outside this major line of development, yet nowhere else in *The Cantos* is it so easy to pick out the combined influences of Propertius, Gourmont, and the troubadours. The canto begins with an account of a woman who used her sexual attractiveness to satisfy personal ambition, and who in the end

---

[1] For an exhaustive account of the sexual elements in *Mauberley*, cf. J. J. Espey's *Ezra Pound's 'Mauberley'* (1955).

brought destruction on the man who allowed himself to be
controlled by her:

> Pearl, great sphere, and hollow,
> Mist over lake, full of sunlight,
> Pernella concubina
> The sleeve green and shot gold over her hand
> Wishing her son to inherit
> Expecting the heir ainé be killed in battle
> He being courageous, poisoned his brother puiné
> Laying blame on Siena
> And this she did by a page
> Bringing war once more on Pitigliano
> And the page repented and told this
> To Nicolo (ainé) Pitigliano
> Who won back that rock from his father
> 'still doting on Pernella his concubine'.

Against this selfishness and calculation, Pound juxtaposes the
joyous, heedless, and generous sexuality of Propertius:

> The sand that night like a seal's back
> Glossy beneath the lanthorns.
> From the Via Sacra
> (fleeing what band of Tritons)
> Up to the open air
> Over the mound of the Hippodrome:

And then, as one who has inherited the spirit of Propertius,
Cunizza da Romano is introduced in a lengthy passage, part of
which I have already quoted in connection with Canto IV. She,
it will be recalled, inspired some of Sordello's finest poetry.
Pound then shifts abruptly to a provincial American context
characterized by a lack of sexual curiosity or vigour:

> Languor has cried unto languor
>   about the marshmallow-roast
> (Let us speak of the osmosis of persons)
> The wail of the phonograph has pentrated their marrow
> (Let us ...
> The wail of the pornograph ...)
>   The cicadas continue uninterrupted.

This is the provincial counterpart of the society depicted in
Canto VII, and an American counterpart of the British society

depicted in *Mauberley*. The imagery does seem to me brilliantly
Poundian: the implication is clearly that the popular music,
like acid, is eating away individual identity and vitality—sub-
liminal disintegration. But the imitation of the phonograph
with a stuck needle and the pun on 'phonograph' are surely
sophomoric. Perhaps they are intended to be excruciating, yet
the tone seems to me quite uncontrolled:

> With a vain emptiness the virgins return to their homes
> With a vain exasperation
> The ephèbe has gone back to his dwelling,
> The djassban has hammered and hammered,
> The gentleman of fifty has reflected
> > That it is perhaps just as well.
> Let things remain as they are.
> The mythological exterior lies on the moss in the forest
> And questions him about Darwin.
> And with a burning fire of phantasy
> > he replies with 'Deh! nuvoletta ... '
> So that she would regret his departure.
> > Drift of weed in the bay:
> She seeking a guide, a mentor,
> He aspires to a career with honour
> To step in the tracks of his elders;
> > a greater incomprehension?
> There is no greater incomprehension
> Than between the young and the young.
> The young seek comprehension;
> The middleaged to fulfill their desire.

The first four lines, clearly, are not ironic; then irony takes
command (except for 'Drift of weed in the bay') up to the last
five lines; but what is the tone of the last five lines? The observations are certainly banal and Pound distrusts generalizations;
but the quality of insight in the rest of the passage, ironic or not,
isn't much better.

> Sea weed dried now, and now floated,
> > mind drifts, weed, slow youth, drifts,
> Stretched on the rock, bleached and now floated;
> Wein, Weib, TAN AOIDAN
> Chiefest of these the second, the female
> Is an element, the female

Eros: An Instigation

Is a chaos
An octopus
A biological process
        and we seek to fulfill ...
TAN AOIDAN, our desire, drift ...
           Ailas e que'm fau miey huelh
           Quar noi vezon so qu'ieu vuelh.
Our mulberry leaf, woman, TAN AOIDAN,
'Nel ventre tuo, o nella mente mia,
'Yes, Milady, precisely, if you wd
have anything properly made.'
'Faziamo tutte le due ...
'No, not in the palm-room.' The lady says it is
Too cold in the palm-room. Des valeurs,
Nom de Dieu, et
        encore des valeurs.

The quality of the wit here is poorer than in 'pornograph'. The Provençal commentary ('Alas that my eyes still see, for I do not see what I wish') is Pound's commentary by way of Sordello. No doubt Cunizza would have found the 'palm-room' too hot. The Italian formula ('In your belly, or in my mind') is Pound's way of putting a blue-stocking in her place: the sensuality and humour of *Propertius*, the bawdy but scalpel-like wit of *Mauberley*—these have very little in common with the droll 'down-to-earthness' of Canto XXIX. Concerning this canto Miss Marianne Moore once observed that Pound's 'unprudery is over-emphasized':[1] this seem to me a just criticism of the deliberate coarseness which appears in this passage, seemingly as an inevitable adjunct to the earlier uncertain irony. It has the kind of disagreeableness which Pound once repudiated in 'The Condolence'. However, agreeable or not, the passage is evidently of some importance in establishing the nature of Pound's views on women and poetry. I think that we must try to grasp what, in this passage, Pound's views are, and then compare these with the views expressed elsewhere in *The Cantos*.

The words 'the female is an element, the female is a chaos' unquestionably reflect Pound's interest in and speculations about Gourmont's *Physique de l'amour*, translated by Pound in

---

[1] *Predilections* (1956), p. 68. The essay from which this is quoted originally appeared as a review of the first thirty cantos (in *Poetry*, October 1931).

1926 with an epilogue by himself which he later saw fit to use as an introduction. This work by Gourmont, as Mr Espey pointed out, had some influence on *Mauberley*; its influence on *The Cantos* was even more important. However, we must be careful to distinguish two kinds of influence: in the passage quoted from Canto XXIX we have a versification of Pound's own speculations about the sexual basis of reality:

> There are traces of it in the symbolism of phallic religions, man really the phallus or spermatozoid charging, head-on, the female chaos; integration of the male in the male organ. Even oneself has felt it, driving any new idea into the great passive vulva of London, a sensation analogous to the male feeling in copulation.[1]

On the other hand, there is the influence of Gourmont's own speculations, which, though of course related, are nevertheless different.

The 'it' referred to in the passage quoted above is Pound's (not Gourmont's) remarkable idea that the human brain is literally a 'great clot of genital fluid, held in suspense or reserve'.[2] This somewhat startling proposition has the advantage of linking sexual and artistic activity more closely than Propertius, Gourmont, or the troubadours, I imagine, ever dreamed possible. The composition of the female mind is not very clearly worked out in Pound's system, but it is sufficiently clear from what has been quoted that a woman is, at most, rather like Bertrans de Born's Maent in *Near Perigord*:

> She who had nor ears nor tongue save in her hands,
> Gone—ah, gone—untouched, unreachable!
> She who could never live save through one person,
> She who could never speak save to one person,
> And all the rest of her a shifting change,
> A broken bundle of mirrors ... !

Here indeed the male artist (Bertrans in the famous *canso* in which he constructs a 'Maent' by borrowing the best features of other ladies) gives form to a female chaos.

In the passage last quoted from Canto XXIX we also find that the poet, as male, gives form to the human female chaos ('nel ventre tuo'); but, at the same time, she ('our mulberry

---

[1] Introduction to *The Natural Philosophy of Love* (London, 1957), p. viii.
[2] *Natural Philosophy*, p. vii.

leaf') provides him with the sustenance he needs as an artist to give form to non-human, female chaos (to spin a song—'TAN AOIDAN'). The female, whether human or non-human, is on this reckoning capable only of receiving the form given her by the male—because she is 'a chaos, an octopus, a biological process'. This is not to say that the female is inferior to the male; she is the 'Chiefest', an 'element' without which the masculine form-creating capacity would come to nothing. Nevertheless, there seems to me a kind of male stupidity in this conception, inherent in any crude version of the Platonic theory of form applied to matter or chaos. Mere 'chaos' or 'matter', however elementally necessary, if of course incapable of significant response or participation.

There is, however, an interesting development of these ideas in the next few lines of Canto XXIX:

> She is submarine, she is an octopus, she is
> A biological process,
> So Arnaut turned there
> Above him the wave pattern cut in the stone

Through the artist the elemental sexual nature of the female is translated into, in this case, an abstract decorative motif. This is, of course, a Poundian version of the troubadours' idea that 'fin amors' is the instigator of art. Nor does Pound fail to mention Propertius and the troubadours in his appendage to Gourmont's study:

> Perhaps the clue is in Propertius after all:
> *Ingenium nobis ipsa puella fecit.*
> There is the whole of the twelfth century love cult … 1

There is little doubt, therefore, that Canto XXIX is based on speculations which were triggered by Gourmont's book. Most of these, at least as they appear in Canto XXIX, are familiarly Poundian; in most respects, indeed, the statement of Canto XXIX is merely a crude variation of what is stated or implied in *Propertius*, *Mauberley*, and Cantos XXXIX and XLVII. But such crudeness makes all the difference between good and bad poetry. So far as poetry is concerned, the ideas in Canto XXIX are not the same as those in XLVII.

1 *Natural Philosophy*, p. xvii.

Moreover, while it must be allowed that Pound's ideas about human relations are often alarmingly simple, I believe that the brutal simplification of Canto XXIX is clearly uncharacteristic. His women are usually more than a 'chaos' or matter capable of receiving form:

> Dark shoulders have stirred the lightning
> A girl's arms have nested the fire,
> Not I but the handmaid kindled
>
> (Canto XXXIX)

His characteristic view is, like Gourmont's, fundamentally Aristotelian:

'The male,' says Aristotle, in his *Treatise on Generation*, 'represents the specific form, the female, the matter. She is passive, inasmuch as she is female; the male is active.'

… The moment will come for the female to be in her turn active and strong, when she has been fecundated and when she must give birth and food to the posterity of her race. The male then becomes inert; equable sharing of the expense of forces, just division of labour …

The female waits or flees, which is but another way of waiting, the active way; for not only *se cupit ante videnti* but she desires to be taken, she wishes to fulfill her destiny. It is doubtless for this reason that in species where the male is feeble or timid, the female resigns herself to an aggression demanded by care for future generations. In short, two forces are present, the magnet and the needle. Usually the female is the magnet, sometimes she is the needle.[1]

The image of the needle and the magnet might be compared with:

> To that is she bent, her intention,
> To that art thou called ever turning intention,
> Whether by night the owl-call, whether by sap in shoot,
> Never idle, by no means by no wiles intermittent
> Moth is called over mountain
> The bull runs blind on the sword, *naturans*
> To the cave art thou called, Odysseus,
>
> (Canto XLVII)

The difference between the Aristotelian and Platonic conceptions of the male-female relationship—and all that is implied

---

[1] *Natural Philosophy*, pp. 60-1.

about the relationship between the artist and his materials—is
profound and significant, in Pound's as in anybody else's usage.

It is for this reason that I object to the following comment on
Canto XLVII by Mr Espey:

> The references are specifically sexual throughout ... Here is the
> very bedrock of *The Cantos*, the creation of order (τὸ καλὸν for
> Pound) out of the formless, the male organ informing the female
> chaos.[1]

This remark might with more accuracy be applied to Canto
XXIX, though of course I agree with Mr Espey that XLVII,
not XXIX, is the 'bedrock' of *The Cantos*. In any case, it seems
to me a matter of some importance to insist that the male/female
relationship envisaged in Canto XLVII is based on mutual
attraction and mutual will, as does not seem to me implied in
Mr Espey's formulation. I realize that, to some readers, this
distinction will appear to be a quibble. But it appears to me the
simplest and clearest way of distinguishing what is permanent
and valuable in Pound's attitude toward, and poetry about,
sexual experience. The sexual act and also the artistic act are in
Pound's view a matter of the male releasing the potential of the
female: 'the god is inside the stone, *vacuos exercet aera morsus*. The
force is arrested, but there is never any question about its
latency, about the force being the essential, the rest "accidental"
in the philosophical technical sense. The shape occurs'. Pound
is often (and often rightly) charged with arrogance, but the
attitude expressed here is one of masculine and artistic humility:

> stone knowing the form which the carver imparts it
> the stone knows the form
> Sia Cythera, sia Ixotta, sia Santa Maria dei Miracoli
> (Canto LXXIV)

This passage from Canto LXXIV was previously quoted in
connection with Canto XLVII. Its most direct connection,
however, is with the Malatesta Cantos (VIII–XI); and since
Sigismondo Malatesta is (in Pound's portrait) a descendent of
the troubadours—

> 'Ye spirits who of old were in this land
> Each under Love, and shaken,

[1] *Ezra Pound's Mauberley*, p. 110.

Go with your lutes, awaken
The summer within her mind,
Who hath not Helen for peer
     Yseut nor Batsabe.'

            (Canto VIII)

—I close this account of the troubadour's influence in *The Cantos* by referring the reader to the cantos in which Sigismondo's heroic struggles are recorded. These struggles were important, in Pound's view, because they were directed toward the construction of the Tempio Malatestiano in Rimini. And Pound is quite unambiguous about what he regards as the motive behind that construction:

> '*et amava perdutamente Ixotta degli Atti*'
> e '*ne fu degna*'
>   '*constans in proposito*
> '*Placuit oculis principis*
> '*pulchra aspectu*'
> '*populo grata* (*Italiaeque decus*)
> 'and built a temple so full of pagan works'
>   i.e. Sigismund
> and in the style 'Past ruin'd Latium'

            (Canto IX)

In this case it is the Tempio with its 'pagan works' that 'gives youth to' a mortal maid. Landor is not quite in the song tradition celebrated in the 'Envoi' of *Mauberley*, but both he and Sigismondo might well join that immortal and immortalizing company.

3. Helen-Tellus and Miss Tudor

If 'fin amors' was an instigation of poetry, of good manners, of the Tempio Malatestiano, and even of chastity, the passion inspired by Helen of Troy was an instigation of destruction— and of the *Iliad*. Certainly the official pagan attitude toward erotic passion was that it was a form of madness—not, certainly, a refining agent of great public utility! Nevertheless, in Canto II Pound embarks on the story of Helen, and the implications of her career are underscored by a quotation from Aeschylus:

'Eleanor, ἑλέναυς and ἑλέπτολις!'
    And poor old Homer blind, blind, as a bat,

Ear, ear for the sea-surge, murmur of old men's voices:
'Let her go back to the ships,
Back among Grecian faces, lest evil come on our own,
Evil and further evil, and a curse cursed on our children,
Moves, yes she moves like a goddess
And has the face of a god
          and the voice of Schoeney's daughters,
And doom goes with her in walking,
Let her go back to the ships,
          back among Grecian voices.'

Helen is indeed the 'destroyer of ships' and the 'destroyer of cities', and in Canto VII Pound adds 'Ἕλανδρος', destroyer of men. In Canto XLVI, though describing the effects of usury, he coins 'helarxe', destroyer of government, after the same pattern. Since Aeschylus himself makes a great (and unscholarly) issue of the derivation of Helen's name, Pound has a distinguished precedent for playing this word game. It is a very serious game indeed, because both Pound and Aeschylus are vitally interested in civic order, and both condemn the immoderate passions which disrupt and plague the state.

But here the parallel ends, for Aeschylus' condemnation draws strength not only from taboos on adultery but also from the dramatic context of his own play, in which the adulterous Clytemnestra is about to slaughter her king and husband. Pound does not, of course, subscribe to any taboo on adultery ('each in his nature'?—Canto XIII); and he has forsaken the advantages which a narrative situation affords: no Clytemnestra, who is known by the audience to be about to kill her lord, has just left the scene when, in *The Cantos*, Pound says 'Eleanor, Ἑλέναυς and Ἑλέπτολις'. The fact is that Pound's attitude toward Helen is a good deal more ambivalent than that of Aeschylus' chorus of citizens or Homer's Trojan elders. Pound's dilemma here is fundamental and its implications bear on the entire poem: as the poet of civic order he cannot keep Helen in his ideal state; as a modern troubadour he is intoxicated by her ideal beauty.

The tension which this dilemma creates—a dilemma inherent in the figure of Helen—might have resulted in great poetry, as it did in the *Iliad* or, to take the modern instance which undoubtedly influenced Pound, in Yeats's poems to Maud Gonne.

In *The Cantos*, however, this tension is an embarrassment, because Pound does not really believe in the traditional figure of Helen. It appears to me that he simply likes and admires the adventuress in particular, and women in general, too well to take the Helen theme very seriously. In Canto VI, for example, he called attention to the parallel between Helen and Eleanor of Aquitaine:

> Eleanor (she spoiled in a British climate)
> Ἔλανδρος and Ἑλέπτολις, and
> poor old Homer blind,
> blind as a bat,
> Ear, ear for the sea-surge,

And there are indeed good historical reasons for viewing Eleanor as a second Helen, a matrix of creation and destruction. (For instance, the presence of Eleanor and her courtly equipage on the Second Crusade is reputed to have cost the lives of many French knights.) But Pound fails to develop the parallel fully: like Helen, Eleanor is pursued vigorously, and possession of her is politically important:

> Divorced her in that year, he Louis,
> divorcing thus Aquitaine.
> And that year Plantagenet married her
> (that had dodged past 17 suitors)
> Et quand lo reis Lois lo entendit
> mout er fasché.

> (Canto VI)

And her connection with poetry and song is given prominence in Canto VI. But the Eleanor who may have encouraged the strife between her own and Henry's sons, who may have spurred her courtly favourite Richard to revolt against his father, and whose dowry of quarrelsome Aquitaine and Poitou proved to be a curse to the Plantagenets[1]—this Eleanor, who might have fascinated an Aeschylus, is eliminated with an Anglophobe parenthesis. Indeed, Pound's Eleanor emerges as a Cunizza-like figure, a rather jolly adventuress who disappeared in a London fog.

There are, however, a number of *femmes fatales* in *The Cantos* who might be regarded as daughters of Helen, such as the Pernella of Canto XXIX, a vampire figure who is contrasted

[1] Cf. Amy Kelly, *Eleanor of Aquitaine, and the Four Kings* (London, 1952), pp. 73 ff.

with Cunizza, the amorous and generous. There are, inevitably, bad women in the Chinese history Cantos. But the daughters of Helen disappear in the Pisan sequence, to be replaced by Pound's goddesses, who, for the first time in the poem, have distinct 'personalities'. In the following passage the characteristic attitudes of Artemis and Aphrodite are reversed, for Artemis is 'compassionate' and Aphrodite is called 'egoista'.

> At Ephesus she had compassion on silversmiths
> revealing the paraclete
> standing in the cusp
> of the moon et in Monte Gioiosa
> as the larks rise at Allegre
> Cythera egoista
> But for Actaeon
> (Canto LXXX, p. 534)

The lines which immediately follow develop the idea of waning and disintegration, so that (as Mr Kenner has pointed out)[1] we have compassionate revelation—of the paraclete, of the larks rising—followed by a cruel withdrawal of the favour. This, however, is a distinctly new development of the *femme fatale* theme: Helen (and even Circe) represent an ambivalent force actively at work in the affairs of men; but the goddesses of the Pisan sequence and Canto 90, though friendly with Pound and ultimately in control, are not directly implicated in human affairs. It is hard to escape the conclusion that Pound's interest in the Helen theme—of glorious yet destructive passion, repeating itself in concrete human terms—did not survive the early cantos (e.g. II and IV). Yet the curious interchange of divine attributes which we see in the last passage quoted prepares the way for a later reconciliation of Helen, Artemis, and Aphrodite.

In fact the transfer of Aeschylus' epithets from Helen to usury in Canto XLVI marks their last appearance in the poem until Canto 91, where they acquire an entirely different significance. Pound's sleight of hand is worthy of close examination.

> Aurum est commune sepulchrum. Usura, commune
> sepulchrum.
> helandros kai heleptolis kai helarxe.
> Hic Geryon est. Hic hyperusura.
> (Canto XLVI, p. 245)

[1] Kenner, *The Poetry of Ezra Pound*, pp. 200–1.

Aeschylus' grave censure fits usury quite well; but, her epithets transferred, Helen the semi-divinity, the legendary queen, vanishes from *The Cantos*. She is translated into 'Helen-Tellus', an entity unlikely to be regarded as the prototype of any particular woman (though she is the prototype of womankind); she has now only her symbolical properties:

> Mist covers the breasts of Tellus-Helena and drifts up
> > the Arno
> (Canto LXXVII, p. 503)

Helen has become Mother Earth—ambivalent as the earth is ambivalent, not as Helen was in the eyes of the Trojan elders: one cannot ship Tellus away!—

> Forked shadow falls dark on the terrace
> More black that the floating martin
> > that has no care for your presence,
> His wing-print is gone with his cry.
> So light is thy weight on Tellus
> > (Canto XLVII, p. 248)

This is by no means a reduction in status. It is, however, a strange procedure for a poet who makes so much of individual qualities, of irreducible particularity.

There is, however, in Canto 91, a resolution of the courtly and the pagan ideas of Eros as an instigation, of creative activity on the one hand, and of destructive activity on the other. It is a resolution made possible, appropriately, by a Renaissance figure:

> Our science is from the watching of shadows;
> That Queen Bess translated Ovid,
> > Cleopatra wrote of the currency,
> Versus who scatter old records
> > (Canto 85, p. 3)

Elizabeth is by no means the only heroine of Canto 91; this canto is, indeed, Pound's 'Legend of Good Women'—including (though sometimes only by implication) the Virgin Mary, Eleanor of Aquitaine, Ondine, Helen of Tyre, the Empress Theodora, the goddesses Artemis and Aphrodite, Cleopatra and Helen of Troy. But Elizabeth is the central figure in the canto, and one cannot do better than quote this poem by Ralegh as a gloss for what is to be discussed:

Praisd be Dianas faire and harmles light,
Praisd be the dewes, wherewith she moists the ground;
Praisd be hir beames, the glories of the night,
Praisd be hir powre, by which all powres abound.

Praisd be hir Nimphs, with whom she decks the woods,
Praisd be hir knights, in whom true honor liues,
Praisd be that force, by which she moues the floods,
Let that Diana shine, which all these giues.

In heauen Queene she is among the spheares,
In ay she Mistres like makes all things pure,
Eternitie in hir oft chaunge she beares,
She beautie is, by hir the faire endure.

Time weares hir not, she doth his chariot guide,
Mortalitie belowe hir orbe is plaste,
By hir the vertue of the starres downe slide,
In hir is vertues perfect image cast.

A knowledge pure it is hir worth to kno,
With Circes let them dwell that thinke not so.

After a brief invocation in Provençal, Pound addresses these lines to Elizabeth:

that the body of light come forth
            from the body of fire
And that your eyes come to the surface
            from the deep wherein they were sunken,
Reina—for 300 years,
                and now sunken,
That your eyes come forth from their caves
            & light then

The image of the body of light coming forth from the body of fire is frequently encountered in *The Cantos* (in IV, XXXIX, XLVII, for example).[1] Its appropriateness as an image of the transfiguring of sensual passion into devotional and creative energy is clear enough. (As, for instance, the *cansos* of the troubadours eventually became hymns to the Virgin.) The image of light coming from eyes lately submerged in sea caves is not so immediately intelligible; but if the source of the light which

[1] Cf. as well note (1), Chapter II.

comes from the body of fire, is, ultimately, Aphrodite, then the source of this light is Artemis, the virgin goddess who, as the Moon, controls the tides. It is not clear whether the light of Artemis is the same as the light of Aphrodite, but it may well be since there seems to be, in this canto, an attempt to reconcile Artemis and Aphrodite in the figure of Elizabeth (as they were once reconciled, in a way, in the figure of the Virgin).

Besides being the goddess of the Moon and controller of the tides, Artemis is also, of course, goddess of the chase; and this attribute is also of some importance in Canto 91. It will be recalled that in Canto XXX Pound attacks 'Pity', and that this attack takes the form of a 'Compleynt' by Artemis. The seed for that canto, in which Mars also complains that Venus 'hath pity on a doddering fool', can be found in the *Pervigilium Veneris*, where the nymphs for a moment turn their attention from Venus (called Dione there, as in Canto XLVII) to Diana:

> 'One thing which we pray thee, Virgin Diana,
> Let the grove be undefiled with the slaughter of wild things.
> Yea, She bids us ask thee if thy strictness might waver,
> She wills that thou deign to come—an thou deemst it
>   maid befitting—
> Where thou mightest see the gay chorus singing, for three
>   full nights amid the herds and wandering through
>   thy glades,
> Through the flowery crown of fields, mid the lodges of
>   myrtle;
> And the whole night long will be watched out with con-
>   tinuing song.'
>   'Dione reigns in the woodland,
>   Give place, O Delian Maid.'[1]

Canto XXX is not a simple inversion of this, but it is similarly based on the neat opposition of Diana the huntress and Venus the protectress. Reduced to a biological principle, this opposition maintains the balance of nature; reduced to a literary principle, it becomes a defence of criticism. But a simple dualism of this kind (however useful) cannot satisfy the imagination indefinitely.

That Spenser's Faery Queen and Ralegh's Diana also had a

---

[1] Pound's translation in *The Spirit of Romance*, p. 11.

Cleopatra side to her has been noticed by Eliot; and it is in fact
Elizabeth's remarkable ambivalence (real and imaginary) as
well as her historical greatness, which makes her such an ideal
figure for the reconciliation of Artemis and Aphrodite.

> Miss Tudor moved them with galleons
> from deep eye, versus armada
> from the green deep
> > he saw it,
> in the green deep of an eye:
> > Crystal waves weaving together toward the gt/
> > > healing
>
> ...
>
> Light & the flowing crystal
> > never gin in cut glass had such clarity
> That Drake saw the splendour and wreckage
> > in that clarity
> Gods moving in crystal
> > ichor, amor

The imagery in the second passage is reminiscent of the imagery
in Canto 90, with which this canto is closely related:

> Wei and Han rushing together
> two rivers together
> > bright fish and flotsam
> torn bough in the flood
> > and the waters clear with the flowing

Of more immediate interest, however, is the movement toward
action which has been instigated by 'Miss Tudor'. Like the
instigations of Helen of Troy and Cleopatra, this leads to
destruction; but, as with the instigation of Sigismondo's Isotta,
the destruction is a way toward constructive effort: the English
Renaissance. But the central image, which is indeed based on
the relationship between Antony and Cleopatra, is not directly
by way of the greatest figure of the English Renaissance; it is
by way of an archaeologist like Pound—Hérédia:

> Et sur elle courbé, l'ardent Imperator
> Vit dans ses larges yeux étoilés de points d'or
> Toute une mer immense ou fuyaient des galères.[1]

Of course Pound has altered the image and conception considerably. In his version Elizabeth seems to be in touch with

---

[1] J. M. Hérédia, 'Antoine et Cléopatre', *Les Trophées* (Cambridge 1942), p. 33.

powers more permanent and profound than exist within the realm of human passion and ambition.

The next development of the image recalls, at last, Helen of Troy:

> 'Ελέναυς That Drake saw the armada
> & sea caves

Destructive passion has at last been translated into constructive action. And, what is equally important, chastity is also defended (resisting unlawful and undesired invasion):

> in the Queen's eye the reflection
> & sea-wrack—
> > green deep of the sea-cave
> ne quaesaris.
> > He asked not
> nor wavered, seeing, nor had fear of the wood-queen,
> > > Artemis
> > that is Diana
> nor had killed save by the hunting rite,
> > > sanctus.

Drake, as Actaeon, becomes both defender and victim of forces greater than himself, or, for that matter, Elizabeth, who translated Ovid and was herself translated by more than one 'mythopoetic' imagination.

So it is that Pound achieves at least a partial reconciliation of the pagan and courtly views of Eros. It is a reconciliation which Elizabeth's career made uniquely possible, for she was a figure at once grand and ambivalent enough to represent Aphrodite compounded with Artemis, subsuming Cleopatra and Helen of Troy. So far as Eros in *The Cantos* is concerned, this is surely Pound's most remarkable conception.

NOTES TO CHAPTER V

(1) In his admirable *In Praise of Love* (New York, 1958), pp. 228–9, Maurice Valency has this to say about Cavalcanti's canzone: 'the dark words of *Donna mi prega*, couched in the style of the *trobar clus* and further obfuscated by the rigors of a complex rhyme-pattern and a technical terminology, seem to have had the greatest influence upon Cavalcanti's contemporaries ... it was one of the prime vehicles of scholastic love-theory and, though it cannot be said to have clarified its subject in any substantial way, it formed the nucleus of a considerable literature.'

Eros: An Instigation

A further comment on the 'trobar clus' by Valency has obvious modern applications, though more to the poetry of Eliot than to *The Cantos*. 'The best of the *trobar clus* is characterized by a parabolic quality, the result of a studied ambiguity which implies a reserve of meaning beyond the comprehension of the average intelligence. The poem communicates a feeling that more is meant than meets the eye, and what meets the eye is by no means certain. We are thus aware of penumbral significances which may or may not have been intended, as well as of a general exasperating breakdown of communication. Such poetry teases the mind into poetic activity on its own account. It elicits an athletic response which is in pleasant contrast with the more passive pleasure of easy poetry, and thus brings about an enhanced participation on the part of the listener or the reader, who has a feeling, if he succeeds in penetrating the poet's meaning, of greater intimacy than less exclusive types of poetry can afford. Of those who practiced the closed style among the troubadours none was able to compose a masterpiece of the magnitude of Donne's "A Nocturnall Upon S. Lucie's Day," but the seventeenth poet's relation to his predecessors in the closed style is unmistakable' (*In Praise of Love*, pp. 125–6). And so is Eliot's relation to the Donne of the closed style unmistakable. I have insisted that, at least until the Rock-Drill Cantos, Pound is not a practitioner of 'trobar clus'; but it is clear that, from the time of *Mauberley*, he has quite intentionally required an 'athletic response' from his reader. And the 'enhanced participation', the 'greater intimacy' which Valency describes (with an eye on the contemporary scene?) also describes the experience of an adept reader of *The Cantos*. In this sense Pound's work is not a poem, it is a conspiracy. This, I think, accounts for the uncritical enthusiasm of many of Pound's disciples: *The Cantos* is as much their poem as it is Pound's. Perhaps, in some cases, Pound has produced 'trobar clus' in spite of himself; but whereas 'trobar clus' is an aristocratic art that instils aristocratic self-satisfaction, Pound's method is supposed to require the sort of 'athletic response' which promotes action or, at any rate, dissatisfaction with the extent of one's own present knowledge.

SECTION TWO

Pound's Arcanum

And they kicked me into the fore-stays.
I have seen what I have seen.

(Canto II)

Bright hawk whom no hood shall chain,
They who are skilled in fire

shall read tan the dawn

Waiving no jot of the arcanum
(having his own mind to stand by him)
(Canto 91)

VI

CAVALCANTI'S CANZONE
D'AMORE AND CANTO XXXVI

1. The Romance of Romance Scholarship

IN 1910 POUND PUBLISHED *The Spirit of Romance,* a work which
pretended to little scholarship and which, generally, has been
treated rather kindly by scholars. Today it hardly attains to the
status of *haute vulgarisation,* for Romance scholarship has advanced enormously since the days when Pound was fresh from
graduate school. It is now a 'Pound document', a reminder of
times when he could speak even of Milton with a modicum of
deference. In 1910, however, it was not merely precocious and
apologetically iconoclastic; its scholarship was then less patently unreliable, and, what is more to the point, it arrived on one
of the last surges of the flood of Victorian popularizations. How
nearly spent that flood was may be gauged by the fact that
the last general book on the troubadours in English was published by H. J. Chaytor in 1912.[1]

The first relatively authoritative account of the troubadours
in English was written by Ford Madox Ford's father, Dr
Francis Hueffer,[2] a product of the great nineteenth-century
German school of Romance philology. He was related by marriage to the Rossettis; and D. G. Rossetti, Pound's too little
appreciated predecessor in the field of early Italian translation,
was the son of a noted Dante scholar. It is interesting to note,
too, that the first and only anthology of troubadour poetry to
appear under English or American editorship[3] is dedicated to

---

[1] *The Troubadours* (Cambridge, 1912).   [2] *The Troubadours* (1878).
[3] *Anthology of Provençal Troubadours,* ed. R. T. Hill and T. G. Bergin (New Haven,
Conn., 1941).

Pound's old teacher, W. P. Shepard (whose 'refined and sympathetic scholarship' Pound mentions in the preface to *The
Spirit of Romance*).

The Spirit of Romance, then, is very much a period piece; and
its author is rather a slightly eccentric member of the family
of Romancers than an outlaw. Though the book still has a
certain novelty, even charm, it is clear that Pound then saw
early Italian poetry mostly through Rossetti's eyes. In particular, he makes only a glancing reference to Cavalcanti's
Canzone d'Amore 'Donna me prega'. His effort to see the troubadours through Dante's eyes is noteworthy. But in any case the
faith in popularization of which this work is a manifestation
did not survive Pound's days as an apprentice poet; and, indeed,
the faith in popularization in general seems, as I have suggested,
to have died out in scholarly circles (in English-speaking
countries anyway). Romance scholarship became much more
professional, as it is today; on the other hand, Pound, perhaps
the most professional poet since Pope, never got beyond the
apprentice stage as a Romance scholar, the stage marked
'promisingly' in *The Spirit of Romance*. His views on mediaeval
poetry and his understanding of it did certainly mature, and his
zeal as a popularizer most certainly continued; but his further
scholarship was unsystematic to say the least, and his approach
to popularization changed radically.

He had long shaken off the poetic influence of Rossetti when,
in 1928, his essay and translation of Cavalcanti's 'Donna me
prega' was first published. But that publication did mark once
and for all Pound's break with the tradition of Romantic
mediaevalism, which often made the 'dolce stil nuovo' synony-
mous with the Lucy lyrics and which rejected that part of
mediaeval poetry which could not be made to fit nineteenth-
century canons of taste. For this is what Rossetti says about
Cavalcanti and 'Donna me prega':

As a poet, he has more individual life of his own than belongs to
any of his predecessors; by far the best of his pieces being those
which relate to himself, his loves and hates. The best known,
however, and perhaps the one for whose sake the rest have been
preserved, is the metaphysical canzone on the Nature of Love,
beginning 'Donna mi priega', and intended, it is said, as an answer
to a sonnet by Guido Orlandi, written as though coming from a

lady, and beginning, 'Onde si muove e donde nasce Amore?'
On this canzone of Guido's there are known to exist no fewer than
eight commentaries, some of them very elaborate and written by
prominent learned men of the middle ages and *renaissance*; the earliest
being that by Egidio Colonna, a beatified churchman who died in
1316; while most of the too numerous Academic writers on Italian
literature speak of this performance with great admiration as Guido's
crowning work. A love-song which acts as such a fly-catcher for
priests and pendants looks very suspicious, and accordingly, on
examination, it proves to be a poem beside the purpose of poetry,
filled with metaphysical jargon, and perhaps the very worst of
Guido's productions. Its having been written by a man whose life
and works include so much that is impulsive and real, is easily
accounted for by scholastic pride in those early days of learning.[1]

It may well be wondered why anybody interested in poetry
would bother with such a work, but the answer is not hard to
discover:

Certainly Cavalcanti's most famous canzone, the didactic poem
on the nature of love, exerted a powerful influence upon Dante,
as upon all their contemporaries. He quotes it twice in his *De
Vulgari Eloquentia* as an example of the solemn style, wholly in
hendecasyllables. Solemn it is, indeed, and with its inner rhymes
and complicated fourteen-line stanzas so elaborate, and with its
intricate deductions so obscure and difficult, that, although in the
middle ages and Renaissance no less than eight commentators and
in recent times a whole series of Italian scholars have explored its
meaning, we still stand before it in bewildered admiration.[2]

Pound shares Vossler's 'bewildered admiration', but he does
not see why one need be satisfied with merely standing before
the poem.[3] What chance Pound had of penetrating the mysteries of such a work can be imagined all too readily. But before
examining Pound's treatment of the canzone, it will be well to
establish a little more exactly what, in the scholars' view, is the
significance of the poem. Fortunately, there is in English a
detailed exegesis of the poem by Professor J. E. Shaw which
anyone can consult who is interested rather in Cavalcanti's

[1] *The Early Italian Poets*, Muses Library (London, 1905), p. 158.
[2] Karl Vossler, *Medieval Culture, An Introduction to Dante and his Times*, trans.
W. C. Lawton (1929), vol. II, pp. 150–1.
[3] Pound, 'Cavalcanti', *Literary Essays*, p. 173.

poem than in Pound's treatment of it.[1] Here is Professor Shaw's
definition of the canzone's place in Cavalcanti's work:

> The love poems other than *Donna me prega* are concerned with the
> full actuality of love, with individual passions for women who come
> and go, but the *Canzone d'Amore*, a complete though condensed
> theory, deals also with the substratum which is the permanent
> source of those passions.[2]

In other words 'Donna me prega' is essentially a work of mature
generalization, based on the particular experiences treated in
Cavalcanti's ballete and sonnets. One may, therefore, to some
extent at least, arrive at a general understanding of the poem
by an examination of the minor poems; and this was one of
Pound's main approaches.[3] But this, obviously, is an inadequate
approach to any poem—and apt to be very misleading. What
is involved in achieving a relatively complete understanding of
the poem is suggested by Professor Shaw's apology for his own
translation of the poem:

> The translation that follows the commentary is my own but a
> poor thing. Any faithful translation of the condensed sentences of the
> original could not help but be obscure. To be clear, it would have to
> include much of the interpretation already given.[4]

What it would have to include, that is, is some eighty-eight
(88) pages of commentary—so many pages merely to fill in the
philosophical background necessary to give depth to the bland,
two-dimensional surface of the translation.

Extraordinarily interesting Professor Shaw's book is. Informed, cogent, sympathetic, it makes Pound's essay on
Cavalcanti seem like a very shabby performance indeed. Yet at
the end of his study he feels obliged to append this palinode:

> The modern view is different. We do not value erudition or pol-
> ished language for their own sakes in poetry; they are acceptable to
> us only when combined with the direct expression of real feeling.
> In the great volume of early Italian verse there are many passages
> and some whole poems in which the words seem to us to well up
> from the poet's heart like fresh water from a spring. We put our

---

[1] *Cavalcanti's Theory of Love* (Toronto, 1949). It should, however, be noted that
Professor Shaw's reading has been attacked by Guido Favati, Cavalcanti's latest
editor, in *Studi petrarcheschi*, IV, 1951, pp. 285–93.

[2] Shaw, p. 114.   [3] Pound, *Literary Essays*, pp. 149–50.   [4] Shaw, p. vi.

finger on these passages and say 'Here is true poetry,' and we judge that the *Rosa fresc'aulentissima* and Rinaldo d'Aquino's *Giamai non mi conforto* are better poems than Guinizelli's *Tegnol di folle 'mpresa* and Cino's *Si mi stringe l'Amore*, not to mention Cavalcanti's *Donna me prega*, which to most moderns is not poetry at all.[1]

That this is merely a restatement of Rossetti seems to me obvious. Yet it is disheartening, for this concession to 'modern' taste concedes much more than the most inveterate romantic could reasonably expect: whatever the deficiencies of 'Donna me prega', whatever the deficiencies of Professor Shaw's study of the poem, his lengthy analysis establishes quite unanswerably that, in Cavalcanti's case at least, erudition and polished language do not exist 'for their own sakes'. Yet here Professor Shaw solemnly repeats the very clichés which, for scholarly purposes, had been argued against with considerable force. Perhaps a fellow Romance scholar's reaction to this split will be of interest:

> However, moved as I am by Professor Shaw's warm defense of the poem, I note that even while insisting that it is something more than versified prose he does not explicitly claim that it is poetry—in a later essay he concludes that to most moderns 'it is not poetry at all.' And one cannot help thinking, as he lays aside these verses, how much more beautifully Leopardi portrayed what seems to be the core of Cavalcanti's thought. In fairness, however, to Cavalcanti, we should not overlook another point made by Professor Shaw: the reader, thinking in terms of the *dolce stil nuovo* and of Dante is not prepared for the unconventional point of view expressed in the *Canzone*. Romanticism, to say nothing of Renaissance Neo-Platonism, have prepared us all too well for Leopardi's lines.[2]

There can be no question of reproving such scholars as Professors Shaw and Bergin, whose acknowledgment of their own dilemma is admirably candid: they are the scholars whom Rossetti would have despised; yet they share Rossetti's views of poetry! And my impression is that this romantic split is fairly typical of specialists in mediaeval poetry—not at all surprising in view of the fact that mediaeval studies and the Romantic movement were interlaced throughout the eighteenth and nineteenth centuries.

[1] Shaw, p. 144.
[2] T. G. Bergin, *Romanic Review*, vol. XLI, no. 4 (1950), p. 279.

From the standpoint of philology this bias probably makes little difference, and the importance of Romance philology no one can doubt who has compared Pound's edition of Cavalcanti[1] with the latest critical edition by Guido Favati.[2] Pound's text of the *Canzone* is so corrupt that his translation of this infinitely subtle poem—so subtle that a misplaced comma is disastrous—can have no claim to accuracy whatever: even if his intuitions were profound, his command of old Italian impeccable, and his knowledge of mediaeval philosophy thorough.

2. *Pound as a Translator of Mediaeval Poetry*

Yet is there not something to be said for a translator about whom Mario Praz has written as follows?

> No matter how much serious scholars may laugh at Pound's amateurishness and inaccuracy (and whoever has seen his pretentious and futile edition of Cavalcanti … is likely to underrate Pound's merits), he had the power of bringing to life the Provençal and early Italian poets, of seeing them 'as contemporary with himself.'[3]

But this praise (the last phrase of which is quoted from Eliot's introduction to his selection of Pound's poetry)[4] would not have been entirely welcome to Pound; for his effort has not been to see Cavalcanti 'as contemporary with himself', but to make his own contemporaries see something of Cavalcanti's mediaeval quiddity—something of the poetic quality which led Dante to cite the *Canzone d'Amore* as a perfect example of the solemn style.

Rossetti was well able to see Cavalcanti 'as contemporary with himself' (or, perhaps, contemporary with Blake, Keats, and Shelley), and Swinburne was well able to see Villon as Swinburne. Neither is there anything wrong with this, and it is even to a large extent unavoidable: such an admission by Pound is implied, I believe, by the gradual replacement of translations in the later cantos by direct quotations. How nearly impossible

---

[1] Pound, *Guido Cavalcanti: Rime*, Edizioni Marsano (Genova, 1931).

[2] Guido Favati, *Guido Cavalcanti: Le Rime* (Milano, 1957).

[3] Mario Praz, 'T. S. Eliot and Dante', *Southern Review*, vol. II, no. 4 (1937). Reprinted in *T. S. Eliot: A Selected Critique*, ed. Leonard Unger (New York-Toronto, 1948).

[4] *Selected Poems of Ezra Pound*, ed. T. S. Eliot (1928), p. 11.

to achieve is Pound's goal for his translations seems to be suggested in this passage from Canto 93:

> how shall philologers?
> A butcher's block for biographers,
> quidity!
> Have they heard of it?
> 'Oh you,' as Dante says
> 'in the dinghy astern there'
> There must be incognita
> and in sea-caves
> un lume pien' di spiriti
> and of memories,
> Shall two know the same in their knowing?
> You who dare Persephone's threshold,
> Beloved, do not fall apart in my hands.

This passage obviously involves a good deal more than the near, or perhaps absolute, impossibility of translation, but it will serve here as an index to Pound's ambition for his translations. Admirable as Rossetti's translations sometimes are, one cannot imagine him taking this view of mediaeval poetry; and though I am persuaded that 'Donna me prega' has suffered less damage in Professor Shaw's hands than in Pound's, it is a rare scholar who has 'cared' for mediaeval poetry as Pound has. Nor, even in the case of 'Donna me prega'—where the odds are so heavily against success—has Pound's been merely another good intention; for on occasion Pound has some awareness of his own limitations, and he is (after all) rather more talented than most of his critics.

Pound divides his translations into two categories: the 'interpretive' and the 'other sort'. The 'other sort' refers to those translations which he has included among his original work in *Personae* or which he has incorporated in *The Cantos*. Pound's own words are required here:

In the long run the translator is in all probability impotent to do *all* of the work for the linguistically lazy reader. He can show where the treasure lies, he can guide the reader in choice of what tongue is to be studied, and he can very materially assist the hurried student who has a smattering of a language and the energy to read the original text along-side the metrical gloze.

This refers to 'interpretive translation'. The 'other sort', I mean in cases where the 'translator' is definitely making a new poem, falls simply in the domain of original writing, or if it does not it must be censured according to equal standards, and praised with some sort of just deduction, assessible in the particular case.[1]

Besides these categories, there is of course simply literal translation. It is obvious that in practice these categories often overlap, but the objective of each is, in theory anyway, distinct. Though the argument in favour of 'interpretive' translation (which Pound inherited from Rossetti) has never seemed to me convincing, it is pointless to require literal exactness of, say, Pound's metrical translations of Arnaut Daniel.[2] In this case he has consciously sacrificed that kind of exactness in favour of another kind (which, it can easily be argued, mattered more to Arnaut than precision of thought). The argument that his 'interpretive' translation of Arnaut reveals a misunderstanding on the literal level will not bear examination, since his essay shows that he had (grateful) access to both Canello's and Lavaud's scholarly literal translations.[3] Yet the Arnaut Daniel translations remain something of a stunt, grotesque in themselves, nearly useless to a student, at best a training ground for *Mauberley*; and the suspicion also remains that the comparative scarcity of literal translations in Pound's repertoire implies, all too clearly, that he is busy at interpreting before he has mastered the fundamentals.

This is certainly true in the case of the translation of 'Donna me prega' which appears in Pound's Cavalcanti essay and again in *Personae*. That it appears in both of these places suggests something about its nature: it is both an 'interpretive' translation and a translation of 'the other sort'. What business this sort of translation has in a semi-scholarly essay on the *Canzone d'Amore*, ostensibly an introduction to the Italian text, may well be wondered at. Here is Professor Shaw's reaction to the essay and translation:

… [Pound's] Italian text is … unreliable. The translation in English verse is more obscure than the original in any version, and the 'Partial Explanation' contributes no light on the meaning; nor do the desultory remarks entitled 'The Vocabulary' and 'Further Notes.'[4]

[1] Pound, *Literary Essays*, p. 200.
[2] Pound, 'Arnaut Daniel', *Literary Essays*, pp. 109–48.
[3] Pound, *Literary Essays*, p. 115.   [4] Shaw, p. 213.

But there is a charitable explanation to be given for the essay and translation: the 'interpretive'-poetic translation is surely a desperate attempt to compensate for the lack of scholarly underpinnings which Pound confesses to throughout this essay. His arrogance in this case consists in having attempted the subject at all, and not in pretending that he has arrived at definitive answers. A partial defence of his 'pretentious and futile' edition of Cavalcanti's poems is that he was quite right and apparently rather advanced in his belief that Cavalcanti needed a major re-editing; at least, since his own ill-starred edition, there have been *two* critical editions of 'Donna me prega'.[1] But why did he take it upon himself to meddle in a matter where, by his own admission, he was unqualified to act with real authority?

Applied generally (as well it might be), this is of course one of the jackpot questions about Pound and *The Cantos*. But for the present it may suffice to say that 'Donna me prega' was of crucial importance to Pound because it seemed to contain a justification of his conviction that he must make excursions into any number of fields outside his obvious field of competence. This being so, it is easy to see why he made such a spectacle of himself trying to establish a reliable text of the poem and trying to puzzle out its meaning: nobody else at that time, apparently, was willing to undertake the job. And besides, there was one respect in which, as a translator, Pound excelled all the Romance philologists put together, whereby to some extent at least he could make good acknowledged scholarly deficiences by a rendering of the poem which gave a hint of why Dante admired the verse craftsmanship of the original. It is chiefly on this that I shall focus attention for the next few pages, as it applies to both the *Personae* and Canto XXXVI translations. Then I shall tackle the larger problem.

In the following passage from the *Personae* version the subject is 'Love':

> Yea, resteth little
> > > > yet is found the most
> Where folk of worth be host.

[1] Besides Favati's edition of all Cavalcanti's poetry, there appeared in 1944 M. Casella's 'La Canzone d'Amore di Guido Cavalcanti', *Studi di Filologia Italiana*, vol. VII, pp. 97–160. Professor Shaw follows Casella's text.

And his strange property sets sighs to move
And wills man look into unforméd space
Rousing there thirst
                that breaketh into flame.
Nor can imagine love
                that knows not love;
Love doth not move, but draweth all to him;
Nor doth he turn
         for a whim
                to find delight
Nor to seek out, surely,
                great knowledge or slight.

Even a passage of this length fails to convey the remarkable sharpness and lightness of touch in this verse. The diction is far from colloquial ('breaketh', 'unforméd'), but it is rather *dry* (as opposed to *juicy*): the scientific air of 'property', for instance, neutralizes 'sighs'. The single striking image in the passage is 'Rousing there thirst / that breaketh into flame'; and for this image the reader will look in vain if he hunts through the Italian text. (Pound's Italian text agrees here with later readings.) What he will find is 'destandos' ira la qual manda foco', or 'while anger rises flashing fire'.[1] Pound's textual notes indicate that he was perfectly aware of the literal meaning of the line (which, apart from the exact thirteenth-century connotation of 'ira', is available to anybody with a smattering of Italian).[2] Pound's elaboration of the metaphor is not an 'improvement' on the line as it stands in the *Canzone*, but it does, certainly, vivify the twentieth-century English poem; and it suggests the liveliness implicit but, as it were, suspended in the obsolescent mediaeval terminology.

Such, it seems to me, are the typical virtues of the *Personae* translation. But the very fact that it was originally intended as an 'interpretive' translation (in which it fails, I hardly need demonstrate) tends to reduce its value as a translation 'of the other sort'. What, for example, does one make of the following?

And save they know't aright from nature's source
I have no will to prove Love's course
                or say

---

[1] In cases where direct translations from the Italian text are necessary, I have preferred to give Professor Shaw's rather than my own.

[2] Pound, *Literary Essays*, pp. 173–4.

> Where he takes rest; who maketh him to be;
> Or what his active virtue is, or what his force;
> Nay, nor his very essence or his mode,
> What his placation; why he is in verb,
> Or if a man have might
>   To show him visible to men's sight.

The first two lines are an extremely hazy paraphrase of:

> che, senza natural dimostramento,
> non o talento di voler provare ...

> (For, without natural demonstration,
> I am not inclined to try to prove ...)

As an interpretive translation this may be all right, i.e. with the Italian text as a gloze for the interpretation (!); but without it, it seems to me that 'to prove Love's course' is extremely opaque. The exact meaning of 'why he is in verb' is available only to the reader with a knowledge of Pound's essay, for it is rather an interesting, extremely compressed bit of exegesis than a translation. There are several other places in this poem where, to follow the meaning properly, it is necessary to refer to the Italian original. Thus, it seems to me, this translation falls between two stools: it is satisfactory neither as an 'interpretive translation' nor as a translation 'of the other sort', which must, one assumes, be an independent poem, requiring no reference to its 'original'.

3. Canto XXXVI as a 'Translation'

The translation which appears in Canto XXXVI is an entirely different matter. It is not a revision of the *Personae* version, but an entirely new work. And it is clearly a translation of 'the other sort'. As a matter of fact it is at many points a much more literal translation than the earlier version, and for this reason it is often clear where the other was obscure:

> Wherefore I speak to the present knowers
> Having no hope that low-hearted
>   Can bring sight to such reason
> Be there not natural demonstration
>   I have no will to try proof-bringing
> Or say where it hath birth

> What is its virtu and power
> Its being and every moving
> Or delight whereby 'tis called 'to love'
> Or if man can show it to sight.

There is no attempt at interpretation here: 'whereby 'tis called "to love" ', for example, is a relatively close translation of 'che 'l fa dire amare', whereas, as previously noted, 'why he is in verb' is not a translation at all. But there are other points in the Canto XXXVI translation where Pound deviates, not merely from the Italian original, but also from his own earlier version:

> And with such uneasiness as rouseth the flame.
> Unskilled can not form his image,
> He himself moveth not, drawing all to his stillness,
> Neither turneth about to seek his delight
> Nor yet to seek out proving
> Be it so great or so small.

The striking image 'thirst/ breaketh into flame' has been sacrificed here, though not, I think, in the interests of a more literal translation. The reason for this change is surely related to the change in the third line, where 'Love doth not move, but draweth all to him' becomes in the later version 'He himself moveth not, drawing all to his stillness'. The point is that the Canto XXXVI version is (in accordance with the characterization given by Dante) much more solemn that the *Personae* version:

> Nor doth he turn
>   for a whim
>   to find delight
> Nor to seek out, surely,
>   great knowledge or slight.

The later version of this passage involves not only a marked change in mood, but also a manifestly conscious departure from the literal meaning of the original:

> e non si giri per trovarvi gioco,
> ne certamente gran saver ne poco.

The line 'ne certamente gran saver ne poco' is Cavalcanti's rebuttal of the troubadour idea (inherited by the early Italian predecessors of Guido) that Love, whatever its ill effects, is a good thing because it is the source of knowledge, refined manners, etc. The Canto XXXVI version sacrifices entirely this signal instance of Cavalcanti's lack of respect for *idées reçues*; and it does so in spite of the fact that the *Personae* version records this heresy quite faithfully. The new line—'Nor yet to seek out proving'—reinforces the passage which we have just examined:

> Be there not natural demonstration
> I have no will to try proof-bringing

Pound's choice of words and meanings depends, then, not on the literal or even the implicit meaning of a specific line in 'Donna me prega', but rather on what will strengthen and unify his twentieth-century poem in English. For this is a translation of 'the other sort', and it must be read and judged accordingly. What I have said about its relation to the Italian poem is, however, by no means irrelevant to my purpose here.

I have noted that in many cases the Canto XXXVI translation is clearer than the 'interpretive translation' in *Personae*; and I have suggested that this greater lucidity is gained by keeping closer to the surface, i.e. literal, meaning of the original. Compare, however, the following:

> In Memory's locus taketh he his state
> Formed there in manner as a mist of light
> Upon a dusk that is come from Mars and stays.
> > (*Personae* version)

> Where memory liveth,
> > it takes its state
> Formed like a diafan from light on shade

> Which shadow cometh of Mars and remaineth
> Created,
> > (Canto XXXVI, p. 182)

The visual quality of the first passage is admirable, and the image of 'a mist of light / Upon a dusk' gets around the difficulty of 'diafan', which, though it is obviously related to the modern 'diaphanous' and 'diaphaneity', strikes one as a very odd word indeed.[1] It gets around the difficulty, however, by

---

[1] There is in fact an early essay (1864) by Pater entitled 'Diaphaneitè' (*Miscellaneous Studies* (London, 1910), pp. 247–54). But this essay is so obscure in every way that it does nothing to familiarize the term or its meaning.

ignoring the difficulty (which, as a glance into mediaeval philosophy will discover, is extremely great). The second version simply recognizes the difficulty: 'diafan' is the word used by Cavalcanti and there is no contemporary equivalent for it, nor is there any satisfactory paraphrase for it (short of a treatise, that is). And most fortunately, there is no *common* term 'diafan' or 'diaphan' in contemporary usage which might, like our 'accident', obscure its special meaning. This is not, of course, to say that the normal reader, upon discovering the word 'diafan', would recognize it as a term from scholastic philosophy. But the oddity of the word, its air of precision, should alert him to depths of meaning which the bland surface of Pound's earlier translation conveys not at all. And Pound has a right to expect his reader to be conscious of the fact that Canto XXXVI is, for the most part, a translation of a notoriously erudite and difficult mediaeval poem; and this consciousness should make him all the more alert.

The same may be said for a number of words present in both versions: the noun 'affect', 'name sensate', and 'virtu'. At one point (rather as with 'diafan') he deviates from a straightforward and literal translation of 'loco'—'place' in the *Personae* version—in favour of a term, 'locus', which thanks to geometry has retained an air of scientific precision. At another point he drops an 'interpretive translation' of 'possible intelletto'—'latent intellect' in the *Personae* version—in favour of 'intellect possible', which may be closer to the original, but is even more *obviously* opaque than 'latent intellect'.

Comparisons of this sort, though necessary for the purpose of demonstration, are very misleading; for, as I have said, the translation in Canto XXXVI is an entirely new poem, in no sense a correction of the *Personae* translation. The question of fidelity to the original in any literal sense is also, as I have argued, largely irrelevant. My comparisons have one main object: to establish how Pound has quite consciously written a 'translation' which, while developing and emphasizing certain ideas quite clearly, succeeds in communicating one primary quality of the original—its impenetrability. And by 'impenetrability' I mean something more important than 'obscurity'; for any critic could prepare an obscure translation of this obscure mediaeval poem. Only Pound could have written verse of such grace and with such pellucid diction, so that although one does not understand fully, one feels that one *should* understand. And that, so far as I can tell, is the effect of the *Canzone d'Amore*.

An achievement of this kind depends, of course, on two things: the balance between what is communicated (quite a bit) and what is incommunicable must be kept fairly constant, lest the reader be entirely thwarted on the one hand or too sure of his comprehension on the other; and the verse must move with so much authority in its own right that the reader retains confidence in the poet even when the meaning appears to be impenetrable:

> Being divided, set out from colour,
> Disjunct in mid darkness
> Grazeth the light, one moving by other,
> Being divided, divided from all falsity
> Worthy of trust
> From him alone mercy proceedeth.

We may be fairly confident that the division of light from colour is a sign of ultimate purity, from which 'alone mercy proceedeth'. And a few lines above this passage there is a line distinctly reminiscent of the Paradiso: 'But taken in the white light that is allness.' 'Ultimate purity', yes, but how much is implied about the mediaeval faculty for vision! Behind the surface simplicity, but with no strain whatever, we feel the weight of scholastic philosophy; and the beauty of that philosophy is manifested by 'Donna me prega'.

The poem, then, is finally impenetrable; but it is at points and in its general import extremely clear. What is clear counts for a good deal in *The Cantos* as a whole, and it is, perhaps, only in the context of the other cantos that Pound's translation of 'Donna me prega' can be fully justified. For as an independent work, it is something of a *tour de force* in rigorously controlled obscurity.

VII

POUND'S ARCANUM

1. 'Deeming intention to be reason's peer and mate'

CANTO XXXVI IS PRECISELY in the centre of the seventy-one
cantos which precede the Pisan sequence. This centrality
serves to emphasize its significance as a target, both for reader
and author, of refinement in expression and comprehension
which Pound thinks should be aimed at. It does, as well,
supply a rationale for his poetic method in *The Cantos*.

> Go, song, surely thou mayest
> Whither it please thee
> For so art thou ornate that thy reasons
> Shall be praised from thy understanders,
> With others hast thou no will to make company.

'Ornate'? This is not merely a mistranslation of Cavalcanti's 'adornato' (which on previous occasions Pound had
translated rather more closely as 'fair attired' and 'adorned')
but the most violently inappropriate description of his own
utterly unornate, translation. Cavalcanti's poem is indeed a
dazzling display of rhyme, a masterpiece of its kind (according
to a greater expert in these matters than Pound or Rossetti):
'ornate' is surely Pound's tribute to Cavalcanti's untouchable
mastery and a confession of the inadequacy of his own *ersatz*.
This translation of 'Donna me prega' is, then, especially a way
of referring the reader of *The Cantos* to the original. Popularization this is, but it is a far cry from the enthusiastic vulgarization
which Pound produced in *The Spirit of Romance*—which as-
sumed, as Pound so often assumes in his prose writings, that it is
all very easy, that the heart of the mystery can be plucked out
by the well-intentioned amateur. For the 'invitation' issued in

the envoi to Pound's translation is as much a warning to the reader as it is a commentary on Rossetti and his twenty-five-year-old disciple of 1910.

The tone which Cavalcanti adopts in the envoi, and throughout the poem for that matter, was not suitable even in his own time, when aristocratic privilege covered a good deal of haughtiness; but his was the voice of the specialist, as Dante's was when he praised the canzone, and as Pound's was when he commented wryly on his own translation: 'ornate'—where the suggestion of vulgarity implicit in our contemporary usage of 'ornate' is partly a judgment on the translation and partly an admission that, after all, the virtuosity in 'Donna me prega' is likely to seem merely ostentatious to a reader unused to mediaeval verse. Is it not this kind of subtlety which provoked this comment by another specialist?

Pound's 'erudition' has been both exaggerated and irrelevantly under-estimated; for it has been judged chiefly by scholars who did not understand poetry, and by poets who had little scholarship.[1]

Mr Eliot's formulation is admittedly rather cavalier, but not too cavalier in 1946 or even today if it is used with discretion; and one is justified in contemplating with some satisfaction its logical extension to the majority of Pound's critics, who are neither poets nor scholars, but who might have been more useful than either in eradicating the vicious partisanship that has obscured Pound's actual achievement.

At any rate, it is with the voice of the specialist that Cavalcanti speaks in the *Canzone d'Amore*; and in so far as Pound's translation is, besides a translation, also Canto XXXVI, Cavalcanti is as certainly a persona for Pound as Sextus Propertius was in 1917. The tone is haughty, but what Cavalcanti-Pound says openly is what most specialists think and feel very frequently. What Cavalcanti says about the understanding of Love might well be applied to any discipline—musical composition, nuclear physics, Romance philology—with the reservation, of course, that a man without an aptitude for any of these disciplines is not necessarily 'low-hearted':

> Who denys it can hear the truth now
> Wherefore I speak to the present knowers
> Having no hope that low-hearted

[1] T. S. Eliot, 'Ezra Pound', *Ezra Pound*, ed. P. Russell, p. 35.

Can bring sight to such reason
Be there not natural demonstration
I have no will to try proof-bringing

This is not just true for an advanced specialist in, say, mathe-
matics who (with a private despair, which he is paid to keep
private and to overcome as far as possible) addresses a crowd of
freshmen on the 'theory of numbers'. It is true to some extent
for everybody, as every parent or teacher must be aware. And
yet one is aware, too, that the experiential gap will in time be
closed and that education is as possible as it is desirable—but,
considering the 'available' body of knowledge, possible only to
a very limited extent. One specializes as one must, and it is
especially in such a society that literature comes into its own as
the discipline which cuts across specializations, dealing with
humanity in its non-specialized aspects.

What happens to a poetry actually addressed to a cult is
illustrated all too clearly by the fate of 'Donna me prega'; and
the same thing, it had better be faced, is likely to happen to the
majority of very late cantos, where Pound has transferred his
allegiance from poetry to the Pound cult. (This is certainly true
in *Thrones*.) But when he wrote Canto XXXVI, and for a good
many years after, he was not only confident that the experiences
treated in the *Canzone d'Amore* were still experienced (of which
he is still confident, no doubt); but he laboured with great
conviction and great energy to confront the problem posed by
Wordsworth in 1800 and, for good reasons, never faced squarely
since:

Poetry is the first and last of all knowledge—it is as immortal as
the heart of man. If the labours of Men of Science should ever create
any material revolution, direct or indirect, in our condition, and in
the impressions which we habitually receive, the Poet will sleep then
no more than at present, he will be ready to follow the steps of the
Man of Science, not only in those general indirect effects, but he will
be at his side, carrying sensation into the midst of the objects of the
science itself. The remotest discoveries of the Chemist, the Botanist,
or Mineralogist, will be as proper objects of the Poet's art as any upon
which it can be employed, if the time should ever come when these
things shall be familiar to us, and the relations under which they are
contemplated by the followers of these respective sciences shall be
manifestly and palpably material to us as enjoying and suffering

beings. If the time should ever come when what is now called science, thus familiarized to men, shall be ready to put on, as it were, a form of flesh and blood, the Poet will lend his divine spirit to aid the transfiguration, and will welcome the Being thus produced, as a dear and genuine inmate of the household of man.[1]

To a certain extent, it is true, Wordsworth is simply putting the discussion on a level lofty enough for him to dismiss the 'transitory and accidental ornaments' of eighteenth-century verse. And the world has indeed changed since he wrote these ambitious, but carefully hedged, words. That the 'material revolution' (more than one?) has happened, there can be no doubt whatever; and poetry has perhaps gone as far as reasonably possible in dealing with the change: for as the effects of science become every day more 'manifestly and palpably material to us as enjoying and suffering beings', the 'objects of science itself' and its 'remotest discoveries' become more and more remote. How little Wordsworth dreamed that, instead of putting on, 'as it were, a form of flesh and blood', science would bring about the possible elimination of all flesh and blood.

The time is gone when it is possible to regard this division of labour with Wordsworth's tranquillity, let alone his sublime confidence:

The knowledge both of the Poet and the Man of Science is pleasure; but the knowledge of the one cleaves to us as a necessary part of our existence, our natural and unalienable inheritance, the other is a personal and individual acquisition, slow to come to us, and by no habitual and direct sympathy connecting us with our fellow-beings. The man of science seeks truth as a remote and unknown benefactor, he cherishes and loves it in his solitude: the Poet singing a song in which all human beings join with him, rejoices in the presence of truth as our visible friend and hourly companion. Poetry is the breath and finer spirit of all knowledge; it is the impassioned expression which is in the countenance of all Science. Emphatically may it be said of the Poet, as Shakespeare hath said of man, 'that he looks before and after'. He is the rock of defence for human nature; an upholder and preserver, carrying everywhere with him relationship and love. In spite of difference of soil and climate, of language and manners, of laws and customs: in spite of things silently gone out of mind, and things violently destroyed; the Poet binds together by passion and knowledge the vast empire

[1] Wordsworth, Preface to the Lyrical Ballads, *Poetical Works*, p. 738.

of human society, as it is spread over the whole earth, and over all time.[1]

Though this is in some respects a peculiarly Wordsworthian analysis ('knowledge ... is pleasure'), and though some of the images are rather rhetorical than analytical, the basic argument is sound, and the last few clauses are Wordsworthian in the very best sense. When he speaks of 'the Poet', he certainly has in mind a sort of composite figure, in whom are united Homer and Shakespeare as well as Wordsworth and Coleridge; and he is certainly right in calling this figure 'the rock of defence for human nature'. He is right, too, in calling the scientist a 'remote and unknown benefactor'—though the scientist is (rightly) less unknown today, and though his role as a benefactor is not so clear-cut. But the very 'human nature' for which the poet is 'the rock of defence' is today threatened with mutation, and, so 'remote' is the knowledge of the biochemist and geneticist (and apparently so uncertain), that it is not possible even to legislate intelligently, let alone deal poetically with anything except the dilemma. That, clearly, is just about all a poet can do; and since the abuse of knowledge is rooted in 'human nature' (as Wordsworth realized with considerable shrewdness), the poet's social function is as crucial as ever.

But the society of specialists (not merely scientists) which has developed since Wordsworth's time, and especially since World War I, is nevertheless a society in which each of us is at the mercy of other specialists, with whom we have no choice but to co-operate. The chain-reaction effect of a labour strike is perhaps the most familiar example of our maddening lack of self-reliance and independence. But this arrangement, which certainly has advantages, works well enough—unless we have reason to doubt, as we often do, the responsibility and good will of the specialists, say politicians, who are serving us. Yet we do not then attempt to become politicians; for we are, ourselves, specialists, and we would not presume to interlope: partly from an informed conviction about the complexity and subtlety of any corner of knowledge, partly from a well-founded fear of appearing ridiculous, and partly from a despair at affecting this uniquely muscle-bound society.

[1] Wordsworth, Preface to the Lyrical Ballads, *Poetical Works*, p. 738.

What all of this has to do with *The Cantos* should be apparent. Pound begins his career, in *The Spirit of Romance*, convinced of the value of a first-hand examination of the materials which form his subject:

> As to my fitness or unfitness to attempt this treatise: Putnam tells us that, in the early regulations of the faculty of the University of Paris, this oath is prescribed for professors: 'I swear to read and to finish reading within the time set by the statutes, the books and parts of books assigned for my lectures.' This law I have, contrary to the custom of literary historians, complied with. My multitudinous mistakes and inaccuracies are at least my own.[1]

This is admirable in its way, and, though one might pause over the assumptions implied in the last sentence, I go on to this statement of purpose:

> The aim of the present work is to instruct. Its ambition is to instruct painlessly.[2]

That a deep belief in the value of first-hand knowledge does not lead, logically, to a work whose 'ambition is to instruct painlessly' seems to me obvious. This is the inherent contradiction in any work of popularization, which every specialist must feel and which, it seems, often cripples the will to instruct any except those who promise to become specialists themselves.

From 1910 onwards Pound wrestled with this contradiction, which was for him, as a translator, a moral and aesthetic problem of the first importance. I think it must be admitted, in the first place, that the problem cannot be solved: there is no translation, poetic, 'interpretive', or literal, which does justice to its original; and there can be no popularization which does not degrade the body of knowledge which it seeks to illuminate. But some compromises are better than others, and it must be admitted that many of Pound's attempts in prose are among the worse. As for his translations, I think that his most brilliant (perhaps unrepeatable) solution was in *Homage to Sextus Propertius*, where his 'translation' is at its wildest: only a fool (or Robert Graves) would regard it as a translation, only a very incurious reader would fail to look into Propertius' *Elegies*

---

[1] Pound, *Spirit of Romance*, p. vii.
[2] Pound, *Spirit of Romance*, p. vii.

after reading Pound's 'Homage'. But it is clearly a triumphant evasion of the problem, not even a near solution.

The widening of interest announced in *Mauberley* multiplied Pound's difficulties, but his basic problem remained the same: how to square the need for first-hand information with the need for popularization. Besides the technical problem—a problem, I have argued, that cannot be given a final solution—Pound was faced with the dilemma that faces anybody today who loses confidence in the specialists who, as the custodians of knowledge and power, control our lives as never before.

That Pound was right, around 1918, to lose confidence in the politicians, economists, and American historians is obvious enough; and it is yet more obvious that he failed practically in his successive roles as political scientist, economist, and historian (to which may be added sculptor, composer, art critic, music critic, mediaevalist, anthropologist, etc.) The undertaking was indeed preposterously ambitious, though it must be added that a breakdown such as I have given is necessarily misleading: Pound is essentially a poet-historian. The *ideal* historian would be a master of all these subjects, and the *ideal* poet would discover, first, the permanent element in all that was impermanent, and, second, a means of fixing it poetically.

Pound's 'solution' to all these difficulties, the so-called ideogrammic method as practised in *The Cantos*, is a most remarkable working compromise—which, however, does not always work. An example of the method when it does work is the following, taken from Canto VI:

> 'Send word I ask you Eblis
>   you have seen that maker
> 'And finder of songs so far afield as this
> 'That he may free her,
>   who sheds such light in the air.'
>
> E lo Sordels si fo di Mantovana,
> Son of a poor knight, Sier Escort,
> And he delighted himself in chançons
> And mixed with the men of the court
> And went to the court of Richard Saint Boniface
> And was there taken with love for his wife
>   Cunizza, da Romano,
> That freed her slaves on a Wednesday

Masnatas et servos, witness
Picus de Farinatis
and Don Elinus and Don Lipus
    sons of Farinato de' Farinati

The first unit in this passage is a pastiche of Bernart de Ventadorn's songs, the second a quotation and paraphrase of Sordello's troubadour biography, and the third a quotation and paraphrase of the document by which Cunizza freed her slaves. In this passage Pound is concerned chiefly with two things: the liberating power of Love (cf. Canto 90) and the curious attachment to place which goes along with mediaeval universality. Both of these concepts matter a good deal to Pound: he is, himself, a poet who has gone far afield in order to free his beloved country.

Any reader willing to do a little work can find these things out for himself, and Pound means him to work: his ambition is no longer 'to instruct painlessly'. For the respect for the materials from which knowledge is derived demands a first-hand examination not merely by the poet, but, as nearly as possible, by the reader as well. The discursive or narrative links which one might expect are not present—but why? Mainly because, if, as Pound believes, the materials themselves cannot be honestly transformed into blank verse or couplets or whatever, neither can they be linked together by narrative or discursive means. Moreover, each passage quoted or paraphrased has one or both of two functions: to refer the reader to the original in its own context *where alone* it has a full life and meaning (as in the case of Bernart de Ventadorn, who is certainly a great lyric poet); and second, each such passage is Pound's guarantee that he has personally examined the subject (hence the direct quotation—'E lo Sordels si fo di Mantovana').

This question of preserving the integrity of his materials (like the good Confucian historian) is so important that I should interrupt my main argument for a moment to quote Mr Kenner in this connection—he is discussing Canto II—

The entire Canto is concerned with the sea, Aphrodite's native element. It is the blue-gray liquid in which seals disport and snipe bathe; but the right kind of eyes bent upon its depths are rewarded with anthropomorphic glimpses, the sea-god's 'Lithe sinews of water,' or 'The smooth brows, seen, and half seen.' Hence the sequence of

images near the end of the Canto; in alternate lines the empiric flux
and the form it conceals:

> Lithe turning of water,
>> sinews of Poseidon,
> Black azure and hyaline,
>> glass wave over Tyro,
> Close cover, unstillness,
>> bright welter of wave-cords

The key to Pound's method throughout *The Cantos* is his convic-
tion that the things the poet sees in the sea of events are really there.
They are not 'creations' of his. Similarly, the values registered in the
poem are ... not even values created by Confucius or Erigena or
Malatesta or anyone else. Their origin is not human, but divine.
In the words of a formulation that comes very late in the poem,

> it is not man
> Made courage, or made order, or made grace.[1]

This is very well said. Another way of saying much the same
thing is that the poet, like the sculptor, like the male, releases
the form which is immanent in his materials; he does not
impose a form on them: 'the god is inside the stone, *vacuos
exercet aera morsus*. The force is arrested, but there is never any
question about its latency, about the force being the essential,
the rest "accidental" ... '[2] What is implied is a co-operation
between the artist and his materials in which the artist's job is to
realize what, in a way, was already there, not to remould them
nearer to the heart's desire. However, as Mr Kenner points out,
the artist is one who has 'the right kind of eyes' to discover what
is there in the sea of events: 'I have seen what I have seen',
says Acoetes to Pentheus in this same Canto II—pointing out
(like a specialist) that unless there is a shared experience there
can be no real communication, only vulgarization. This ex-
plains the chunks of relatively untampered-with materials and
the gaps between them which force the reader to see for himself
the form in the flux—or to see nothing at all.

I have suggested that each passage quoted or paraphrased
in *The Cantos* (whether a snippet, an entire poem, or the history
of China) has two existences: it is fully alive only in its original

---

[1] 'The Broken Mirrors and the Mirror of Memory', *Motive and Method in the
Cantos of Ezra Pound* (New York, 1954), pp. 13–14.
[2] Cf. my discussion in Chapter V, pp. 96–97.

context, where often it is alive only to the specialist; its ghost, often very lively, is present in *The Cantos,* where it is given new life by association with other lively ghosts from other fields of knowledge. And behind this colossal effort lies a conviction that there must be such interpenetration of specialized knowledge if there is to be a real civilization, and further that poetry alone, in this uniquely muscle-bound age, could liberate the knowledge so industriously collected and stored away by others.

It may be objected that in the process Pound has violated Wordsworth's very sound first principles and, as well, the principles of sound scholarship; that the result (with a few notable exceptions) is a work which is neither scholarly nor poetic. This certainly seems to me true of a major portion of the poem. Yet, though I am not ready to prefer Pound's failure (so far as he has failed) to the general failure of contemporary poetry to be as great in scope as it is splendid in detail, I believe that it is important to recognize that *The Cantos* represents the only major twentieth-century claim for the civilizing force of poetry. It may again be objected, and with truth, that Pound himself was not fully civilized, and that the claim might have been made more fortunately by somebody else. But it was not made by somebody else.

Whether poetry can effectively civilize by importing into its fabric, on a large scale, materials from a great variety of times, places, and disciplines is certainly open to question. Of course any civilization *is* made up of such materials, but they have been worn smooth, adjusted to each other by a process of gradual increment and usage. This is a truism worth insisting on in the face of rampant exoticism, among whose derelictions are Romantic mediaevalism and orientalism. But if exoticism is debilitating because it is onanistic (which it is), it should not be confounded with attempts to make that damage good by importations from foreign sources. The form of argument which the following commentary takes seems to me particularly telling:

> Standing as he [Pound] does at the latest point of Orientalism, emerging through his career into a literature of full renascence in which he becomes a dictator of poetic convention, he illustrates at least one fact of art antithetical to the whole nature of exoticism. This fact was simply stated by Ferdinand Brunetière in 1888, in an

essay on European decadence: 'Ce n'est pas enfin l'homme qui est fait pour art, c'est l'art qui est fait pour l'homme.'[1]

Mr Baird does not pretend to understand *The Cantos* fully, and he has other, less complimentary things to say about Pound. But what he points to here, by way of Brunetière, is certainly true of Pound as it is not true of any other important twentieth-century poet writing in English. And it had better be underscored that exoticism is not merely a loss of contact with one's own best tradition, but a loss of contact with what is best outside that tradition. The Chinese history cantos, so far from being examples of exoticism, make up an attempt to cure precisely that disease.

Concerning translation (or importation of the sort that Pound is aiming at), it must from one point of view be regarded as a necessary make-shift, never a substitute for the original. Only in original composition, in one's own language, is perfect communication possible; and that is not achieved very often. Moreover, perfect comprehension of a foreign literature (which is the ideal basis of translation) is not achieved very often either. This is obvious and true. But civilization is built out of make-shifts, as human relations are. When Pound claims that each great period in English literature has been, as well, a great period of translation, he is demonstrably right. This is not to say that the relationship between translation and original work is as simple as Pound often suggests or that the relationship, simple or complex, is the same in each great age; but the conjunction is a fact of English literary history, and it is a manifestly important fact. Pound's chief claim to importance as a historian of our literature is based on his having stressed this fact, rudely and egotistically and single-mindedly, but unforgettably.

The demands for perfection of communication which lead on the one hand to the conclusion that one should study only one's own literature (or, at most, English and French),[2] or which lead on the other hand to the very late cantos—where Pound seems to say, 'This is untranslatable, this is too good or too big

---

[1] James Baird, *Ishmael* (Baltimore, 1956), p. 49.

[2] Cf. F. R. Leavis, *How to Teach Reading: A Primer for Ezra Pound* (Cambridge, 1932). Dr Leavis's criticism of the essay 'How to Read' is basically sound; his own recommendations are another matter. Pound's *ABC of Reading*, though it incorporates much of 'How to Read', is a notable improvement.

to absorb in my poem'—come to the same thing in the end: the thing to which Cavalcanti's 'Donna me prega' is perhaps literature's greatest monument. It is, indeed, only within such a closed system, where the assumptions and experience and language are held in common, that perfect increments of perception can be made. And so far as these are the desiderata (which to some extent they must be) one had better not place much reliance either on Mr Eliot's 'remarkable little book' on Dante[1] or on Pound's vast and often inexpert importations from other cultures, other fields of knowledge. But what lies before or after the perfectly articulated work of art is a series of coarse compromises, of which the coarsest are often those made in the name of discrimination or integrity.

2. Further Reservations

What is wrong finally with Pound's method is that it is based on a translator's, not a poet's, approach to the world. Few would deny that at his best Pound is both a distinguished translator and a distinguished poet, and often both at the same time. But the man who invented the method used in *The Cantos* was a translator so obsessed, in principle, with the integrity of his materials—so sure that apparent rocks, by crafty selection and arrangement, could be persuaded to reveal their latent form and significance—that he rarely gave the poet a chance, or, in the end, even the translator. In actual practice Pound did not preserve the integrity of his materials, and he could not; for, taking into account his conviction that he could speak with authority only on matters of which he had a first-hand knowledge (so far as possible), it is clear that the scope of his project placed an impossible burden on him. Although there is much to be said for this radically unacademic approach to reality, in this extreme form it is rather the way of Hemingway than of Chaucer or Shakespeare or Milton.

Pound is, in fact, so untrustworthy[2] that his 'documentation'

---

[1] Leavis, *How to Teach Reading*, p. 43.

[2] Among many, many errors of scholarship in *The Cantos*, one in particular ought to be pointed out here: the line 'Lo Sordels si fo di Mantovana' apparently exists only in Pound's faulty transcription (cf. *Sordello: Poesie*, ed. M. Boni (Bologna, 1953), which records all known versions of Sordello's biography). Pound's version resembles several extant versions (e.g. 'Sordels fo de Mantoana'). His mistake is in itself negligible—though typical—but considering the function of this phrase in Canto II, the mistake acquires some significance.

is hardly more than a form of rhetoric, which sometimes, as in the Malatesta Cantos, produces a kind of marginal poetry. For Pound (who resembles the late Senator MacCarthy in more than one respect) suppresses or ignores 'evidence' that happens not to suit his theories. This might not seem to matter in the case of poetry, and indeed it would not matter if Pound accepted the responsibilities and limitations of a fictionalist. But he does not accept them, and what he offers as a substitute for fiction is often a peculiarly Poundian oleo which is not quite poetry and not quite history—but which pretends to be both. That it occasionally has some value as literature I do not wish to deny, but the reader of, say, the Malatesta Cantos ought to bear in mind that Pound's version of Sigismondo leaves out whatever Pound considers 'irrelevant' or 'probably invented by Sigismondo's enemies'. This is not to say that Pound is dishonest; but he is obsessed with the idea that history has everywhere been falsified by the ruling interests, and that the honest investigator must always read between the lines. There is some truth in this of course; but a mind bent on *investigating* everything under the sun, or rather everything hidden from the sun, is a mind bent on its own corruption: it projects whatever forms it desires on to the flux of experience. For instance, there is no proof whatever that the armaments king Sir Basil Zaharoff (Pound's Sir Zenos Metevsky) was a Jew, but that Pound preferred to believe the rumours is demonstrated in Canto XVIII. His portrait of Zaharoff is in fact ludicrously inadequate:

> And Metevsky, 'the well-known philanthropist',
> Or 'the well-known financier, better known',
> As the press said, 'as a philanthropist',
> Gave—as the Este to Louis Eleventh—
> A fine pair of giraffes to the nation,
> And endowed a chair of ballistics,
> And was consulted before the offensives.
>
> (Canto XVIII, pp. 85–6)

What Zaharoff did endow was a chair of French literature in England, and a chair of English literature in France.[1] But this is too much for Pound, whose computer doesn't solve that sort

---

[1] Richard Lewinsohn, *The Man behind the Scenes: the Career of Sir Basil Zaharoff* (1929), pp. 134–5. Zaharoff received a great deal of publicity immediately after World War I, especially in France and Germany.

of problem and whose poem doesn't absorb that sort of information. The pity is that, if Pound had been capable of something
more than simple-minded caricature, the subtle and sinister
Zaharoff might have seemed really dangerous and evil—an
enemy worthy of the heroic Odysseus-Pound. Here, as so often
in *The Cantos*, one readily grants the importance of Pound's
subject, but questions the importance of his treatment.

Another aspect of Pound's method that must be commented
on is the lack of any plot or formal scheme in *The Cantos* within
which every particular fits and contributes towards an ordered
development. This is not to deny sequaciousness within a canto
or a group of cantos; but it is to deny that there is (or was
intended to be) any predetermined pattern which extends from
Canto I to, say, Canto LXXI. Events are prepared for (there is,
for example, an elaborate preparation for the 'Hell' Cantos),
but there is no way for the reader to anticipate with any accuracy what is likely to happen. The advantage of this method is
that each new image, quotation, or whatever, *is* unexpected,
a discovery; and therefore each new particular has the force of
an event significant in itself, though often intelligible only in
relation to what has preceded it. But to justify this focus on
details and to justify the constant vigilance required of the
reader, Pound must always, or nearly always, keep his details
charged with significance; the method leaves little room for
dull or inferior writing. In a poem like *Paradise Lost* Milton can
be—and sometimes is—dull and impoverished, because his
narrative gains enormous momentum from the parts that are
well written: enough to carry him over the parts where his
invention failed. But there is nothing to carry Pound when his
invention fails; he is then intolerably boring.

There are, of course, many cantos to which these generalizations do not apply, i.e. those in which Pound distills poetically
the ideas contained or implied in all of his particulars. Such
cantos, it is true, are but parts of a sequence, and often they
seem intended to polarize the materials surrounding them (the
famous 'Pull down thy vanity' passage in LXXXI does have this
effect). But my experience in reading *The Cantos* is that the individual cantos which form the most successful aesthetic wholes
tend to acquire a life of their own which is greater than that
of the entire poem. That is to say, Canto XLVII is brilliantly

self-sufficient, it exists aesthetically in a way that Cantos
XLVI and XLVIII do not. The images, the thematic fragments
out of which it is built do indeed recur and reverberate in other
parts of the poem, thereby giving the poem a certain measure
of coherence; the canto itself, however—there are others like it
—not only disrupts the unity of the poem as a whole, but it also,
because it is different in kind, fails to function properly in
its immediate context. Therefore I find it difficult to accept a
description of this kind, put forward by Mr Emery:

> Cantos 45–6: These state and rest the case against usury,
> the former 'poetically,' the latter in 'a more natural language.'

> Cantos 47–52: Canto 47 restates the nekuia-regeneration theme
> as the conditions for escaping the degradation of 45–6, and it adds
> another condition (*via* Hesiod's *Works and Days*): the need to impose
> ritual order upon natural creative process (already, of course,
> implied in 13, the Kung canto).[1]

Mr Emery has mapped out the relationships between these
cantos very competently; but, contrary to Mr Emery and all
who believe in the unity of the poem, the qualitative difference
between Cantos XLV and XLVI, and again between XLVI
and XLVII, is not the difference between a 'poetical' and 'a
more natural' language: it is the difference between what is
immediately apprehended as a poetic unit (not quite an independent poem) and what is, by courtesy, accepted as something
more than a passage of prose. The difference is absolute, the
communication is on a different and, in XLV and XLVII,
superior level. If we respond to Cantos XLV and XLVII as
we should, we shall not—without some other kind of response—
feel that Canto XLVI has much to do with them.

Thus, it seems to me, Pound's finest poetic achievements
work against the success of *The Cantos* almost as much as do the
passages which the reluctant translator fitted together. Only
in the Pisan Cantos does he escape from this difficulty, for
there the cantos are so long, diverse and interrelated as to force
one to view the sequence as a whole. There, moreover, he
seems to me to transform his translator's ethic into a really
workable poetic. For along with his staggering faith in the value
of first-hand examination of objects, poems, and documents,

[1] Emery, *Ideas into Action*, p. 126.

went an almost equal faith in the value of personal contacts with the great figures of his time: in the Pisan Cantos he was able to recapture these contacts and write his strange elegy for 'things silently gone out of mind, and things violently destroyed'.

If *The Cantos* did by some miracle form a successful poetic whole, then of course it would deserve any amount of detailed attention; for it would certainly be an unprecedentedly great and original achievement. But since it does not, I can only conclude that it is best to concentrate attention on those cantos which seem likely to survive. This is not to suggest that the reader should ignore the rest of the work (for the better cantos often acquire even greater force if one is familiar with the others), or that Pound's demands on his reader's time and attention are wholly unreasonable. Indeed, I am not sure that the reader, *qua* reader, has any 'rights' except the all-important right to refuse to read Pound's poem. But a critic, though he may have no rights either, does have a responsibility to literature in general as well as to the author he is discussing. Pound at his best seems to me as good or nearly as good as any twentieth-century poet writing in English; but when he is not at his best, he is certainly inferior to many less celebrated poets, past and present, who deserve our attention.

Time and Tradition in Pound's Poetry

This is not to damn incontinent all that intervenes, but I think the chief question addressed to me by people of good-will who do not, but are yet ready and willing to, read James, is: Where the deuce shall I begin? One cannot take even the twenty-four volumes, more or less selected volumes of the Macmillan edition all at once, and it is, alas, but too easy to get so started and entoiled as never to finish this author or even come to the best of him.

The laziness of an uncritical period can be nowhere more blatant than in the inherited habit of talking about authors as a whole. It is perhaps the sediment from an age daft over great figures, or a way of displaying social gush, the desire for celebrity at all costs, rather than a care for letters.

Ezra Pound, *Literary Essays*, p. 304

VIII

PROPERTIUS, MAUBERLEY, AND THE CANCELLED CANTOS

1. Homage to Sextus Propertius

THOUGH THE EARLIEST CANTOS were published before the complete *Homage to Sextus Propertius*, the latter is so far the masterpiece of Pound's early period, in the literal sense of 'masterpiece', that it may be taken as the representative and definitive achievement of the volume *Personae*. It precedes *Mauberley* chronologically, but it follows *Mauberley* in Pound's arrangement of his early poems. This arrangement has caused some confusion,[1] and I am inclined to think that *Mauberley* ought to be printed as an appendix to *Personae*. But the arrangement is clear enough for those who give the matter any thought: *Propertius*, not *Mauberley*, is the consummation of the volume as a whole; whereas *Mauberley*, however great it may be, is something of a sport in this context. To this extent, Dr Leavis is right in singling out *Mauberley* as an uncharacteristic achievement; but he is certainly wrong when he supposes that *Mauberley* is necessarily uncharacteristic because it is great, and great because it is uncharacteristic.

Propertius is representative of the early poetry in terms of approach and technique, and it is definitive in terms of its attitude toward, and apology for, the poet whose work is collected in *Personae*. The approach and technique are uniquely Pound's, but the attitude and apology locate him very clearly

---

[1] Among others, Mr Fraser was led by this arrangement to suppose that *Propertius* was written before *Mauberley*. (Cf. Fraser, *Ezra Pound*, p. 63.)

within a specifically English literary tradition (which might be called the Outcast tradition, unbroken from Byron down to our own day) and within a timeless community of minor masters—e.g. Propertius, Cavalcanti, Landor, Corbière—after whom no Age could be named, yet who are worthy of our admiration just the same. It is, of course, in Pound himself that these are joined: for the poems which precede *Propertius* are a record of his devotion to the Victorian literature of aestheticism and revolt, and of his exploration of poetry largely foreign to the English tradition; but in the elegies of Sextus Propertius Pound discovered a body of poetry which was at once firmly a part of the Classical tradition yet, by comparison with Horace or Virgil, definitely eccentric—but none the less valuable for being so.

For *Propertius* is not, like *Mauberley*, a poem of protest and contempt; and to read it by the lamp of *Mauberley*, written several years later, after a major shift of attitude towards his medium and the world, is to distort its significance very much indeed. *Propertius* is mellow, leisurely, and often playful (how much of this belongs to Propertius, how much to Pound, is not a strictly relevant consideration, since Pound has elected to endorse everything that be brings over from the *Elegies*); but it is deeply serious in its defence of a poet's right not to be a respectable citizen, a bulwark against immorality, and author of Birthday Odes, or a Classic. If this defence were at all strident, it would be intolerable today, as most such defences are. But it has the same attitude as these lines from Hardy's 'A Singer Asleep', which have a poise and ease that their subject, Swinburne, could never have achieved:

> —It was as though a garland of red roses
> Had fallen about the hood of some smug nun
> When irresponsibly dropped as from the sun,
> In fulth of numbers freaked with musical closes,
> Upon Victoria's formal middle time
> His leaves of rhythm and rhyme.

But *Propertius* is not (nor is 'A Singer Asleep') a plea for rebelliousness; it is a plea for the poet's right to observe that the king is naked, to treat the pomp of empire irreverently, or to take no interest in these matters. In so far as Propertius is inescapably a Classic and Pound's use of Propertius is inescapably irreverent, this attitude is built into the texture of poem; and to the extent that this irreverent use of a notably irreverent classic actually serves Propertius best, Pound's attitude is brilliantly vindicated and *Homage to Sextus Propertius* is a major triumph of wit and invention.

To mention wit and invention, particularly in connection with a poem which is essentially a paraphrase from Latin, is to invite comparison with Dryden or Pope. But it would be misleading to call *Homage to Sextus Propertius* an Augustan poem: it is in many ways an anti-Augustan poem, as it is also an anti-Romantic poem. It belongs to no party, and that is its point. It implicitly repudiates the Romantic doctrine of originality (though it is a very original poem indeed), and it repudiates much of the Augustan ethos. For the purposes of poetry, anyway, Pope could look back on Augustan Rome as a golden age, the age of an ideal Establishment which sponsored the finest artistic talent: but that, precisely, is what Pound doesn't believe. The Augustus referred to in *Homage to Sextus Propertius* is not quite a George I:

> Make way, ye Roman authors,
> > clear the street, O ye Greeks,
> For a much larger Iliad is in the course of construc-
> > tion
> (and to imperial order)
> Clear the streets, O ye Greeks!

but he is closer to the Empress Victoria than he is to Pope's ideal Roman Emperor. And whereas the axes of Pope's poetry are public and moral, the axes of Pound's first mature poem are private and aesthetic (the title of the poem contains a pun which should warn us that Pound's primary object is not to castigate vice or, even, the Empire).

Certainly there is nothing flippant about the poem, though it is important to realize that, in 1917, a comparably serious European couldn't have written it. Its author was an American and an admirer of Swinburne and Pater, Browning and Landor; and yet, even so, it seems unlikely that he could have achieved the same confident, mellow tone, at that time, if he hadn't been immersed in a Latin author. His memoir of Gaudier-Brzeska had appeared the year before, and it leaves no doubt that he was already disturbed by the war. Nevertheless, there is nothing evasive about *Propertius*: on the one hand, what Pound 'means' is perfectly clear and straightforward once one has grasped the convention of the poem; and, on the other hand, the very convention of the poem constitutes an assertion that 'the times' had not changed so far as to make Propertian (or Flaubertian) disengagement impossible. In fact, however, the times had worsened greatly—or so, at any rate, is the message of *Mauberley*, written three years later. In spite of its chronology, then, *Propertius* is essentially a pre-World War poem:

> Annalists will continue to record Roman repu-
> > tations,
> Celebrities from the Trans-Caucasus will belaud
> > Roman celebrities
> And expound the distentions of Empire,

This would apply as well to Kaiser's empire as to the British Empire of pre-World War days, but it does not fit the situation in 1917.

However, it is the essence of *Propertius* that it is not 'contemporary' except in so far as Sextus Propertius himself is. The closing lines of the poem give us a list of Propertius' antecedents:

> Varro sang Jason's expedition,
> > Varro, of his great passion Leucadia,
> There is song in the parchment; Catullus the highly
> > indecorous,
> Of Lesbia, known above Helen;
> And in the dyed pages of Calvus,
> > Calvus mourning Quintilia,
> And but now Gallus had sung of Lycoris.
> > Fair, fairest Lycoris—
> The waters of Styx poured over the wound:
> And now Propertius of Cynthia, taking his stand
> > among these.

The list of Pound's antecedents which this serene conclusion invites us to compile would certainly include Propertius himself, the troubadours, Cavalcanti, Waller, Landor, Swinburne, Browning, and early Yeats. Other names might be mentioned (for instance, Pound likes to contrast Sappho with Pindar), but the principle of selection is the important thing to note. The poets named appear as 'influences' in the post-Victorian poems collected in *Personae*, for which *Propertius* is the apology. It is also the apology for the earliest draft of cantos, which are as private and uncontemporary as possible.

2. *The Cancelled Cantos*

The earliest cantos immediately precede *Propertius* in composition and publication; and in *Quia Pauper Amavi* (1919) they are not placed, as one might expect, at the end of the volume, but rather immediately before *Propertius*. This arrangement has a more than chronological significance, as all such arrangements have in Pound's books of verse; for, as I suggest above, though *The Cantos* were intended to be Pound's major 'work-in-progress', *Propertius* was intended to be (among other things) an apologia for the private, uncontemporary, 'uncommitted' nature of the long work he was embarking on. Actually this early version of *The Cantos* was not so totally unlike the final version as this description might suggest: Pound was able to salvage about two-thirds of it by judicious cutting and rearrangement, so that the first seven cantos of the early version have much in common with the corresponding section of the final version. Nevertheless, the differences between the two versions are far more important than the similarities.

The early version begins:

> Hang it all, there can be but the one 'Sordello,'
> But say I want to, say I take your whole bag of
>   tricks,
> Let in your quicks and tweeks, and the thing's an art-
>   form,
> Your 'Sordello,' and that the 'modern world'
> Needs such a rag-bag to stuff all its thought in;
> Say that I dump my catch, shiny and silvery
> As fresh sardines flapping and slipping on the marginal
>   cobbles?

Here Pound is clearly addressing the ghost of Browning, just as he does at the beginning of Canto II in the received text; but in this earlier version he continues to do so (intermittently) at least through the first two cantos. As the first canto develops, it becomes clear that Pound's subject is the poem itself: what form is it to take, what is it to contain, where is it to begin?

> We let Ficino
> Start us our progress, say it was Moses' birth year?
> Exult with Shang in squatness? The sea-monster
> Bulges the squarish bronzes.
> Daub out, with blue of scarabs, Egypt,
> Green veins in the turquoise?
>   Or gray gradual steps
> Lead up beneath flat sprays of heavy cedars:
> Temple of teak-wood,

This passage occurs well inside Canto I, but the 'progress' never really begins; for here the art really is an 'art of reverie', of association after association moving up to the foreground of the poet's mind and then being replaced by another out of a rich and seemingly inexhaustible hoard:

>   Your palace step?
> My stone seat was the Dogana's vulgarest curb,
> And there were not 'those girls,' there was one flare,
> One face, 'twas all I ever saw, but it was real …
> And I can no more say what shape it was …
> But she was young, too young.
>   True, it was Venice,
> And at Florian's under the North arcade
> I have seen other faces, and had my rolls for breakfast,
> Drifted at night and seen the lit, gilt cross-beams
> Glare from the Morosini.
>   And for what it's worth
> I have my background; and you had your background,

In fact Pound's 'background' is worth just about everything, so far as these earliest cantos are concerned. The intimate, casual tone, as of an old man reminiscing, often sentimentally but more often vigorously, could be very easily parodied. It is not Eliot's 'Mind of Europe', but an American literary tourist rambling genially about things that are more pleasant to think about than current affairs and contemporary landscapes.

Speaking of the world he takes as his own, he asks rhetorically:

It is a world like Puvis'?
>   Never so pale my friend,
'Tis the first light—not half-light—Panisks
And oak-girls and the Maelids have all the wood;
. . .
'Non é fuggi.'
>   'It is not gone.' Metastasio
is right, we have that world about us.

In a somewhat modified form this passage later becomes part of Canto III, and the subject remains of central importance in the final version. In a slightly later section of this first version of the poem,[1] there is an early draft of what was to become Canto VII, which suggests that Pound from the very beginning intended to deal, to some extent, with the contemporary loss of contact with non-material values. Indeed, the ideas and some of the language of the present Canto VII date back at least to 1915:

We find the men whose minds have petrified at forty, or at fifty, or at twenty, more resolutely against us ... it is, perhaps, a matter of the will ... The age of the closure varies but the effect is the same. You find a man one week young, interested, active, following your thought with his thought, parrying and countering, so that the thought you have between you is more alive than the thought you may have apart. And the next week (it is almost as sudden as that) he is senile. He is anchored to a dozen set phrases ... You look sadly back over the gulf, as Ut Napishtim looked back at the shades of the dead, the live man is no longer with you ... He has gone from Elysium into the *basso inferno*. The speed of light, the absolute power of the planes in Egyptian sculpture have no charm left for such men. And the living move on without them.[2]

However, the dominant tone of the cancelled cantos is perhaps best indicated by this curious bit of self-portraiture dating from 1916: Pound is talking about himself and young Gaudier-Brzeska:

I knew that many things would bore or disgust him, particularly my rather middle-aged point of view, my intellectual tiredness and

[1] Cf. *Poems 1918–21* (New York, 1921). Cantos IV–VII (first version) are printed in this volume; they are somewhat closer in tone to the final version than are the cantos (I–III) in *Quia Pauper Amavi*.

[2] Pound, *Gaudier-Brzeska: A Memoir* (new edition, Marvell Press, Hessle, East Yorkshire, 1960), pp. 108–9.

exhaustion, my general scepticism and quietness, and I therefore opened fire with 'Altaforte,' 'Piere Vidal,' and such poems as I had written when about his age ... He even tried to persuade me that I was not becoming middle-aged, but any man whose youth has been worth anything, any man who has lived his life at all in the sun, knows that he has seen the best of it when he finds thirty approaching; knows that he is entering a quieter realm, a place with a different psychology.[1]

In view of his subsequent career, this account is incredibly lacking in self-knowledge; but this role was one which he was apparently studying in all seriousness at that time. Speaking of ancient China and mediaeval Italy, he confesses:

> I have but smelt this life, a whiff of it,
> The box of scented wood
> Recalls cathedrals. Shall I claim;
> Confuse my own phantastikon
> Or say the filmy shell that circumscribes me
> Contains the actual sun;
>   Confuse the thing I see
> With actual gods behind me?
>   Are they gods behind me?
> Worlds we have, how many worlds we have.
>   If Botticelli
> Brings her ashore on that great cockle-shell,
> His Venus (Simonetta), and Spring
> And Aufidus fill all the air
> With their clear-outlined blossoms?
> World enough.
>
> . . .
>
> Such worlds enough we have, have brave decors
> And from these like we guess a soul for man
> And build him full of aery populations,
>   (Panting and Faustus)

This is really appallingly bad, so bad as to make one agree with Yvor Winters that this early version of *The Cantos* often seems to belong to Pound's earliest work.[2]

[1] Pound, *Gaudier-Brzeska*, pp. 45–6.

[2] Cf. Yvor Winters, *In Defence of Reason* (London, 1960), pp. 493–6. Winters's habit of over-simplification makes his discussion of Pound unsatisfactory, but there are important insights into Pound's weaknesses to be found in Winters's scattered remarks on this subject.

This early version is, however, easier to understand than the received text, partly because of the imaginary conversation with Browning (and sometimes, perhaps, with the reader: in either case, Pound proceeds by 'anticipating' and then answering questions—a clumsy and irritating device which nevertheless makes the motions of his thought easy to follow). Probably more important, his thought is easier to follow because the method *is* that of reverie-like association: by no means so free and uncensored as Molly Bloom's day-dreams, but still plausibly casual and, like most reverie, relatively connected. Moreover, Pound is often willing to incorporate footnotes and stage directions into his text:

> Lie quiet Divus, *plucked from a Paris stall*
> *With* a certain Cretan's '*Hymni Deorum*';
> *The thin clear Tuscan stuff*
>   *Gives way before the florid mellow phrase,*
> Take we the goddess, Venerandam
> Auream coronam habentem, pulchram ...

The information and judgments italicized are not present in the corresponding passage in the final version, with the result that we do not know (1) that Pound plucked his copy of Divus from a Paris stall; (2) that the lines quoted and paraphrased are taken from a Cretan's 'Hymni Deorum' which was 'with' Divus's translation of Homer; and (3) that Pound considers Divus's Latin to be far less florid than the Cretan's. All of this information seems to me irrelevant and distracting, for the primary meaning of the passage is that Pound's loving labours of translation are rewarded with a glimpse of Aphrodite. How Pound obtained his copy of Divus, how Divus and the 'Hymni Deorum' were associated, are personal accidents of little or no significance; but this sort of association is to be found frequently in the first version, where Pound's 'personality' is almost suffocatingly present. The third point, that the Cretan's phrase is florid, appears to me about equally irrelevant; but it is possible that when Pound eliminated this judgment from the final draft, he did so partly in order to force his reader to see for himself (or not at all) that the language was somewhat overripe.

When Pound revised this early draft, then, he removed most of the transitional elements and so unclogged the movement from image to image, with the result that the appearance and (for the reader) convenience of reverie were largely eliminated. And when Pound shifted the translation of Homer from the back of Canto III to the front of Canto I, he was announcing a radical change of purpose and method: the poem would now hurdle forward towards discovery (it would not primarily draw on a rich background); it would force the reader to keep up with the poet (it would not lure him into a comfortable study where he could sink back and drift with the poet's fascinating but apparently goalless conversation); and it would have as one of its chief ends the restoring of the poet's lands to order and well-being (it would not presuppose that one should be contented with a private aesthetical-mystical salvation: 'World enough'). Some of the reasons for this major reorientation are stated in *Hugh Selwyn Mauberley*.

3. *Hugh Selwyn Mauberley*

The most celebrated of Pound's poems, *Mauberley* has received at least five commentaries worthy of mention: Dr Leavis's and Mr Kenner's, taken together, form a good introduction; Mr Espey's is perhaps a little too exhaustive, but is invaluable for information on background and especially difficult points; Mr Rosenthal's provides an excellent model for classroom discussion of the poem; and the most recent, Dr Davie's, besides advancing some new and interesting readings, defines many of the critical problems which the poem presents.[1] Given these commentaries, each of them valuable in its own way, I do not see that there is much to be gained by my supplying yet another detailed commentary. On the other hand, I imagine that other commentaries are forthcoming; for the exact significance of *Mauberley* has not been settled, and probably never will be.

The firmest ground is possibly the 'Envoi' which concludes the first section of the poem. Here Pound seems to be speaking with his own voice, though he is borrowing language and concepts that go back through (among others) Waller, Herrick, and Shakespeare to the troubadours. He is, in other words, doing much the same thing that he did in *Propertius*—a matter of some

---

[1] Donald Davie, 'Ezra Pound's "Hugh Selwyn Mauberley"', *The Modern Age* (Pelican Guides to Literature, 1961), pp. 315–29. The other commentaries appear in works cited above.

importance if we read *Mauberley* in the light of Pound's past and future career as a poet. Although his use of the 'Envoi' corresponds roughly to familiar English usages (Chaucer's, for instance), it is nevertheless odd that the *envoi* to this uncourtly sequence should itself be a very elegant courtly song; and I therefore believe that Pound must have had two other traditional uses of the *envoi* in mind. In troubadour usage the *envoi* (or *tornada*) normally contains personal allusions and topical references, which are not permitted in the main body of the song; but in *Mauberley* this procedure is exactly reversed, which is in itself a disdainful commentary on 'The Age' and its sense of literary priorities. A second, though related, traditional usage is exemplified by Cavalcanti's:

> Go, song, surely thou mayest
> Whither it please thee
> For so art thou ornate that thy reasons
> Shall be praised from thy understanders,
> With others hast thou no will to make company.

The *envoi* was the place, that is, where after a fine performance the poet expressed his contempt for his enemies and any potential detractors of the poem. (It should be remembered that *Propertius* had received obtuse and insulting reviews when it first appeared.) While the function of the 'Envoi' is clear enough without our being aware of these traditional usages, there is every reason to suppose that Pound was aware of them and expected his informed readers to be, too. In any case, they help to bring the 'Envoi' and its relation to the preceding sequence into a sharp focus.

The 'Envoi' is elaborately, but meaningfully, ambiguous:

> *Go, dumb-born book,*
> *Tell her that sang me once that song of Lawes:*
> *Hadst thou but song*
> *As thou hast subjects known,*
> *Then were there cause in thee that should condone*
> *Even my faults that heavy upon me lie,*
> *And build her glories their longevity.*

Now the colon at the end of the second line would seem to indicate that what follows is the actual message which the 'dumb-born book' is to deliver, i.e. a direct quotation in which 'thou' refers to the lady. But most readers, I think, would quickly decide that the punctuation of slightly misleading, and that 'thou' refers to the 'dumb-born book'. This reading would be in harmony with the second and third stanzas, in which there is no direct quotation. And besides, there are no quotation marks around the passage in question. Accordingly, the meaning of the first stanza seems to be fairly straightforward: if the 'dumb-born book' contained as much song as learning (of which it has plenty), then there would be cause in the book not only to condone the poet's faults but also to immortalize the lady's beauty. (The word 'cause' seems to be used in two of its senses: as something which provides an occasion for an action of some kind, and as something which acts; and the 'cause' in each case is the missing 'song'.) On this reading, then, the first stanza, like the entire poem, is an ironic confession of poetic inadequacy.

But this reading is not entirely satisfactory, partly because of Pound's punctuation and partly because of the absence of irony in the rest of the 'Envoi', where the poet's confidence in his own powers is quite unambiguous:

> *Tell her that sheds*
> *Such treasure in the air,*
> *Recking naught else but that her graces give*
> *Life to the moment,*
> *I would bid them live*
> *As roses might, in magic amber laid,*
> *Red overwrought with orange and all made*
> *One substance and one colour*
> *Braving time.*
>
> *Tell her that goes*
> *With song upon her lips*
> *But sings not out the song, nor knows*
> *The maker of it, some other mouth,*
> *May be as fair as hers,*
> *Might, in new ages, gain her worshippers,*
> *When our two dusts with Waller's shall be laid,*
> *Siftings on siftings in oblivion,*
> *Till change hath broken down*
> *All things save Beauty alone.*

On a second reading the meaning of the first stanza is something quite different: if you [the lady] had but known song as you have known worshippers, then there were cause in you [i.e. you would know enough] to condone even the faults of the 'dumb-born book' (since it *does* have song) and to build *her* glories their longevity. But to whom does 'her' refer in this case? It refers to the immortal female beauty of tradition who lies behind all of the ambiguous and slightly confusing personal pronouns in the third stanza. The lady addressed, like the 'some other mouth ... in new ages', is but a temporary embodiment of immortal beauty, i.e. Aphrodite (cf. 'Medallion', which is a sort of parody of the 'Envoi').[1] It seems probable, moreover, that she would 'build her glories' by giving the poet materials, i.e. herself, out of which to build a poem. But the main points are that the 'Envoi' answers Pound's critics in the very words which seem to confess failure, and further that the 'Envoi' itself, like the lady addressed, is but the contemporary embodiment of the immortal beauty of tradition. Everybody, I suppose, recognizes the melodic beauty of the 'Envoi'; the exploitation of ambiguity (especially in the reference of pronouns) seems to me almost as impressive.[2]

The 'Envoi', then, is concerned with what is 'timeless' and, in the most meaningful sense, 'impersonal'. The sequence which precedes it, on the other hand, is what Pound once described as an attempt to condense a Jamesian novel:

He has left his scene and his characters, unalterable as the little paper flowers permanently visible inside the lumpy glass paperweights. He was a great man of letters, a great artist in portrayal; he was concerned with mental temperatures, circumvolvulous social pressures, the clash of contending conventions, as Hogarth with the cut of contemporary coats.[3]

Certainly one of Pound's major concerns was to 'fix' the Age in the manner described in the first sentence of this passage. However, he was able to do so by virtue of two un-Jamesian

---

[1] In connection with this reading, see Chapter V, pp. 88–90.

[2] However, it must be owned that such ambiguity leaves room for rather too much interpretation. Donald Davie's attractive reading of the 'Envoi' is based on the conjecture that 'her' refers to England; but while this reading fits the first and third stanzas brilliantly, it does not seem to me to fit the second without some forcing. And I do not see how it is possible to combine Mr Davie's and my reading of the 'Envoi'.

[3] Pound, *Literary Essays*, p. 339.

devices: first, by keeping his subjects in a wide historical frame of reference; and second, by constantly shifting the speaker's point of view and attitude. The difficulties of interpretation created by the latter are usually overcome by reference to the subject's historical 'placing'; while the tendency of Pound's historical view to make everything modern uniformly bad and dead is overcome by the constant shifts of attitude and point of view, which give the effect of a lively and sensitive intelligence responding actively to the variety of experience. We have no warrant for saying that the experiencing intelligence must be regarded as that of Ezra Pound, author of *Cathay* and *Lustra*; we have excellent reason to suppose that the intelligence is *not* that of the fictional Mauberley: it suffices, surely, that the various responses—given the variety of subjects—might well be those of a single mind representing the literary conscience of the age.

This seems to me true, at any rate, of the poems numbered II through XII. The 'Envoi' falls outside the sequence; its subject, the author's point of view and style, are 'timeless'. For when the poet says 'Tell her that sang me once that song of Lawes', he is quietly informing us that he (the ambiguous 'me') is the timeless, placeless Poet, just as she (the ambiguous 'her') is the timeless, placeless Beauty. All of this is in the sharpest contrast to the preceding sequence; it is a defence of the poetic concerns and methods embodied in *Propertius*; and it is a definitive answer to the 'indictment' of E. P. which is delivered in the first poem of the sequence:

> For three years, out of key with his time,
> He strove to resuscitate the dead art
> Of poetry; to maintain 'the sublime'
> In the old sense. Wrong from the start—
>
> No, hardly, but seeing he had been born
> In a half savage country, out of date;

Mauberley is in fact a savage attack on the kind of criticism which is based on the accidents of biography, though it is at the same time an account of how the finer but weaker spirits of an age are destroyed by a thoroughly materialistic environment. The reference to Villon in the last stanza is, however, an assertion that environment cannot kill the true poet:

Unaffected by 'the march of events',
He passed from men's memory in *l'an trentiesme*
De son eage; the case presents
No adjunct to the Muses' diadem.

The concluding statement is delivered, as Mr Rosenthal puts it, 'in the voice of the chairman of some imaginary committee of literary stuffed shirts'.[1] The sequence which follows leaves little doubt that E. P.'s era, in its way, was as bad as or worse than Villon's era. When out of this sequence of the 'dated', particular, and local (each fixed historically) the 'Envoi' at last emerges, it seems indeed to be a miracle of art—like Botticelli's Venus emerging from the flux of the sea, herself unhistorical, immortal. (Even Pound's italicizing the whole of the 'Envoi' underscores the foreignness of this courtly song in the context of *Mauberley*.)

This seems to me, generally, to be the correct way of reading the first sequence. Even allowing for numerous difficulties of interpretation (especially in the case of the first poem), the sequence must surely be rated among the finest poetic achievements of the century. It is true, as Mr Davie has pointed out, that Poem IV seems to have the voice of the author of *The Cantos*, while (among other variations) Poem XII has an almost Prufrockian voice at times; but it seems to me that these shifts do not blur the poetic/moral focus, and further that these shifts of attitude contribute as much as the variety of subjects to our sense of the adequacy of Pound's portrait of the age. Moreover, these modulations seem to me prepared for in Poem II, where in the third stanza the voice suddenly changes, as though the speaker grew impatient with his own coy diction:

The age demanded an image,
Of its accelerated grimace,
Something for the modern stage,
Not, at any rate, an Attic grace;

Not, not certainly, the obscure reveries
Of the inward gaze;
Better mendacities
Than the classics in paraphrase!

[1] Rosenthal, *Primer of Ezra Pound*, p. 34.

> The 'age demanded' chiefly a mould in plaster,
> Made with no loss of time,
> A prose kinema, not, not assuredly, alabaster
> Or the 'sculpture' of rhyme.

However, the first sequence is but part of an extremely complex and ambitious poem which Dr Leavis and others have insisted is a whole. 'The whole is great poetry, at once traditional and original.'[1] The second sequence, which is Mauberley's biography, is intricately related to the first sequence and is, if anything, more dazzling technically. Although the first sequence comes close to being a whole by itself, it is not one because the first poem ('E. P. Ode pour l'Election de Son Sepulchre') carefully introduces misconceptions about 'E. P.' which are not really cleared up in the first sequence—although the 'Envoi' is in its way Pound's eloquent and conclusive rejoinder. The point is that, having introduced himself as a literary personality, he must somehow—since 'his true Penelope was Flaubert'—purge this personality. And, for a poet already undertaking a great Odyssean poem,[2] what better way than to create a diminished analogue of himself, an imaginary poet who embodies Poundian traits which Pound recognizes as the liabilities of a minor artist? The resultant poet, though a sympathetic fictional character in his own right, might almost be the author of the earliest cantos:

> And his desire for survival,
> Faint in the most strenuous moods,
> Became an Olympian *apathein*
> In the presence of selected perceptions.

To this we might add:

> Not, not certainly, the obscure reveries
> Of the inward gaze;
> Better mendacities
> Than the classics in paraphrase!

This, though from the first sequence, applies about equally well to Mauberley and Pound himself: 'obscure reveries of the inward gaze' is not a bad description of much of the early draft

---

[1] Leavis, *New Bearings*, p. 150.

[2] The *new* version of *The Cantos* is hinted at (it seems) in these Homeric allusions. Cf. the discussion which follows.

of cantos; 'mendacities' would not seem to fit Mauberley's productions, but they fit parts of *Lustra* well enough; 'classics in paraphrase' are the sort of thing that Mauberley might indulge in, and its sounds like an obtuse reviewer's tag for *Homage to Sextus Propertius*. It should be apparent, then, that Pound and Mauberley are not always to be clearly differentiated. Perhaps the single characteristic which most distinguishes Mauberley from Pound is the former's sexual blindness and timidity.

> He had passed, inconscient, full gaze,
> The wide-banded irides
> And Botticellian sprays implied
> In their diastasis;
>
> . . .
>
> The sleek head emerges
> From the gold-yellow frock
> As Anadyomene in the opening
> Pages of Reinach.

The second quotation, from Mauberley's 'Medallion', has been glossed by Donald Davie as follows: 'Venus Anadyomene, the mythological expression of how sexual and other vitality is re-newed, hardens under Mauberley's hand into the glazed frontispiece to a book on Comparative Religion. (We note that it is the head which, for Mauberley, is rising Venus-like from the sea, not the breasts or the loins.)'[1] And Mr Espey has noted (though Mauberley did not) that the 'gold-yellow frock' has the colour of Hymen. The author of *Homage to Sextus Propertius* is of course quite aware of such things; yet, even so, there was a curious blindness in this parallel passage from the earliest cantos:

> If Botticelli
> Brings her ashore on that great cockle-shell,
> His Venus (Simonetta), and Spring
> And Aufidus fill all the air
> With their clear-outlined blossoms?
> World enough.

On the one hand, Pound seems to be saying what he says in the 'Envoi'; but, on the other, he also seems to be implying that,

---

[1] Davie, 'Ezra Pound's "Mauberley" ', *The Modern Age*, p. 329.

for him, there would be 'world enough' in a state of aesthetic receptivity—Botticelli having, as it were, translated and captured sexual vitality in his art. Pound, in other words, is purging in the person of Mauberley a specifically Paterian tendency in himself.

Such, in general terms, seems to me the relationship between Pound and Mauberley. To say that 'Mauberley' was the author of the earliest cantos would be to simplify grossly, yet it is a simplification which has the advantage of emphasizing the transitional nature of *Mauberley* and of emphasizing the difference between it and *Propertius*, which is, as I have suggested above, a defence of the poetic preoccupations revealed in the early cantos. This is not to say, however, that *Mauberley* is in any sense a repudiation of *Propertius*; on the contrary, the 'Envoi' is certainly a defence of *Propertius*, which Pound himself regards as a better poem than *Mauberley*. Since I share Pound's view, I had best explain why *Mauberley* does not seem to me the poetic whole that others have taken it to be.

I have pointed out that the first sequence is not quite a poetic whole, largely because the opening poem introduces a detailed but distorted portrait of Pound as a literary personality; and since the first sequence deals with 'the age', not with the poet's personality, something remains to be said. The opening poem, then, prepares the way for the second sequence; but the trouble is that the first sequence nevertheless achieves remarkable coherence and, in the supremely impersonal 'Envoi', dramatic finality. Brilliant as it is, therefore, the second sequence is an appendage, and no amount of interconnection with the first sequence can make it anything else. *If* the first sequence were less complete, or *if* the speaker of the first sequence were clearly Mauberley rather than Pound, then the second sequence (where Pound seems clearly to be the speaker) would perhaps complete a poetic whole. As the poem stands, however, the second sequence is an issue, not of the sequence which is resolved in the 'Envoi', but rather of the opening poem of that sequence; and to my mind the result of this organization is a poem lacking fully coherent development and final unity.

There are, moreover, other reasons not to be completely satisfied with *Mauberley* generally and with the Mauberley-Pound sections particularly. For one thing, the full irony which

Pound intended (i.e. that the poem is anything but a confession of literary failure, that it contains but little severe self-criticism) is communicated adequately only to those who are able to share Pound's own view of the matter. Those who do not share his view, Dr Leavis for example, simply do not read the poem which Pound had in mind and which, perhaps, he wrote. I say 'perhaps' because in places, especially in the crucial opening poem, it is far from clear what Pound did mean. To show what this obscurity amounts to, I shall quote two quatrains from 'E. P. Ode pour L'Election de Son Sepulchre' and then four commentaries by critics who admire *Mauberley*. It should be kept in mind that the meaning of *Mauberley* as a whole and the range of Pound's irony, hinge to a fairly large extent on the meaning of this opening poem.

> Ἴδμεν γάρ τοι πάνθ᾽, ὅσ᾽ ἐνὶ Τροίῃ
> Caught in the unstopped ear;
> Giving the rocks small lee-way
> The chopped seas held him, therefore, that year.
>
> His true Penelope was Flaubert,
> He fished by obstinate isles;
> Observed the elegance of Circe's hair
> Rather than the mottoes on sun-dials.

Here is Dr Leavis's commentary:

The Homeric quotation suggests his romantic addiction to the classics and the past: his ear has been unstopped to too many sirens.

> His true Penelope was Flaubert

—In all his romantic excursions he has remained constant to one faith, the aesthetic: his main concern has been art as represented by Flaubert, saint and martyr of the artistic conscience.

> He fished by obstinate isles

suggests his inveterate eclecticism, his interest in various periods and cultures, Provençal, Italian, Chinese, classical, and so on. He has always

> Observed the elegance of Circe's hair
> Rather than the mottoes on sundials.

He has devoted his life to aesthetic discrimination and technical perfection while life slipped by.[1]

[1] Leavis, *New Bearings*, pp. 141–2.

Mr Fraser comments only on the second quatrain:

Flaubert is ... the patron saint of aestheticism, and Pound ought to have rejoined him in Ithaca, but he has instead spent his time fishing by the islands of pleasure, like that of Circe in the *Odyssey*, which prevent him from reaching his Ithaca. (They are obstinate, I think, because in one's youth they will not allow one to pass them by.) A hedonistic-aesthetic attitude to female beauty ... has absorbed Pound so much that he has not noticed the mottoes on sundials: such mottoes, for instance, as 'It is later than you think.'[1]

Mr Rosenthal has a different view:

[The reference to Capaneus] leads to another classical allusion, this time to Book XII of the *Odyssey*, where the Sirens are shown singing their seductive song to Odysseus. The comparison between E. P. and Odysseus is developed over two stanzas, establishing an identification like that of the *Cantos*. He has lingered in the dangerous, choppy seas of the 'rocks' of English culture; presumably he had cherished hopes that the superficial classical sophistication of the British literary and academic world was the real thing, and that he would find his true home, his Ithaca and Penelope, there. But his 'true Penelope' was not the pretentious show-classicism of England but the dedicated, stylistically precise, unsqueamishly truthful art of Flaubert—the true classicism of the modern world.[2]

And here is the most recent reading, Dr Davie's:

By introducing the line from Homer's *Odyssey*, 'For we know all the things that are in Troy', the speaker of this poem wittily makes Odysseus's own story of Troy into the siren-song which Pound heard and was seduced by. And in fact Pound had already started his version of the story of Odysseus, the long epic poem which has occupied him ever since. In the speaker's view, Circe, representing Pound's epic aspirations, had beguiled him from pursuing his voyage home to his faithful wife, Penelope, to this true objective, which was Flaubertian.

Mr Davie then quotes Mr Kenner, who had pointed out that Flaubert represented (to Pound) the 'ideal of disciplined self-immolation from which English poetry has too long been estranged', while he also represented (to the imaginary author of this Ode) 'a foreign, feminine, rather comically earnest indulger in quite un-British preciosity'.[3] And so Mr Davie concludes,

---

[1] Fraser, *Ezra Pound*, pp. 53–4. [2] Rosenthal, *Primer of Ezra Pound*, p. 34.
[3] Kenner, *The Poetry of Ezra Pound*, pp. 170–1.

'Thus the speaker of the poem says what is true while meaning to say (in identical words) what is false'.[1]

Each of these readings seems to me fairly plausible, and the fourth is (probably) a fairly accurate interpretation of Pound's intended meaning. Mr Fraser follows Dr Leavis's reading generally but attempts, as Dr Leavis does not, to discriminate clearly between the values represented by Flaubert on the one hand and by Circe on the other; but he certainly misses some important ironic implications—that the 'obstinate isles', for instance, are almost certainly the British Isles. Dr Leavis and Mr Rosenthal attempt to interpret the passage in the light of preconceptions about Pound's vices or the vices of the British literary world; and while Mr Rosenthal's reading is closer to the spirit of the poem, both his and Dr Leavis's interpretations overcome difficulties by ignoring them. Mr Davie's reading is very seductive, but his attempt to identify the Sirens with Circe seems to me a convenient but unjustifiable simplification. Moreover, that E. P.'s fascination with 'the elegance of Circe's hair' represents Pound's epic aspirations appears to me wildly improbable—almost as improbable as Mr Rosenthal's contention that it represents Pound's temporary flirtation with 'the pretentious show-classicism of England'.[2]

I believe that these conflicting interpretations do not point to any lack of sensitivity in their authors, although Dr Leavis and Mr Fraser have perhaps paid too little attention to Pound's intentions, while Mr Davie and Mr Rosenthal have perhaps paid too much. The fact is that Pound's notation is extremely imprecise; and so long as the meaning of the opening poem is obscure, the rest of *Mauberley* cannot be interpreted with precision. Having said this, I should immediately add that even the most unintelligible lines move with remarkable poetic authority, that in its parts *Mauberley* is the work of a poetic genius of very high calibre, and that in spite of its defects (which seem to me serious) it is still a very important poem.

However, that *Mauberley* is generally accounted a better poem than *Propertius* is largely due, I think, to the fact that it is what

[1] Davie, *The Modern Age*, pp. 319–20.
[2] My own guess, for whatever it may be worth, is that Mr Davie is right about the Sirens and Flaubert, but that the lines about Circe and the sundials refer (with Mauberleyan blindness) to the period when Pound wrote *Homage to Sextus Propertius*.

'the age demanded': 'an image of its accelerated grimace'. The age did not demand the mellow wit, the leisurely rhythms, the unpretentious dignity of the earlier poem. Unlike *Mauberley*, *Propertius* does not invite endless explanation; once we have grasped its basic conventions, it speaks for itself remarkably well. Parts of *Mauberley* and *The Cantos* are perhaps greater than any part of *Propertius*. At any rate, they speak more directly to our time. But *Propertius* is a poetic whole, brilliantly sustained and unified. It seems to me Pound's most complete poetic success and one of the finest poems of the century.

IX

THE FIRST SEVENTY-ONE CANTOS

1. Cantos I–XLI

THE EARLIEST CANTOS, as we have seen, date from 1916 or perhaps even earlier, and *Homage to Sextus Propertius* (1917) was intended to be, among other things, an apologia for the pre-occupations of these cantos. This series of cantos continued to appear even after the publication of *Mauberley* (1920), but *Mauberley* reveals a wider and deeper awareness of the relationship between literature and society than Pound had heretofore shown. Moreover, the Odyssean motifs in *Mauberley* suggest that Pound had already decided to recast the early cantos into a far more vigorous form. At any rate, when the first sixteen cantos of the new version were first published in 1925,[1] it became clear that the poem was to be a great Odyssean voyage through time and space, with, apparently, no limits as to what might eventually be encountered (no limits, that is, except the poet's tact and sense of relevance). The following resumé of Cantos I–XLI, in which the emphasis is on continuity rather than variety and disparateness, may prove helpful by indicating the range of Pound's voyaging without overwhelming the reader with detail.

The scheme, roughly, is this: Cantos I–VII, general poetic, moral, and historical principles; Cantos VII–XII, creative and destructive intelligence in action; Canto XIII (Confucius), transitional—practical counsel and clean state-of-mind; Cantos XIV–XVI, emphasis on states-of-mind—infernal, purgatorial,

---

[1] *A Draft of XVI Cantos of Ezra Pound* (Paris, 1925).

paradisal; Canto XVII, distinction between live (Ovidian) and dead (Venetian) visions of other-than-phenomenal-reality; Cantos XVIII–XXX, intermixture of previous materials with special emphasis on Italian Renaissance (usurious) decadence and twentieth-century internationalism in aspects amusing (e.g. American tourism) and sinister (cartels, etc.); Cantos XXXI–XXXIV, major shift to early years of the American Republic—with special emphasis on the qualities of a statesman (Jefferson) and the necessity of avoiding European entanglements; Canto XXXV, Mitteleuropa—European decadence, cheap goods, breeding ground of wars; Canto XXXVI, Cavalcanti's *Canzone d'Amore*—ultimate achievement of a mediaeval tradition uniting music, philosophy, and verse—a supremely non-commercial effort; Cantos XXXVII–XLI, decline of American fiscal integrity and consequent involvement of U.S. with European finance, international arms, etc.—appearance of Mussolini as latest (1933) constructive force; and Canto XXXIX (Circe-Odysseus) appearing in the midst of these largely distressing and indeed daunting events as an image of the creative intelligence regaining vigour and direction.

These cantos, then, are chiefly Pound's attempt to account historically for twentieth-century occidental civilization, which is characterized by an internationalism at once sham (e.g. VII), comical (e.g. XXVIII), and positively evil (e.g. XLI). Against this there is, of course, the internationalism of *The Cantos* itself, which is dedicated to breaking down provincial ignorance as the only possible way to combat the international evil. Consequently, Pound feels free, in fact obliged, to voyage through space and time—to Renaissance Italy, Ancient China, nineteenth-century America, contemporary Europe—to any place or time that seems to offer information about the origins of contemporary troubles or their possible remedy. Throughout this section, too, there are images of the poet or some other constructive figure consulting an expert: Sigismondo talking with Gemisthus Plethon about Plato (VIII); Pound travelling to Freiburg to consult the great Provençal scholar Emil Levy (XX); Jefferson writing to Washington to inquire about the terrain west of the Atlantic seaboard (XXXI). All of these developments are of course prefigured in Canto I, where Odysseus makes a necessary detour in order to speak with Tiresias. Also prefigured, in

Canto II, are the anti-Odyssean figures: the pirates 'mad for a little slave money' who kidnap Dionysus and take Acoetes' ship 'off her course ... ' Thus Canto I dramatizes the inquiring intelligence, which must detour frequently; while Canto II dramatizes the moral will, which must stay on course. The anti-Odyssean figure, the usurer, is one whose moral will has gone off course but whose intelligence never detours: 'Baldy's interest / Was in money business./ "No interest in any other kind uv bisnis" ' (Canto XII). And finally there are those who have ample intelligence but no will whatever—the lotophagoi of Canto XX.

This, then, is a brief account of the contents and poetic strategy of Cantos I–XLI. Since I have already explained why, in my view, such a sequence lacks poetic unity and, regarded as a sequence, also lacks much poetic interest, and since I have already discussed in detail most of the individual cantos which seem to me of enduring value, I shall not undertake a detailed criticism of Cantos I–XLI; a brief commentary should suffice. Cantos I and II seem to me among the greatest, and though at first glance they appear to be merely brilliant paraphrases of Ovid and Homer, they acquire greater significance and greater beauty as one perceives their connection with each other and with the rest of the poem. They are a great beginning; but the decline in quality thereafter, though not precipitous, is immediate. Cantos III and IV are closely related, III being concerned with the transitoriness of even the most robust civilization, and IV being concerned with the eternal means of renewal which cut across particular civilizations; taken together, they form an impressive unit, but they are uneven in quality and clearly inferior to I and II. Cantos V, VI, and VII develop a sort of three-layer theory of history in which mediaeval Provence, Renaissance Italy, and contemporary Europe correspond to Homeric Greece, late Greece and Early Rome, and Rome in decadence; these cantos are yet more uneven, often cryptic, and sometimes only marginally poetic; but they seem to me interesting and the second half of VII is very powerful indeed. This completes the introductory section. Cantos VIII–XVII, in my view, continue to be interesting poetically, though there are some dead spots in the Malatesta Cantos and in Canto XVI. In fact, a comparison of the treatment of the Great War in XVI with the treatment in *Mauberley* reveals as clearly as possible what is wrong with so many cantos: refusing to generalize, Pound always runs the risk of becoming diffuse, and to counter this tendency he often resorts to cryptic allusion; seeking a 'more natural language', he often sacrifices rhythmic intensity. These criticisms do not apply to Cantos XIII and XVII, the second of which is especially remarkable because it reveals Pound responding sensitively to the beauty of Venice and Venetian painting in spite of the fact that they represent, in his scheme of things, decadence and the evil of usury. The result is a portrait at once beautiful and sinister:

> Borso, Carmagnola, the men of craft, *i vitrei*,
> Thither, at one time, time after time,
> And the waters richer than glass,
> Bronze gold, the blaze over the silver,
> Dye-pots in the torch-light,
> The flash of wave under prows,
> And the silver beaks rising and crossing.
> > Stone trees, white and rose-white in the darkness,
> Cypress there by the towers,
> > Drift under hulls in the night.
>
> > > 'In the gloom the gold
> > Gathers the light about it.' ...
>
> > > > > (p. 82)

It is not very often that one praises Pound for understanding and appreciating the Enemy.

Cantos XVIII–XXX bring the first sequence to a close, and with the exception of the first half of XXX they seem to me the worst part of the poem. This is not to deny that there are moments of beauty; humour, and insight; the treatment of the lotophagoi in Canto XX (pp. 96–8), for example, has the same excellence as the treatment of Venice in Canto XVII. But taken as a whole, these cantos are incredibly diffuse: one knows well enough why Pound communicates his meaning through pages of exemplary anecdotes and extracts from state documents or private letters, but after a while one begins to feel that this method disguises an actual poverty of meaning which would become apparent if Pound once resorted to the poetry of abstract summary statement. And throughout these cantos we are made to feel the presence of Pound himself—the irrepressible personality of 'Ole Ez', private investigator and cracker-barrel philosopher. Those who prefer Pound to poetry will undoubtedly enjoy these cantos. The first part of XXX I have already praised; if it does not represent Pound at his very best, it is still very distinguished poetry.

Cantos XXXI–XLI (1934) are somewhat better than most of the cantos which immediately precede them. For in Cantos XXXI–XXXIV the intelligence of Jefferson, John Adams, and James Madison suddenly shines:

> With respect to his motives (Madison writing) I
> $\qquad\qquad\qquad\qquad\qquad$ acknowledged
> I had been much puzzled to divine any natural one
> without looking deeper into human nature
> than I was willing to do.
> $\qquad\qquad\qquad\qquad$ (Canto XXXI)

This extract sums up a good deal of eighteenth-century sensibility (in the twentieth-century sense of the word). It is not poetry but it is 'language charged with meaning'. Pound's mannerisms are sometimes distracting and annoying in these cantos, but in Canto XXXI especially he pieces together a portrait of these American statesmen worthy of attention. Of the remaining cantos in this sequence, XXXVI and XXXIX are valuable as poetry, though the latter seems to me less good than other critics have supposed. One interesting approach to XXXIX is to read it as an answer to *The Waste Land*:

> Eurilochus, Macer, better there with good acorns
> Than with a crab for an eye, and 30 fathom of fishes
> Green swish in the socket,

Then there is the fine passage inspired by the *Pervigilium Veneris*:

> $\qquad\qquad$ there in the glade
> To Flora's night, with hyacinthus,
> With the crocus (spring
> $\qquad\qquad\qquad$ sharp in the grass)
> Fifty and forty together
> $\qquad\quad$ ERI MEN AI DE KUDONIAI

Betuene Aprile and Merche
>   with sap new in the bough
With plum flowers above them
>   with almond on the black bough
With jasmine and olive leaf,
To the beat of the measure
From star-up to the half-dark
>   Unceasing the measure
Flank by flank on the headland
>   with the Goddess' eyes to seaward
By Circeo, by Terracina, with the stone eyes
>   white toward the sea
With one measure, unceasing:
>   'Fac deum!' 'Est factus.'
Ver novum!
>   ver novum!
Thus made the spring,
Can see but their eyes in the dark
>   not the bough that he walked on.

'ERI MEN AI DE KUDONIAI' is a fragment from Ibycus on which Pound based an early (though impressive) Yeatsian poem, 'The Spring'. 'Ver novum! ver novum!' is from the *Pervigilium Veneris*, a late Latin poem sung in connection with the festival of Venus Genetrix. Pound notes in *The Spirit of Romance* that the poem is remarkable for a metric which expresses 'tendencies indigenous to the Italian peninsula, which had been long suppressed by the imitation of Greek scansion'.[1] And since it was a Greek festival transplanted to Italy which reawakened the native metric, it is possible that Pound's translation of Homer into a meter based on the Anglo-Saxon was a conscious parallel. However that may be, one should recall that a phrase from the *Pervigilium Veneris* appears at the end of *The Waste Land* as one of the fragments which Eliot had 'shored against ... [his] ruins'; but, as Pound charged in Canto VIII, Eliot merely 'shelved' this fragment by associating it with Tennyson's 'O swallow swallow'. Pound, on the other hand, seeks here to 'unshelve' the *Pervigilium Veneris* by providing a vigorous new context. Unfortunately, other parts of the canto are extremely cryptic and, I think, marred by Poundian horse-play—something that might be called 'unsolemnity'.

---

[1] *Spirit of Romance*, p. 10.

2. *The Fifth Decad of Cantos*

Cantos XLII–LI were first published as a complete sequence in 1937. They begin unpromisingly enough with a pastiche and paraphrase of documents dealing with the foundation and operation of a Sienese bank, the Monte dei Paschi, whose credit was based on public grazing lands. The banking provisions appear to be sensible and humane:

> and 6thly that the Magistrate
> give his chief care that the specie
> be lent to whomso can best use it USE IT
> (*id est, più utilmente*)
> to the good of their houses, to benefit of their business
> as of weaving, the wool trade, the silk trade
> And that (7thly) the overabundance every five years shall
> the Bailey
> distribute to workers of the contrade (the wards) holding in
> reserve a prudent proportion as against unforeseen losses
> though there shd. be NO such losses
> and 9th that the borrowers can pay up before the end of
> their
> term whenso it be to their interest. No debt to run more
> than
> five years.
>
> (Canto XLII, pp. 217–18)

This is the prose of Pound's bread-and-butter cantos, interesting perhaps, but remote from poetry. A few lines later, however, the following appears:

> wave falls and the hand falls
> Thou shalt not always walk in the sun
> or see weed sprout over cornice
> Thy work in set space of years, not over an hundred.

Then Pound returns to his bank and other economic matters, and continues without a poetic interruption until Canto XLV. But these four lines announce the recovery of Pound's major poetic voice. They look like a fragment broken loose from Canto XLVII, yet in fact they fit very well into the present context. For of course economics do matter to us, and they matter precisely because we have only a 'set space of years, not over an hundred' in which to realize our human potential. Pound in his way is as much concerned with the eternal verities as anyone else is; but, perhaps more than any other twentieth-century poet except Hardy, Pound knows the importance and the poignancy of the passing of time:

> Time is the evil. Evil.
> A day, and a day
> Walked the young Pedro baffled,
> a day and a day
> After Ignez was murdered.
> Came the Lords in Lisboa
> a day, and a day
> In homage. Seated there
> dead eyes,
> Dead hair under the crown,
> The King still young there beside her.
>
> (Canto XXX)

Of course four lines of poetry cannot bring pages of Poundian economics to life, though they should increase our respect for Pound's economic concerns. The four lines are worth quoting again:

> wave falls and the hand falls
> Thou shalt not always walk in the sun
> or see weed sprout over cornice
> Thy work in set space of years, not over an hundred.

The simplicity of the language is striking, as is the absoluteness with which Pound identifies human life and death with the primordial motion of the sea. That man's destiny is bound up with the motions and seasons of the natural world is a source of joy for him (cf. XLVII and 90), but it also makes man terribly vulnerable. The slow, solemn rhythm of these lines, which enforces their meaning, is typical of all the great cantos of the 'Fifth Decad'. And all of these must be read in the light of Pound's concern with the place of man in a natural order which gives and takes life and allows man but a 'set space of years' in which to accomplish his work. This is particularly true of the 'Usura' cantos, XLV and LI:

> Usury rusts the man and his chisel
> It destroys the craftsman; destroying craft
> Azure is caught with cancer. Emerald comes to no
> Memling

Usury kills the child in the womb
And breaks short the young man's courting
Usury brings age into youth; it lies between the bride
and the bridegroom
Usury is against Nature's increase.
Whores for Eleusis;
Under usury no stone is cut smooth
Peasant has no gain from his sheep herd

(LI, pp. 261–2)

The simplicity here is mediaeval; the allegorizing of 'Usury'
reminds one of the morality plays. (It ought to be noted that
the 'Usura' cantos are constructed on the same principles as
Canto XXX, whose mediaeval affiliations are equally important.) Mr Alvarez has rightly noted that these lines are merely a
series of unsupported assertions unrelated by logical development.[1] The principle of organization here is that of the tableau:
the commanding figure of Usury, like the figure of Death in the
mediaeval tableaux, appears in one scene after another,
thwarting the characteristic and necessary activity of each
member of the human community. The effect of such a method
must be stasis, yet also inevitability.

Behind this simplicity there is intense feeling, and there is
more subtlety than meets the eye. In the passage quoted we
have 'Emerald comes to no Memling'; the meaning is clear
enough: Usury intervenes and prevents the emerald from
coming into the hands of a Memling. But the idea is more
complicated than this, as the corresponding line in Cantos XLV
makes clear: 'Emerald findeth no Memling.' Here the verb is
more obviously active in mood: Usury destroys a mystical
affinity between the artist and his materials, between man and
nature, as though some agent cancelled the magnetic fields of
force which draw the compass needle to its North. But a better
analogy is with the sexual imagery of Canto XLVII, where the
male and female attract and seek to fulfil each other:

> Two span, two span to a woman,
> Beyond that she believes not. Nothing is of any importance.
> To that is she bent, her intention,

[1] A. Alvarez, *The Shaping Spirit* (1958), pp. 48–72. Mr Alvarez's essay on Pound
is full of interesting and, I believe, just observations. However, he seems to me to
underrate the achievement involved in Pound's poetic simplicity—an achievement
quite as remarkable as any metaphysical complexity?

To that art thou called ever turning intention,
Whether by night the owl-call, whether by sap in shoot,
Never idle, by no means by no wiles intermittent
Moth is called over mountain
The bull runs blind on the sword, *naturans*
To the cave art thou called, Odysseus,
By Molü hast thou respite for a little,
By Molü art thou freed from the one bed
      that thou may'st return to another
The stars are not in her counting,
      To her they are but wandering holes.

Here again the verse is disarmingly simple. Pound deals here
with the elemental forces of nature, and to communicate this
meaning adequately he exploits the elemental forces of language.
Particularly remarkable is the action he evokes from the
prepositions 'by' and 'to'. This is accomplished by simple
inversions ('to that art thou called ever turning intention') and
by simple parallelism ('by no means by no wiles'): this manipulation of syntax throws the prepositional function into such
prominence that, in the last line of the passage, the preposition
'To' has an almost physical force; and thus the line conveys an
image of almost absolute female subjectivity, drawing the most
remote and detached of things into the realm of her undiffer-
entiating intention. For Odysseus, of course, though he gladly
yields to female attraction, such subjectivity would be suicidal;
after all, the stars' fixed relations are essential to his navigation;
and they are, besides, objects for him to speculate about and explain in various ways—an activity essential to the masculine mind.

    This sexual attraction is indeed the most important of the
magnetic forces in the temporal order of nature. For Pound
it is the basis of art and religion as well as of life:

Emerald findeth no Memling
Usura slayth the child in the womb
It stayeth the young man's courting
It hath brought palsey to bed, lyeth
between the young bride and her bridegroom
                CONTRA NATURA
They have brought whores for Eleusis
Corpses are set to banquet
at behest of usura.
                                  (XLV)

The last lines, recalling as they do Canto XXX,[1] should remind
us that interference with natural union and degradation of the
mysteries are a form of murder; and they warp human nature
just as surely as the murder of Ignez warped King Pedro.
Although Pound here draws strength from the same fund of
mediaeval thought and feeling that Hooker and Shakespeare
drew from, he does not share their Christian faith in an after-
life; and so his concern that the natural order should not be
disrupted is, if anything, more urgent than theirs. Yet it is
not quite true that for him, as for Pedro, 'Time is the evil. Evil'.
This is true only of the society which usura paralyses, where
human potential is not permitted to realize itself. In the agra-
rian society of Canto XLVII, however, Pound finds a resting
place in time, where temporal limits are understood and
honoured:

> By this gate art thou measured
> Thy day is between a door and a door
> Two oxen are yoked for plowing
> Or six in the hill field
> White bulk under olives, a score for drawing down stone,
> Here the mules are gabled with slate on the hill road.
> Thus was it in time.
> And the small stars now fall from the olive branch,
> Forked shadow falls dark on the terrace
> More black that the floating martin
>   that has no care for your presence,
> His wing-print is black on the roof tiles
> And the print is gone with his cry.
>
> So light is thy weight on Tellus
> Thy notch no deeper indented
> Thy weight less than the shadow
> Yet hast thou gnawed through the mountain,
>   Scilla's white teeth less sharp.
> Hast thou found a nest softer than cunnus
> Or hast'ou a deeper planting, doth thy death year
> Bring swifter shoot?
> Hast thou entered more deeply the mountain?

[1] Mr Rosenthal has also pointed out a striking parallel in Blake's:

> But most thro' midnight streets I hear
> How the youthful Harlot's curse,
> Blasts the new born Infant's tear,
> And blights with plagues the Marriage hearse.

Here at last Odysseus-Pound has come temporarily to rest after his prodigious travels to many times and places: here, though in the immemorial rural order which has disappeared or is disappearing from the face of the earth, he finds a place where the temporal order of seasonal birth, growth, and death is felt deeply and allowed for in the scheme of life. Canto XLVII is in fact the pivotal canto in a sequence which acts as a transition from the wanderings of the early cantos to the Chinese and American history cantos (LII–LXXI), where Pound at last submits to the tyranny of place and time. This is a matter of some importance, since it involves the only formal principle of development that I am able to discern in *The Cantos*. In Cantos I–XLI, that is, we find Pound escaping the physical limits of time and place; he gallops up and down and jumps back and forth from the histories of many civilizations; the image he wishes to communicate is that of an active traveller, not that of a mind engaged in reverie. This, for Pound, is a new way of triumphing over the limits of time and place; but it is an old and central concern of his: in *Propertius* he had triumphed by speaking through the mask of a first century B.C. Roman; and in *Mauberley* he had triumphed in the 'Envoi', where, using the language of Shakespeare, Herrick, and Waller, he spoke as the immortal poet of the courtly tradition, thus defying and setting himself apart from the particular era of British letters treated in the opening sequence of the poem. To escape from such limits is not merely the privilege of the artist; it is, in one way or another, what is required of him—otherwise he is a mere journalist. However, it is clear that (apart from any other objections) Pound's method of jumping about in time and place is a method which fails to accommodate his deepest feelings and best insights. We might concede that the liberties of the early cantos were necessary for Pound to discover and reveal the scope of usura's domain; but the tyranny of usura is evil because it destroys the rhythms, the harmonies, the magnetisms of the temporal order of nature to which man belongs and in which, Pound believes, man must seek his salvation. Therefore, Pound gives up his freedom of movement, and, in Cantos LII–LXI, engages himself with the longest continuous history extant, that of China. On the one hand, Chinese history affords him an unparalleled opportunity to study the interconnections between political and economic policies and effects; on the other, it affords an unparalleled perspective—season after season, war after war, generation after generation—on the human condition. And again, in Cantos LXII–LXXI, Pound continues to accept the limitations of time and place; but in these, the Adams Cantos, he restricts his movement still further, dealing only with the early years of the American Republic. Here Pound's emphasis is on the way a great statesman goes about meeting the problems of a particular place and time—as of course any statesman must: the conditions are to a large extent local, peculiar to that place and time; but Adams's approach might serve as a model for any statesman.

The Pisan Cantos were to some extent an accident, since Pound certainly did not foresee the tragic events of 1938–45. Probably he intended that Cantos LXXIII–C should complete the poem; and, probably, he intended to devote most of this concluding section to a statement and poetic demonstration of the eternal principles of order and harmony anticipated in Cantos XIII and XLVII. This is to some extent what actually happens in the Rock-Drill sequence (Cantos 85–95), which first appeared complete in 1955. But in the Pisan sequence (LXIII–LXXXIV), first drafted in 1945 but published in 1948, Pound himself becomes unmistakably fixed in time and place and allows himself the freedom of a reverie which ranges everywhere, though always returning to the concentration camp where he is a prisoner. Here again he triumphs over the restrictions of time and place; but the triumph in this case is explicitly a triumph of memory, which defies the destruction of things inherent in the temporal order. This is something quite different from the active voyaging of the earlier cantos. However, I do not wish to exaggerate the importance of Pound's treatment of time; for it does not provide us with any 'key' to the poem's development. But so far as there is any formal 'plot' in *The Cantos*, these major shifts of the relationship between time and the poetic endeavour seem to be its chief events.

The 'Fifth Decad', then, is the crucial transitional sequence which leads us out of the unchronological muck-raking cantos into the great chronological unfolding of Chinese history. Since it is a transitional sequence, it contains cantos which might almost as well have appeared in an earlier sequence. There is

also a special preparation for the Chinese history cantos in
Canto XLIX:

> Sun up; work
> sundown; to rest
> dig well and drink of the water
> dig field; eat of the grain
> Imperial power is? and to us what is it?
>
> The fourth; the dimension of stillness.
> And the power over wild beasts.

Certainly this is very simple, but it is very effective, too. Each
of the five lines of this primitive little Chinese poem is divided
into two parts: in the first four lines, the first half of each line is a
concrete physical action or event, while the second half contains
its necessary and unquestioned consequence; but the fifth line
departs from this pattern by positing (though doubtfully) the
existence of an abstraction, and by then questioning its consequence. This reveals a habit of mind which Pound sympathizes
with, but I think it is clearly implied that, alas, imperial power
may mean a good deal to us if it should happen to want fuel
for its engines. The closing lines of this canto—'The fourth; the
dimension of stillness./ And the power over wild beasts'—recall
one of the attributes of Dionysus, whose rites are among those
celebrated in Canto XLVII. The 'dimension of stillness' also
recalls XLVII, since it seems to refer to the experience of deep
tranquil satisfaction after hard physical labour or sexual intercourse. These lines serve admirably to bring to repose what is
surely one of the most beautiful cantos:

> Autumn moon; hills rise about lakes
> against sunset
> Evening is like a curtain of cloud,
> a blurr above ripples; and through it
> sharp long spikes of the cinnamon,
> a cold tune amid reeds.
> Behind hill the monk's bell
> borne on the wind.
> Sail passed here in April; may return in October
> Boat fades in silver; slowly;
> Sun blaze alone on the river.

Canto XLIX was written twenty years after *Cathay*, and, not surprisingly, it is considerably finer, especially so far as music is concerned.

3. Cantos LII–LXXI

The historical scheme developed in Cantos LII–LXXI, of American history beginning where Chinese history left off, is not so wild as it seems. As Pound makes quite clear, the American Founding Fathers were by no means revolutionaries of the nineteenth-century variety; they were men of property and education to whom many features of twentieth-century American democracy would have been extremely repugnant. Their roots were in the Enlightenment, and there is no question whatsoever that such leading figures as Jefferson knew of and admired the teachings of Confucius. Since China was then widely considered to have a model government based on Confucian principles (a standing reproach to the Christian princes of Europe), there is every reason to suppose that American statesmen founding their own non-European government did not ignore the example of China. This is not to say that early American government turned out to be very Confucian; its antecedents, in fact, are clearly European—going back to ancient Greece rather than to ancient China. But what Cantos LII–LXXI emphasize is that China, in spite of severe periodic set-backs, always kept alive a tradition of responsible government and thus demonstrated what was not so evident in the history of Europe: that there were permanent principles of sound government to be discovered (whether in China or elsewhere), and that these were the true measure of political institutions. This lesson men of the Enlightenment were delighted to receive, and—especially in North America—it furnished a useful argument against both theocracy and monarchical rule by divine right.[1]

However, if there is some truth in Pound's historical scheme, there is also some reason to question whether *The Cantos* is

[1] A more elaborate account of this aspect of *The Cantos* can be found in Hugh Kenner's 'Ezra Pound and the Light of France', *Gnomon*, pp. 263–79. A scholarly account of the connections between Confucian, French Enlightenment, and early American political thought can be found in H. G. Creel's *Confucius: the Man and the Myth* (London, 1951), pp. 276–301.

really able to assimilate 180 pages of Chinese and American history. Sir Herbert Read has observed, humorously but justly, that Pound's poem has the digestive system of a boa-constrictor: but even boa-constrictors do not try to swallow elephants. Yet I think that in fact *The Cantos* do assimilate the Chinese history cantos without too much difficulty, since Pound's abbreviation of that history moves briskly and fairly clearly in a relatively uncluttered chronological sequence. Though I am not really competent to judge, Pound's Cantos LII–LXI appear to me to provide a fairly reliable and very readable introduction to Chinese history.[1] If nothing else, they provide a necessary change of pace in the poem. If we compare these cantos with an analogous section in *Paradise Lost* (the vision of the future in Books XI and XII), I think we might be less impatient with Pound. For me, at any rate, Pound's Chinese history is more moving and instructive than Milton's story of mankind. I feel, too, that the great cantos of the 'Fifth Decad' prepare the way effectively for this survey of the human condition and the bases of humane government. While I agree that the history is sometimes monotonous, I find that it usually retains my interest:

> Tchang-siun fighting for SOU TSONG had need of arrows
> and made then 1200 straw men which he set in dark
> > under wall at Yong-kieu
> and the tartars shot these full of arrows. And next night
> Colonel Tchang set out real men, and the tartars withheld
> > > their arrows
> > till Tchang's men were upon them.
> To SOU TSONG they sent rhinoceri and elephants dancing
> > and bowing, but when Li-yen
> sent TÉ TSONG a memorial on the nuances of clouds, our
> > > lord
> TÉ SONG replied that plentiful harvests were
> > > prognostications more to
> his taste than strange animals
> or even new botanical specimens and other natural
> > > what-nots
> > > (Canto LIV, p. 300)

[1] Cf. Achilles Fang, 'Notes on China and the Cantos', *Pound Newsletter*, No. 9 (January 1956), pp. 3–5. Mr Fang makes out an interesting case for the value of these cantos as history.

This is a fairly representative passage. It is not poetry of course, but it was a poet who placed the line 'till Tchang's men were upon them' where he did. The only sustained passage of poetry (bits and pieces are scattered throughout) will be found in Canto LII, pp. 268–71, a translation of the *Li Ki*:

> Know then:
>> Toward summer when the sun is in Hyades
> Sovran is Lord of the Fire
>>> to this month are birds.
> with bitter smell and with the odour of burning
> To the hearth god, lungs of the victim
>>> The green frog lifts up his voice
>>> and the white latex is in flower
> In red car with jewels incarnadine
>>> to welcome the summer
> In this month no destruction
>>> no tree shall be cut at this time
> Wild beasts are driven from field
>>> in this month are simples gathered.

It should be clear how this almanac/book of rites carries forward the imagery and concerns of Cantos XLVII and XLIX. Here again Pound is 'in time'.

But the Adams Cantos, I'm afraid, cannot be accepted without major reservations. I am prepared to accept, and indeed I find very interesting, Pound's conception of the American Founding Fathers inheriting the relatively unbroken tradition of Confucian political philosophy and practice. Of course Pound's history of China (since it is based on Confucian sources) largely ignores the fact that Confucians were sometimes as great a curse as blessing to China; and John Adams was not, I believe, always so politically sagacious as Pound's Cantos LXII–LXXI would lead us to suppose. But these are matters which we should be ready to overlook, since Pound's historical scheme has a truly epical grandeur about it: the parallel with Shakespeare's chronicle plays has been pointed out frequently and, I believe, usefully. Unfortunately, however, Pound's conception is a great deal more impressive than the actual product: the Adams Cantos, though they cover only a few years of American history, are as long as the Chinese history cantos; and they seem to be about twice as long.

Mr Kenner, writing of these cantos, has explained that ' ... verbal exactitudes, taken from the correspondence of John Adams, are set in motion in the un-canorous Cantos LXII–LXXI. It is the essence of Pound's praise of Adams, and intimately related to Adams' political efficiency, that his casual phrases are so closely derived from his sense of fact as to permit of this use. The early Chinese editors anthologized Confucian dicta in this way. These cantos are the Analects of Adams, as comparable technical devices in Pound's new translation of the Confucian Analects make plain'.[1] I think that Mr Kenner has divined at least part—and possibly the most important part—of Pound's intentions in these cantos, but it had better be insisted that the Adams Cantos are not at all like the Confucian Analects, either in character or quality. The Analects appear to have been shaped, to some extent anyway, by oral transmission: like the best ballads they are stripped down to essentials and are quite self-contained. Though clearly related to the political situation which existed during Confucius's lifetime, the problems and personalities in the Analects appear to have undergone a salutary simplification—so that they are by no means embedded in the history of a particular province during a particular period. The Adams Cantos are inevitably very different in character: they are, unmistakably, extracts from a fuller context and therefore less self-sufficient than the Analects; and they are very much embedded in the history of a particular province during a particular period.

One of Pound's chief difficulties, in fact, is that Adams's historical context is enormously important and that Adams himself is important chiefly because of his active participation in events of great moment. It is not Occidental provincialism, I think, to insist that this is not at all the case with Confucius: his historical context does not matter very much in the history of China and the world—except is so far as it may have helped to shape Confucius's own very momentous pronouncements. Pound's problem, then, is somehow to liberate Adams from his historical context—and thus give his observations a general significance and force—but, at the same time, to reveal Adams's role in shaping American governmental policy and practice. The difficulty of such a task is manifest, and Pound does not

[1] Kenner, *The Poetry of Ezra Pound*, p. 48.

overcome it. For one thing, he wishes to demonstrate Adams's impressive attention to detail; but to do this he feels obliged to fill the Adams Cantos with details which in themselves are un-impressive:

> Saw ladies take chocolate in Spanish fashion
> > dined on board La Belle Poule
> Galicia, no floor but ground trodden to mire by
> > men hogs horses and mules
> no chimney 1/2 way as you ascend to the chamber
> was a stage covered with straw
> > on which lay a fattening hog
> above, corn was hung on sticks and on slit work
> in one corner a bin full of rape seed or culzar
> in the other a bin full of oats
> > among which slept better than since my arrival
> > > in Spain
> > > (p. 393)

No reader of this passage would ever question Adams's powers of observation and attention to detail, but Pound is not satisfied with a single example: Adams's details are to be found every-where in these cantos. Moreover, there are many, very many passages which, if they do have a general significance, do not yield it to this reader:

> Jurors refuse to take oath
> saying: while Chief Justice of this Court stands impeached.
> Moses Gill has made many justices by lending money.
> > A statue of H.M. (His Majesty)
> very large
> on horseback
> solid lead gilded with gold
> on a high marble pedestal
> We then walked up Broadway
> > magnificent building, cost 20,000 pounds
> > > N.Y. currency
> Ship
> of 800 tons burden lest leveling spirit of New England
> should propagate itself in New York
> > whole charge of the Province
> between 5 and 6 thousand pounds N. York money

185

For Massachusetts about 12 thousand lawful
as wd/ equal about 16,000 of N. York
Advised him to publish
from Hakluyt the voyage of J. Cabot,
              Hudibras
tavern, Princeton, sing as badly as the presbyterians of
                                     N. York
                              (p. 381)

Of course there are admirable or interesting pronouncements
to be found in these cantos:

'Passion of orthodoxy is fear, Calvinism has no other agent
study of theology
      wd/ involve me in endless altercation
to no purpose, of no design and do no good to
               any man whatsoever ...
not less of order than liberty ...
          Burke, Gibbon, beautifiers of figures ...
middle-path, resource of second-rate statesmen ...
                 (p. 357)

This passage might conceivably remind us of the Confucius of
Canto XIII (which is largely a pastiche of the *Analects*) and
there are others like it; for Adams *was* a great statesman and a
remarkably intelligent and honest man (albeit no Confucius).
But the Adams Cantos, though they reveal his honesty very
well, do not do the justice to Adams's intelligence that Pound
must have intended: Adams is very nearly buried in his own
details. I might add that the sequence is often punctuated with
annoying Poundisms:

an' Mr Madison's move wuz DEE-feated.
Maclay and Jim Jackson stood out against dirtiness'
     smelled this stink before Madison
smelt it or before he told long Tom about it.
                 (p. 430)

This is one of Pound's voices—the one with which he reads
Uncle Remus—but it is not the unaffected voice of the Pisan
Cantos. And even the characteristic insertion of thematic
phrases from earlier contexts is reduced here to tic:

                              in quella parte
dove sta memora, Colonel Chandler not conscious
these crude thoughts and expressions
are catched up and treasured as proof of his character.
                                        (p. 370)

This mechanical use of Cavalcanti's *Canzone* compares very
poorly indeed with the use that Pound was to make of it in the
following sequence.

X

THE LATE CANTOS

1. The Pisan Sequence

Where memory liveth,
    it takes its state
Formed like a diafan from light on shade

Which shadow cometh of Mars and remaineth
Created, having a name sensate,
Custom of the soul,
    will from the heart;

Cometh from a seen form which being understood
Taketh locus and remaining in the intellect possible

POUND'S CLAIM TO GREATNESS may well be held to rest with
the Pisan Cantos, which I have discussed hardly at all. They
are the quintessentially Poundian achievement, surely one of the
most impure pieces of poetry every written. If criticism were a
matter of distinguishing models for young poets (as Pound
usually assumes) then a critic might reasonably put the
sequence on his Index. Yet, for my own part, I find the
sequence very moving indeed, and the only part of the poem
where Pound's characteristic obscurity does not annoy me very
much. But it must be owned that these cantos are extremely
obscure, incredibly miscellaneous, and, so far as I can tell, not
organized according to any clear design.[1]

From one point of view, however, all that is essential is that
the reader of the Pisan Cantos know who Pound is, where he is,

[1] However, see Mr Emery's discussion of the Pisan Cantos in *Ideas into Action*.
His notes on the sequence are quite detailed and helpful.

188

and when it is. For if the sequence holds together at all, it does so because it is fundamentally a dramatic monologue, because at last Odysseus-Pound has been trapped in the tragic plot of history, and because he has nothing but his own past and present to make poetry out of. This in itself is a formal advantage which he denies himself elsewhere in the poem except on rare occasions. Obscurity as such, if never a virtue, is much less crippling within a dramatic context. That the situation is potentially dramatic (whatever we may think of Pound for being in it) can hardly be denied. Perhaps following Shelley's argument in the *Defence of Poetry*, Pound once remarked of the Pedro-Ignez da Castro episode retold in Canto XXX, that 'the great poem, "Ignez da Castro", was written in deeds by King Pedro. No poem can have such force as has the simplest narration of the events themselves'.[1] It seems clear to me that Pound did fall into such a situation, and further that he was well aware of it.

Besides offering him a dramatic situation, his predicament allowed him to dramatize to artistic effect what seems to me the chief defect in his poetic gift—a split between the artist and the man, which does not exist when he acts or writes as a man of letters (as in *Propertius* and *Mauberley*), which is healed in several of the 'Fifth Decad of Cantos' and perhaps in the Chinese history cantos, but which crops up frequently and disruptively elsewhere. In the Pisan sequence Pound capitalizes this defect as only a very fine artist could. Besides the great hoard of esoteric objects stored up in his memory, which bejewel his reverie, there are in this sequence those glimpses of the D.T.C. compound and its inmates which reveal Pound responding as a human being, as much at ease as could be expected. These two levels, of the timeless and the temporal, the esoteric and the familiar, are united in the great and not so great artists and poets whom Pound has known and remembered here:

[1] *Spirit of Romance*, p. 230. An interesting confirmation of Pound's claim can be found in an aside by Professor W. J. Entwistle to the effect that, had the ballad then flourished in Portugal, the death of Ignez would certainly have been a likely theme (*European Balladry* [Oxford, 1939], p. 191). Shelley and Pound seem to me obviously right, whether our critical theory can account for it or not. Pound's awareness of such matters is also evidenced by his heroic record of the flight of the transatlantic pilot in Canto XXVIII, pp. 144–5: this, too, might have been celebrated in a ballad if the technology which made the flight possible had not wiped out balladry.

> Lordly men are to earth o'ergiven
> these the companions:
> Fordie that wrote of giants
> and William who dreamed of nobility
> and Jim the comedian singing:
> 'Blarrney castle me darlin'
> you're nothing now but a StOWne'
> (Canto LXXIV, p. 459)

A good example of Pound's ability to make poetry out of the D.T.C. compound is the following passage (Pound has been observing a wasp build a nest):

> It comes over me that Mr Walls must be a ten-strike
> with the signorinas
> and in the warmth after chill sunrise
> an infant, green as new grass,
> has stuck its head or tip
> out of Madame La Vespa's bottle
> mint springs up again
> in spite of Jones' rodents
> as had the clover by the gorilla cage
> with a four-leaf
>
> When the mind swings by a grass-blade
> an ant's forefoot shall save you
> the clover leaf smells and tastes as its flower
>
> The infant has descended,
> from mud on the tent roof to Tellus,
> like to like colour he goes amid grass-blades
> greeting them that dwell under ΧΤΗΟΝΟΣ ΧΘΟΝΟΣ
> ΟΙ ΧΘΟΝΙΟΙ; to carry our news
> εἰς χθονίους   to them that dwell under the earth
> begotten of air, that shall sing in the bower
> of Kore,   περσεφόνεια
> and have speech with Tiresias, Thebae
> (Canto LXXXIII, p. 568)

This immediacy of perception is fairly frequent in the Pisan Cantos, as it is not in other parts of his work. Pound's imagination has always been visual and, in its way, distinguished; but the perception here is as fresh as the best of Hemingway's, yet better because it has humour and learning to complement it.

The element of poetic fantasy is not new in Pound's work, but it is stronger in the Pisan sequence (as it is again, notably, in Canto 91). The bowling alley image which Pound uses to sum up Mr Walls's virile powers is (1) an accurate recollection of one of the mating grounds of urban America; (2) a friendly criticism of the degree of consciousness and chastity which prevails there; (3) a striking variation on the image of the sperm driving into the egg. Whether it does not also record Mr Walls's promiscuous masculine fantasies can be decided by each reader, according to his judgment of Pound's powers of insight and compression.

Such exhibits of a peculiarly Poundian excellence could be multiplied by anybody undertaking a full defence of the Pisan sequence, and many exhibits of a less admirable character could be produced by anybody undertaking an attack. What matters, however, is whether the 'good things' are nuggets glowing in a cave, illuminated by the lamp of an occasional lost critic, or whether the sequence as a whole is luminous, so that the exact contour of nearly every phrase and exact colour of nearly every word are immediately apparent. To my mind the latter is true, but I cannot enter here upon the kind of discussion required to defend this judgment.

What must be emphasized, however, is the sheer range of diction which Pound manages in these cantos. He is as much at ease with this:

> (O Mercury god of thieves, your caduceus
> is now used by the american army
> > as witness this packing case)

> Born with Buddha's eye south of Mason and Dixon
> > (Canto LXXVII)

as he is with this:

> Tudor indeed is gone and every rose,
> Blood-red, blanch-white that in the sunset glows
> Cries: 'Blood, Blood, Blood!' against the gothic stone
> Of England, as the Howard or Boleyn knows.
> > (Canto LXXX)

The one may be 'Poetry' and the other 'prose', but there is the same grip on language, no fondling of exotic words: because at this late stage in *The Cantos*, and in his career, Pound is as much at ease with 'Mercury god of thieves' as he is with the negro prisoner who stole the packing case for him to use as a desk. In the stanza modelled on Fitzgerald's *Rubaiyat*, the first line is so contrived that 'every rose' may be the subject of an implied predicate 'is gone' or, as it turns out, of 'Cries'. Ambiguous syntax of this kind is quite the opposite of decadence or even of decadence illustrated and by implication criticized, as in *Gerontion* and *The Waste Land*. For this ambiguity illustrates not merely the motion of the mind as it first muses upon a 'rose' that is merely conventional, unvisualized, and then upon a rose which, as it gather concreteness, gathers also those historical and symbolical properties which draw the imagination back in time, to the England which Pound is to celebrate in Canto 91; but it illustrates, as well, the power of syntax to renew itself and invigorate poetry. There is a great deal more than mere craftsmanship involved in such poetry; but such poetry does not come into being without 'mere craftsmanship'.

Indeed, the long passage dealing with England, from which this stanza is extracted, may be taken as a text to illustrate the indivisible relationship between Pound's peculiar use of language and his, I should say, not at all peculiar way of recalling and valuing the past. The peculiarity and unrepeatableness of the achievement is, however, something that should be stressed: the Pisan Cantos are as odd as *Tristram Shandy*. I give part of the passage immediately preceding the stanza discussed above.

> and for that Christmas at Maurie Hewlett's
> Going out from Southampton
> they passed the car by the dozen
> who would not have shown weight on a scale
> riding, riding
> for Noel the green holly
> Noel, Noel, the green holly
> A dark night for the holly
>
> That would have been Salisbury plain, and I have not
> thought of
> the Lady Anne for this twelve years
> Nor of Le Portel

How tiny the panelled room where they stabbed him
     In her lap, almost, La Stuarda
  Si tuit li dolh ehl planh el marrimen
     for the leopards and broom plants

There is no point in pretending that all of this would be intelligible to Pound's English reader, much less to his American
reader. It moves, as reverie does move, by association; but it is
the carefully edited reverie of a full mind, and the accidental
element in the association, though to some extent real, is also a
carefully preserved illusion. It is real to the extent that Hewlett
was a romancer and poetical historian of England whom Pound
knew and liked, and to the extent that he apparently visited the
places mentioned. That Pound knew Hewlett and visited these
places does not, in itself, matter to his reader, except in so
far as they stand for something he understands or can understand. Whether Pound can expect his reader to have a necessary
superficial acquaintance with Hewlett's work is a question
which I can't answer; and it may be that the passage is sufficiently clear without that acquaintance. In any case, Pound did
know Hewlett and apparently believed that he embodied
peculiarly English virtues and that the English past was still alive
in him. And what Pound is implying here and throughout the
Pisan Cantos is that, yes, it matters very much to him that he
knew Hewlett and that he took these journeys; for in so far as
the English past is alive and meaningful to him, it is so because
of these concrete associations, with man and rooms and journeys; with the Christmas holly in which tree spirits took refuge
before the Christian era; with 'the leopards and broom plants'
which were the heraldic devices of Richard Cœur-de-Lion
and the Plantagenets; and with a line from Bertrans de Born's
'Planh' for the Young English King, Prince Henry Plantagenet.[1]

---

[1] This Pound once translated, not very closely, yet beautifully:

   If all the grief and woe and bitterness,
   All dolour, ill and every evil chance
   That ever came upon this grieving world
   Were set together they would seem but light
   Against the death of the young English King.
   Worth lieth riven and Youth dolorous,
   The world o'ershadowed, soiled and overcast,
   Void of all joy and full of ire and sadness.

Then begins the stanza in which Pound recalls the English roses to life, roses which are the counterparts of the leopards and broom plants. It is true that he does not develop the earlier images fully, yet it would be foolish to assert that 'leopards' = Richard. The heraldic device recalls Richard in a special way, via the trappings and pageantry of mediaeval chivalry. There are of course many sides to Richard, among them his cruelty and bankrupting ambition and preference for the climate and language of southern France; and young Prince Henry Plantagenet was, besides a gallant knight and patron of troubadours like Bertrans, a wastrel and a renegade against his father, the king who adopted broom plants as his device and who brought about the martyrdom of Thomas, etc. Pound's references, then, have a specific weight and value, as important for what they exclude as for what they include. And there can be no objection if Pound wishes (as most of us do) to recall the chivalric Richard, generous and talented and courageous; for in the Pisan Cantos he is not (or only rarely) trying to 'prove' this or to 'expose' that or even to instruct us very much—though the sequence is certainly instructive.

Behind this procession of anecdotes and heraldic devices and meticulously rendered scenes from the D.T.C. compound, there lies the conception expressed in Canto XXXVI:

> Where memory liveth,
> > it takes its state
> Formed like a diafan from light on shade
>
> Which shadow cometh of Mars and remaineth
> Created, having a name sensate
> Custom of the soul,
> > will from the heart;
>
> Coming from a seen form which being understood
> Taketh locus and remaining in the intellect possible

In Pound's case it is true that 'memory liveth', and the many anecdotes, places, and sayings recorded in the Pisan sequence 'cometh from a seen form which being understood/ Taketh locus and remaining in the intellect possible'. The following example of this process is also a gentle parody of it:

> Well, Campari is gone since that day
> with Dieudonné and with Voisin
> and Gaudier's eye on the telluric mass of Miss Lowell
> (Canto LXXVII)

Like Pound, Gaudier brings a professional eye to bear on the
objects around him, storing the significant details away for
future use. (In context the humour is even greater, for Pound
cuts abruptly from 'the telluric mass of Miss Lowell' to ' "the
mind of Plato ... or that of Bacon" '—p. 498.)

The phrase 'a seen form which being understood' underscores the necessity of actual personal experience accompanied
by a perception of its significance. (Pound is fond of Spinoza's
'the intellectual love of a thing consists in the understanding
of its perfections'.)[1] This approach is based, of course, on the
premise that the observer has had access to significant individuals, events, and works of art—and this Pound certainly has had.
Among these many sought-after contacts, none was more important than his friendship with Gaudier-Brzeska. And ultimately the great elegy which the Pisan Cantos comprise, an
elegy for all that Pound knew and loved before World War II,
is based on his grief and reflections over the death of Gaudier
in World War I. Gaudier's death is recorded very modestly in
Canto XVI:

> And Henri Gaudier went to it,
> and they killed him,
> and killed a good deal of sculpture.

Modest this is, but Pound's grief and outrage are recorded elsewhere (in his *Gaudier-Brzeska* particularly, and, more imper-
sonally, in Poems IV and V of *Mauberley*[2]). How they 'killed a
good deal of sculpture' is, generally speaking, obvious enough;
but Pound has something more specific in mind:

> 'as the sculptor sees the form in the air
> before he sets hand to mallet,
> 'and as he sees the in, and the through,
> the four sides
> (Canto XXV)

[1] Quoted by Pound in *Literary Essays*, pp. 71, 184, and 204.
[2] Echoes of the ideas and phrasing of Poems IV and V can be found in *Gaudier-Brzeska* (new ed., 1961), pp. 17, 54, 110.

Because of the nature of his medium (if he carves or chisels), he simply must 'see the form in the air/ before he sets hand to mallet', because there is no turning back once he begins to sculpt. It is, then, peculiarly true of a sculptor like Gaudier that the work is actually in existence before it receives its concrete embodiment; and from this point of view the Germans did literally 'kill a good deal of sculpture' as well as an enormous potential. The development of this idea can be followed in these images, the first from Canto XXXVI and the second from the Pisan sequence:

> Yet shall ye see of him That he is most often
> With folk who deserve him
> And his strange quality sets sighs to move
> Willing man look into that forméd trace in his mind

>   nothing matters but the quality
> of the affection—
> in the end—that has carved the trace in the mind
> dove sta memoria

When he set out on *The Cantos* Pound was concerned chiefly with wasted potential, the sculptor with the form in the mind, which was destroyed with the sculptor; in the Pisan Cantos he is on this side of World War II, concerned with the passing away of men and things which exist now only in the mind, and there only because he had studied them with affection and taken careful mental note of them. But the cost of war to civilization in general

> is measured by the *to whom* it happens
>   and to what, and if to a work of art
>   then to all who have seen and who will not
>   (Canto LXXVI)

All of these ideas are brought together in the famous passage which closes Canto LXXXI:

> What thou lovest well remains,
>   the rest is dross
> What thou lov'st well shall not be reft from thee
> What thou lov'st well is thy true heritage

> Whose world, or mine or theirs
> > or is it of none?
> First came the seen, then thus the palpable
> > Elysium, though it were in the halls of hell,

The 'halls of hell' are of course the places where Odysseus-Pound has gone to see Tiresias, and there is more than one Elysian Field:

> Romains, Vildrac, and Chennevière and the rest of
> > them
> before the world was given over to wars
> Quand vous serez bien vielle
> > remember that I have remembered,
> > > (Canto LXXX)

Usually the great passage of general statement at the end of Canto LXXXI is anthologized by itself, apart from the many particular recollections which it subsumes. This is perhaps the inevitable fate of a poetry which enshrines so many 'significant details', whose significance is not always generally recognized or comprehended. But it is by the peculiar, individual qualities of men and things that Pound remembers them; and it is the essence of his poetic principles and methods that he should set these particulars down as his testimony that he has 'seen' and 'understood' Yeats or Joyce or whomever—quite the opposite of:

> and Uncle William dawdling around Notre Dame
> in search of whatever
> > paused to admire the symbol
> with Notre Dame standing inside it
> > > (Canto LXXXIII)

It is a modest bit of practical criticism, of the Yeats whose defect of interest in the thing itself led sometimes to embarrassing exaggeration ('On the Death of Major Robert Gregory'), but, under correction, to a mighty transformation ('Easter 1916'). Pound's style rarely transforms, nor is it calculated to. It is perhaps only in the Pisan Cantos that his translator's ethic really bears fruit.

For in that sequence, where he is OY TIΣ, he might well state as his first principle, 'Amo ergo sum, and in just that proportion'

(Canto LXXX). He *is* only in so far as the things and men he loves define his being. They do not exist because of him. But, nevertheless, in the midst of death and destruction, it is Pound's memory and art that preserve the contour and quiddity of the things he loved.

2. Cantos 85–109

The Rock-Drill Cantos (1955) and *Thrones* (1959) bring the poem to within eleven cantos of the end. The main objective of these twenty-four cantos, and presumably of the cantos which will follow, is to enunciate the timeless principles upon which civilizations are built. This is not to say that Pound abandons his historical researches or that splendid lyrical passages are lacking; yet the pedagogical function of both sequences, whatever the subject or style of an individual canto, is far more explicit than before. Unfortunately, however, to communicate the philosophical basis of *The Cantos*, Pound continues to use the extreme elipses and cryptic allusions which were appropriate (if often frustrating) in the Pisan Cantos. At one point in *Thrones* he openly abandons the attempt to communicate with any except his most devoted students:

If we never write anything save what is already understood, the field of understanding will never be extended. One demands the right, now and again, to write for a few people with special interests and whose curiosity reaches into greater detail.

(Canto 96, p. 11)

This, it should be clear, is Cavalcanti-Pound speaking; and here, in the very late cantos, we have Pound's arcanum. In Canto LIII (p. 283) he once wrote, 'Taught and the not taught. Kung and Eleusis / to catechumen alone'. And now anybody who wishes to read Pound must become a catechumen.

I have already said everything that I am able to say in defence of this tendency in *The Cantos*. What must be insisted now is that Cantos I–LXXXIV, however cryptic or deformed in other respects, do represent a serious attempt to communicate with more than 'a few people with special interests'. And even in the cantos under discussion Pound does not give up the attempt entirely: Canto 99, for instance, should be fairly accessible to the lay-reader:

People have bodies
          ergo they sow and reap,
Soldiers also have bodies,
          take care of the body as implement,
It is useful,
To shield you from floods and rascality.

(pp. 57–8)

However, those who wish to gain wisdom will probably do well to look elsewhere, perhaps in the books from which Pound mined these cantos.[1] Even the cantos which have much or some beauty—i.e. 90–3 and 106—are maddeningly cryptic, though I believe that it is possible to defend Pound's cryptic method in the case of some of these cantos, 91 especially, on the grounds that no other method would quite do the job. As for the rest, they do not seem to me to reward the close study which they require. Perhaps when the *Annotated Index* is supplemented to include the post-Pisan Cantos, they will seem less difficult and more rewarding.

But at present I think that the reader's attention had better be concentrated on Canto 91. A full-scale exegesis would be out of place here, and in any case I have already discussed parts of this canto. At this point I merely wish to indicate how Pound's cryptic method actually functions poetically. Canto 91, it will be recalled, is concerned with the recurrence of certain values or artistic insights:

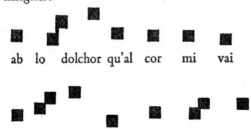

ab   lo   dolchor qu'al   cor   mi   vai

AB LO DOLCHOR QU'AL COR   MI   VAI
that the body of light come forth
          from the body of fire
And that your eyes come to the surface
          from the deep wherein they were sunken,

---

[1] Information about Pound's sources and a more sympathetic account of these cantos can be found in Mr Emery's *Ideas into Action* and Mr Kenner's 'Under the Larches of Paradise', *Gnomon* (New York, 1958), pp. 280–96.

Reina—for 300 years,
           and now sunken
That your eyes come forth from their caves
      & light then
                 as the holly-leaf
            qui laborat, orat
Thus Undine came to the rock,
                       by Circeo
and the stone eyes again looking seaward

The musical annotation seems to recall the 'Song of the Birds' by Janequin, which Pound transcribed in Canto LXXV. According to Pound the song of the birds which was in Janequin's original has survived through many transcriptions for various instruments down the centuries.[1] On the strength of what follows in Canto 91, I should guess that Pound also believes that Janequin (or some unknown predecessor) had such inwardness with the singing of the birds that he discovered once and for all time how to register their music for reproduction by man-made instruments. The Provençal line appears to be Pound's own pastiche of lines taken from Bernart de Ventadorn and Guillem de Poitou.[2] A free translation of the relevant stanza in Guillem's song: 'With the sweetness of the springtime, the woods come into leaf and the birds sing, each in his own tongue, according to the style of the new song.' Bernart's song: 'When I see the lark move his wings joyously in a sun ray, then forgetting himself and letting himself fall, on account of the sweetness that comes into his heart.' Here indeed there is inwardness with nature and, more specifically, with the nature of birds. Nobody, I suppose, will deny the obscurity of these associations; but on the other hand, it is probably only necessary that the reader make the easy association of troubadour language with the idea of Eros as an instigation. If, however, one is fully aware of Pound's associations at the beginning of the canto, one is in a position to see how each cryptic phrase calls to mind a host of analogues from various centuries and various languages. Thus the 'Reina' of the following lines is not merely Elizabeth Tudor: she is the Diana who killed Actaeon; the

[1] Pound, *Guide to Kulchur*, p. 152.

[2] The Provençal lines are these: 'Ab lo dolchor del temps novel' and 'per la doussor c'al cor li vai' (*Anthology of Provençal Troubadours*, pp. 9 and 45). Pound's line: 'with the sweetness that comes into my heart'.

Eleanor of Aquitaine to whom Bernart's song was directed across the English Channel; and the Virgin Mary in whose honour the troubadours sang after their courtly patrons were destroyed by the Albigensian Crusade. A little farther on in the canto we encounter a reference to Helen of Tyre, who is possibly a prototype of 'Our Lady' of the troubadours, of the Christian hymn-makers, and of the Tudor courtiers. These associations, if unavailable to most readers, are perfectly valid; and it is precisely such associations, regarded as recurrences of a permanently valuable concept, that are the real subject of this canto. Though often beautiful and sharply denotative in their own right, the actual words on the page exist chiefly for the sake of suggesting and directing the line of association: thus 'Undine' suggests Hans Andersen's mermaid, Pound's Aphrodite coming to shore, and Ibsen's Lady from the Sea—whose eyes were as remarkable as those of Hérédia's Cléopatre or Pound's Miss Tudor or Bernart's Eleanor.[1]

For Pound's purposes, it should be evident, the normal language of poetry—language with the virtues of prose—would interfere with the rapid interplay of association which is the chief action of this canto. Such poetry can never be very widely understood or appreciated, and it is to be hoped that other poets will not try to follow in Pound's footsteps. However, Canto 91 seems to me the most brilliant example of Pound's poetry of cryptic allusion and the consummation of the poetic attitudes and techniques inspired by Cavalcanti's *Canzone d'Amore*. There will always be a few people (not necessarily Poundians) who will take the trouble to understand it, and in my opinion it is by far the most rewarding of the cantos which follow the Pisan sequence.[2]

3. Cantos 110–?

Canto 120 is now supposed to be the last one, but it is apparent that even the illusion of completion could be achieved only if Pound were capable of a stupendous finale. Whether a poet

---

[1] In the *canso* cited above, Bernart speaks of Eleanor's eyes as mirrors, which suddenly metamorphose into the pool in which Narcissus drowned himself.

[2] Up to the italicized diatribe at the bottom of p. 73. For a tactful and informed reading of this canto, see Donald Davie's ' "Forma" and "Concept" in Ezra Pound's Cantos', *Irish Writing* (Autumn 1956), pp. 160–73.

in his late seventies can be expected to enjoy another resurgence of poetic powers—which have been ebbing since 1948—seems highly unlikely, to say the least. However, it is probably wrong to suppose that Pound intends a real conclusion: probably the poem will end with an exhortation (explicit or otherwise) to the faithful, urging them to continue the never-ending journey after knowledge which Odysseus-Pound got under way. In any event, I see little reason to suppose that the final cantos will alter my present conviction that the poem, as a poem, is a colossal failure. Perhaps its failure might have been less unquestionable if Pound had been willing to end with Canto 100 and if he had been able to suppress his urge to investigate such matters as the career of Thomas Hart Benton and the history of Byzantine coinage and interest rates. But in the end it is with Pound as it was with Ulysses: curiosity counts for more than good judgment, and so the poem itself—which it once seemed possible to end fairly happily—must follow the curve of Ulysses' fortunes.

Pound has suggested that when he finished *The Cantos* he might provide an 'Aquinas-map' for those who failed to see his design. I should certainly like to study such a map; for, as I have already admitted, I am able to discern only one 'plot' whose development has any formal significance—i.e. the major shifts in the relationship between time and the poetic endeavour —and this is so general as to be of very limited importance to the reader who is struggling in a sea of particulars. (Though I should insist that it is a matter of importance, and might have been of still greater importance if the post-Pisan Cantos had been more uniformly and intelligibly concerned with the timeless principles upon which civilizations are founded.) However, if Pound does produce his 'Aquinas-map', I do not see how it could really reveal any great formal design in *The Cantos*: if the design is so thoroughly buried in the particulars as to be invisible to all eyes save Pound's, then it hardly matters. Besides, the analogy with Dante's poem is pointless: useful as the accessory notes and diagrams are, one can perceive the major design of the *Commedia* without them; for the great system is firmly, if not always clearly, implicit in each of the details. Of *The Cantos* this is not and cannot be true.

Pound scholars will undoubtedly continue to write about the poem as though it were successful enough to be regarded as the great American epic, a poem as great as or greater than *Paradise Lost*. Though I do not share this view, I still feel that their researches into the meaning and form of the poem deserve respect and, in certain cases at least, encouragement. On the other hand, there are many readers who will continue to regard *The Cantos* as a poem which is entirely evil, sterile, or incomprehensible, or all three at the same time. And again, though I do not share this view, I agree that there is much in *The Cantos* that falls into these categories. Between these two camps there can be little understanding or sympathy; for while the one mistakes Pound's pure intentions for pure achievements, the other is hardly willing to touch the poem (or let others touch it) for fear of contamination. Of course *The Cantos* encourages such extreme reactions. It is a poem which invites its critic to regard himself as a chivalric defender of civilization, as the poem appears alternately in the guise of a dragon or a lady in distress. It is both, and the critic who thinks it is only a dragon or only a lady distressed by critical dragons, merely joins its author in tilting at windmills.

Therefore, I think that I should state my conclusions as firmly, clearly, and briefly as possible. Although I encourage readers, in justice to Pound, to examine the entire poem, yet I am satisfied that certain cantos are a great deal better than others and that these should be isolated for special attention. The best seem to me Cantos I, II, XVII, part of XXX, XLV, XLVII, XLIX, part of LI, and part of 91. The Pisan sequence must, I think, be taken as a whole, though there are of course several passages which make handsome anthology pieces. Other cantos of merit which are important for understanding the poem are Cantos III, IV, VII, XIII, XXXVI, and 90. To search out the beautiful fragments or passages in other cantos is not a waste of time by any means. But it seems to me vastly more important to isolate the cantos or parts of cantos which are fairly complete poetic wholes: for the best of these will survive; they are among the greatest poetic achievements of this century.

Though certainly very high, Pound's place among modern poets can hardly be fixed during his own life-time or for many years to come. Probably Yeats's brilliant evaluation of Pound, in its entirety, is the best short statement on the subject that we shall ever get; but here it is sufficient to quote only a part:

'When I consider his work as a whole I find more style than form; at moments more style, more deliberate nobility and the means to convey it than any contemporary poet known to me ... '[1] I am not quite sure what reservation, if any, is implied in 'deliberate'; but 'deliberate nobility' is undoubtedly the right characterization of Pound's best work:

> Rathe to destroy, niggard in charity,
> Pull down thy vanity,
> > I say pull down.
> But to have done instead of not doing
> > this is not vanity
> To have, with decency, knocked
> That a Blunt should open
> > To have gathered from the air a live tradition
> or from a fine old eye the unconquered flame
> This is not vanity.
> > Here error is all in the not done,
> all in the diffidence that faltered.

I have seen this described somewhere as (in the modern sense) an apology, much as those with little wit or honesty mention, in passing, *Mauberley* as Pound's confession of literary failure. Since the 'fine old eye' with 'the unconquered flame' perhaps belongs to Yeats, there may be some point in hearing what he has to say about the sort of critics with whom Pound has been commonly plagued, who have commented on his work with more self-righteous snickering than his abundant folly ever deserved, with but cautious recognition of his sometimes great achievements, and with utterly mean and incurious contempt for his titanic, if often misguided, effort:

> Come let us mock at the great
> That had such burdens on the mind
> And toiled so hard and late
> To leave some monument behind,
> Nor thought of the levelling wind.

But there is no reason to quote the rest of this great passage from 'Nineteen Hundred and Nineteen', at the end of which Yeats turns on the mockers themselves. It is the work of a greater poet than Pound, well remembered in the Pisan Cantos, as are so many of the great and fanatic figures of Pound's era.

[1] Yeats, *Oxford Book of Modern Verse* (1936), pp. xxiii–xxvi.

INDEX

Index

Index